B

"If you could only have one book on barbecuing and grilling, this is the one you should have. But if you already had a dozen books, you still ought to have this one.

Joe Phelps, Publisher, National Barbecue News.

"I bought Smoky's first book in the early eighties, it changed my life.That's about all there is to say .... Get his second, it has more great stuff!"

Doug Hulen

"I read it cover-to-cover twice before I put it down!"

Jim Baker, Managing Partner, Owen Brennan's, Memphis, TN and team member of Grand Champions at Memphis-in-May barbecue cook-off.

"This book should be a mandatory gift at every wedding. It is filled with information that will help a bride or husband learn about barbecue, thus preventing the necessity for the newlyweds and others to consume large quantities of creosote while trying to preserve the marriage."

Clifton W. Welch, Kansas City Barbecue Society and Memphis-In-May certified barbecue judge, writer.

"Even a committed vegetarian who never intends to own a grill would enjoy reading this book!"

Evelyn Beard, Food Editor.

© 2000 by C. Clark " Smoky" Hale

Previous books by Author:
The Great American Barbecue Instruction Book, 1985

Manufactured in the United States of America

Library of Congress Cataloging-in-Publication Data

Hale, C. Clark "Smoky," 1935-
The Great American Barbecue & Grilling Manual
Includes illustrations, index, resources.
ISBN: 0-936171-03-0 Hardcover
0-936171-02-0 Softbound
1. Cookery —Barbecuing, Grilling I. Title
2. Cookery, American Outdoor
3. Smoking meat and fish
4. Barbecue and grill designs and plans
TX840.b3H29 199999-90544
641.7'6 CIP

Published by: **Abacus Publishing Company**
8168 Highway 98 E. L3
McComb, MS 39648

The Great American Barbecue and Grilling Manual

Written by

C. Clark "Smoky" Hale

Abacus Publishing Company
McComb, Mississippi

B

Dedicated to

**St. Jude Hospital and those
who developed the St. Jude
artificial aortic valve**

and

Dr. William Holman

**who installed it
and gave me the time to write this book**

and

Dianne

**who protected my time,
fed me when I would not stop to eat
and gave aid and comfort
on the days when
gremlins ruled.**

Edited

by

Sandra Lyon

and for content

by

Bob Lyon
co-founder and Executive Secretary
Pacific Northwest Barbecue Society

who should not be held accountable for the
allowing the often awful alliterations
which follow.

Credits

Luscious cover photo is by T. Douglas Hale

Meat illustrations courtesy of the
North American Meat Processors Association
(NAMP)
Other illustrations are individually identified

Table of Contents

Foreword by Carolyn Wells

Foreword

With hundreds of cookbooks on the market, the outdoor cook faces a dizzying array of choices. Some books talk barbecue, that most time-honored tradition of slow cooking at low temperatures. Others speak to grilling, hot and fast. Volumes exist on hot smoking, cold smoking, camp cooking and chuck wagon cuisine. Guides abound for charcoal and wood cookery, and for gas and electric grills. Encyclopedias, bibles and "complete guides" run the gamut of barbecuing, while many books focus on particular barbecue "hot beds" North Carolina, Memphis, Texas and Kansas City. Few are great, some good, and others just average. This one fits the first category.

As a lifelong student of barbecue and Southern cooking, Smoky Hale has researched the cooking methods, added his experience of preparing and eating barbecue, and incorporated new ideas in this comprehensive thesis. Included in this new volume is information on equipment, meats, woods, seasonings, and sources. His goal was to create a compendium of useful information for both the novice and the experienced outdoor cook. In this book, he achieved that goal.

Food writing is a matter of finding one's own voice— that which sets you apart from all the others, Smoky Hale has definitely found his (if ever it was lost). He is considered by some a guru of barbecue. Those he considers to play fast and loose with the truths about barbecue think he's an equal opportunity offender. He's definitely got an opinion.......and an attitude. Smoky's colorful alliterative phraseology blends factual information into his unique slant on the subject at hand. Draw your own opinions and conclusions as you experience the gospel of barbecue according to Smoky in *The Great American Barbecue & Grilling Manual,* a most comprehensive guide to barbecue.

Peace, love & BBQ,

Carolyn Wells, Ph. B.

Carolyn Wells is a founder and Executive Director of the Kansas City Barbecue Society, Executive Vice President of the National Barbecue Association and Board Member, World Barbecue Society and known to some as the Princess of Barbecue.

Introduction

Somehow, I thought that when *The Great American Barbeque Instruction Book* was published, in 1985, that would be the end of it and I could concentrate on my day job. Actually, it was just a beginning. I had no idea that barbecuing would become so popular, and I was totally unprepared for grilling's explosive growth.

According to the last biennial survey (1997) funded by the Barbecue Industry Association (BIA), 84% of American families own at least one grill and fire them, on average, more than once a week. This means that on any given weekend, more people are cooking and eating in their back yards than watched SuperBowl XXXII! Of course, you **can** do both simultaneously—and I will teach you how.

The BIA survey shows that grilling is, by far, America's favorite way of entertaining at home. It is healthier eating, more relaxing and allows more time for visiting. Barbecue bursts social barriers and economic boundaries and ignores age.

Nor was I prepared for such an increasing demand for more and more accurate information about outdoor cooking. In response, I wrote weekly newspaper columns on outdoor cooking, for several years, and magazine articles along the same lines. Since mid-1996, I have written columns and answered e-mail questions about barbecuing, from around the world, at *Barbecue'n On The Internet* at *www.barbecuen.com,* and began teaching seminars, coast to coast, at the invitation of barbecue associations, demonstrating the old and proven techniques of effortless grilling.

It is though I have been drafted to serve as a conduit for accurate information about the truths of barbecuing. When there were enough "old basters," we could personally reach out and teach anyone who wanted to learn. We only paused to snigger at the modish melanges of meats and faddish fruits, grouped on a grill and artfully glistened with glycerin by fawning food stylists; photographed and pawned off as barbecue. We were content to let them simmer in their own catsup confections. But the metrics of Malthus no longer allow us the luxury of personal contact with all who really want the truth.

Central to the Code of barbecuing is the canon of sharing. It is, in order to share, that barbecuers always cook more than their families can consume. The Code also requires that those of us, to whom the basting mops were passed by the ancient Keepers of the Coals, share our knowledge of the art and science of barbecue.

Therefore, true to the Code, we will pass along the ageless truths about outdoor cooking. I pledge to do that to the best of my ability and let the ashes fall where they may.

We felt a new book was required: one which would more fully explain all the different grilling techniques, equipment, fuels, meat selection and seasonings. The *Great American Barbecue and Grilling Manual* reflects that purpose in its content.

While this book contains lots of recipes, the emphasis is on technique and factual "how-to" information.

I believe that trying to learn to grill from recipes is the equivalent of trying to understand and appreciate the panorama, and the geology, of the Grand Canyon from a collection of random snapshots, taken by an assortment of strangers. A recipe permits you to prepare one dish. Learning technique gives you the skills and knowledge to create your own recipes.

I invite you to take this grand tour of grilling from top to bottom and from beginning to end. Shortly, you will come to look upon your grill as a home entertainment center which seems, by alchemy, to quickly convert ordinary fare into sumptuous food for feasts — easily, and effortlessly.

With this book, you will become the master of this magical box.

As you read, remember the first rule of barbecue, "Have fun."

Smoky Hale
1999

Chapter One
Definitions
"What's in a name . . . ?"

As Billy Bob Shakespeare once wrote, "What's in a name? A *roast* by any other name would smell as sweet." Actually, that is true. Problems arise, however, when some folk begin to call anything done on or near a grill or anything slopped in gooey, catsupy sauce, "barbecue."

A long time ago, when folk started confusing roses with stinkweed, people decided it would reduce confusion if there were a book that had the meanings of words. So they sat down and wrote up a dictionary. Almost immediately people started calling roses, "roses" and stinkweed, "stinkweed."

Sometimes, however, the guys whipping up the dictionaries ran across unfamiliar words and relied upon inaccurate information to form their definitions. It was even more difficult when the word was used several ways as a noun and several ways as a verb. Take the case of "barbecue."

When Mr. Webster produced his first dictionary in 1828, barbecue was already well more than 200 years old. Suffering the disability of living up in New England, Mr. Webster had never had the opportunity to witness barbecuing, much less savor the succulent stuff. He was undoubtedly influenced by the English dictionary of the time which still bore the brand of its creator and literary lion of the previous century, Samuel Johnson. It is unlikely that Johnson, who began his dictionary in 1746, could have escaped the influence of a preceding lion, Alexander Pope. Pope had, about 1735, erroneously defined barbecue prominently in his published works.

According to James Boswell, his biographer, when Mr. Johnson was asked by a lady friend how he came to identify *pastern* as the *knee* of a horse, the great one answered, "Ignorance, Madam, pure ignorance."[1] Mr. Webster can, thus, be somewhat excused for defining barbecue as, "A whole hog or beef roasted or broiled over an open fire." But, it is time for Mr. Webster's successors to recant this grievous error and redeem themselves. Barbecue is neither broiled nor roasted nor cooked over a fire. Let us, therefore, offer the real definitions for the various forms of cooking done on a grill.

After establishing a common language, we will concentrate on explaining how to best use each technique. It's all in the name.

One of the 5 basic barbecue positions

---

[1] *The Life of Samuel Johnson* by James Boswell, p. 106.

A Glossary of Outdoor Cooking Words and Terms

A barbecue: An occasion upon which food is barbecued.

Barbecue: Meat cooked in the dry heat of wood coals at about the temperature of boiling point of water 180-215°. Barbecuing can render tender the toughest lean and the greasiest fat meat into healthy, succulent, savory fare because the long cooking at low temperatures allows heat to be conducted to the center without the exterior drying out. Fat is melted away, basting as it goes, while tissues soften to the consistency of a grandmother's heart. Time on the grill— 3-24 hours. Time in attendance— 10 minutes to a total of two hours. The long cooking period allows for myriad savory seasonings and provides ample opportunity for pleasurable activities. The consummate barbecuer excels in the latter as much as the former.

Barbecuing: The act of rendering ordinary meat into savory succulence. Barbecue has been going on since certain Southerners with a distinct fondness for strict compliance with the laws of conservation of energy discovered that a whole hog could be rendered tender and delicious by long, slow cooking while basting with a seasoned sauce. Southerners who migrated, or escaped, to Texas began to do the same thing with tough old beef.

Barbecue Grill: An appliance for cooking meat in the heat of **wood coals or charcoal** which allows the temperature to be maintained in the 180-225° range.

Baste, Basting Sauce: Along with low temperature, this is the real secret of barbecue. The proper basting sauce flavors and tenders the meat, keeping the exterior moist, while the inside cooks.

Brisket: A tough piece of meat from the front of a cow best used as corned beef. This started out as a Texan joke on tenderfeet Easterners and it backfired on them. They had planned to ship out the tough cuts along with the noxious weed, mesquite, and save the tender steaks and roasts for themselves. They hawked it so highly that folk expected to see it cooked when they went to Texas. Therefore, Texans had to start cooking and eating it. Brisket often costs more than sirloin tip roast, is tougher, less tasty and loaded with fat. For the same amount of time, less money and less bother, you can have a good piece of meat.

Broiling: Cooking tender meat or veggies quickly on a grill at high temperatures — 500-900° Fahrenheit— in dry heat. Only the tenderest cuts of grain- fed beef, tender cuts of pork and lamb are suitable for broiling without considerable alteration of natural characteristics of the meat. Seafood and vegetables are fine broiling fare for the grill. Time on the grill— less than 15 minutes. Time in attendance— 3-5 minutes.

Charcoal: The charred remains of wood which has had the moisture and volatile gasses driven off by being heated in an atmosphere deprived of sufficient oxygen to blaze. It can be had in lump form or in briquettes. Most briquettes contain awful adulterants.

Cooker: See **Barbecue Grill, Barbecue Pit, Grill**

Dry Rub: A mixture of salt and seasonings which is sprinkled on or rubbed into the surface of meat before it is placed on the grill. It may be placed on the meat minutes or hours before cooking.

Grill: 1. A rack, over a heat source, upon which food is placed for cooking. 2. An appliance, constructed of metal, masonry or clay products, used for cooking over a heat source, which contains a rack for meat and a grate for the coals. It may be uncovered and as simple as a brazier or hibachi, or it may incorporate a large firebox, removed from the meat rack which could allow broiling, roasting, barbecuing and smoking to be conducted simultaneously. The price may vary from $2.99 to $9999.99 for a backyard grill.

Grill: To cook food on a grill or grate over a heat source. Grilling may include broiling, roasting, barbecuing, smoking, drying or baking. In normal use among knowledgeable people, it usually means to broil items such as hamburgers, wieners, steaks, shish ka bobs, shrimp, etc.

Grill, Electric: An appliance containing a meat rack or grill over an electric heating element. It works the same as the broiler in an electric stove.

Grill, Gas: An appliance containing a gas-fired burner under a food grill or grate. Clean, convenient gas grills are excellent for broiling burgers and weenies and even steaks, if they produce enough heat. If they have separately controllable, right and left, burners, and enough volume under the lid, they can be used to roast and bake.

With the lid closed, a gas grill works just like a gas oven. With the lid open, it works just like the broiler in a gas stove. You can barbecue on a gas grill to the same degree that you can barbecue in a gas range, i.e., you can't.

Grilling: Anything done in dry heat on a grill. Possibly old English — 'Twas grillig, and the slithy toves . . .. " Comes from " Jabberwocky" by Lewis Carroll.

Marinade: A mixture of seasonings, in a liquid, which is designed to alter the texture and the original flavor of the meat.

Pit Roasting: To cook meat, and/or vegetables, suitably wrapped, in a hole in the ground, under a cover of hot coals. A large pile of hardwood is burned down in a pit and, using various methods, part or all of the coals are removed; the meat is wrapped, placed in the pit and covered with various materials, including some of the coals, and allowed to cook much like a pot roast. It is actually braising, cooking in moist heat, rather than roasting.

Roast: A piece of meat suitable in size, and provenance, to be roasted.

Roasting: Cooking larger pieces of relatively tender meat, or whole smaller animals, in dry heat at temperatures from 250-400°. In an enclosed pit, the effect is the same as baking in an oven. Having less fat interspersed within the muscle, these cuts of meat benefit from roasting, rather than broiling, since the lower temperature, and longer cooking period, allow tougher tissues to become tender. Meat may be basted to prevent drying. Meat from naturally fed animals may require *larding*, introduction of fat through the meat with special needles, and *barding*, covering with layers of fat, to render it tender. Meat may also be injected, by means of a large syringe, with seasonings, which contain some oil to assist in tenderizing these types of meat. This also offers more opportunity for flavoring. Time on the grill—1-4 hours. Time in attendance— 10-15 minutes.

Smoker: 1. A compartment of or a whole railroad car to which gentlemen retire for an after dinner cigar. 2. A seedy night club where elder males of prurient interests congregate. 3. A structure or construction wherein meat is placed after being cured to be further cured and flavored by smoke. 4. One who smokes.

Smoking: 1. Inhaling the smoke from smoldering tobacco leaves— the Native Americans' revenge on the invaders. 2. A buzzy word, of fuzzy meaning, erroneously used as a synonym for barbecuing by newcomers who first tasted barbecue in a restaurant, and learned all they know about outdoor cooking from women's magazines.

Smoking, Cold: Exposing some veggies, meat, fish and fowl, **which have been cured**, to a gentle smoke at temperatures in the 70-90° range, for relatively long periods in preparation for long-term preservation without refrigeration. Examples are hams, bacon, cold-smoked fish, sausages. Time: 6 hours to 6 weeks.

Smoking, Hot: Exposing meat, fish, fowl, **which may or may not have been brined**, and some veggies, to a gentle smoke for a few hours at 170-190°, for seasoning purposes— not preservation. Time: 3 hours to 24 hours.

Water Smoker: A sheet metal appliance which has a bottom rack for fuel, wood or charcoal, a top rack for meat and an open pan containing water, or mixtures thereof, between the meat and heat. In the chapter on **Heat**, read why water in the grill is a waste of time, taste and heat.

Chapter Two

Barbecue from Birth to Present

Origin of the Word *Barbecue*

Barbecue's perpetual popularity presents an irresistible lure to those who are just discovering it — especially food writers. If all the awful offal, published under the guise of barbecue, were gathered on one site, it would represent the greatest collection of compostable material since Hercules cleaned out the Aegean stables.

Embryonic food writers cannot, it seems, escape the temptation to cover their ignorance of the *technique* by blithely describing the *origin* of the word. Inevitably, they repeat H.L. Mencken's assertion that it came from the Spanish word *"barbacoa,"* which, somehow, had its roots in the Taino language somewhere in the Caribbean and it allegedly meant a wooden rack for cooking meat.

The Taino, members of the Arawak tribe, and native to the Caribbean area, were the gentle, handsome people who graciously greeted Columbus when he wandered ashore, on his short cut to the Spice Islands. Enslaved, murdered and infected with European diseases, the Taino, according to normally reliable sources, were extinct by about 1610. This left the question of the origin of "barbecue" open to all sorts of speculation and absurd claims.

Authoritative Spanish dictionaries say that *barbacoa* is an American word meaning a wooden rack. The French word for a wooden rack for cooking is *boucan*. From this, they derived the word *buccaneer,* after the activities of a group of unsavory European castoffs, who congregated on the island of Hispaniola, and apparently, also cooked on wooden racks. However, claiming French origin for barbecue, with "*de barbe et queue*" being translated as "from beard to tail," can be dismissed as flagrantly fatuous franco-poop! In the most recent absurdity, a writer claimed, in a well-known food magazine, that "barbecue" came from a tribe of cannibals that lived on the South American mainland. He may have erroneously confused the Taino, who migrated from South America through the West Indies islands, to eventually reach mainland North America, with South American cannibals— or he may have just been confused.

By persistence and good fortune, I was able to discover the real origin of the word. Peter Guanikeyu Torres, president and council chief of the Taino Indigenous Nation of the Caribbean and Florida, proclaimed that the Taino are alive and well and rumors of their demise should be greatly depreciated. Mr. Guanikeyu holds degrees in Anthropology and Puerto Rican Studies from Rutgers University. He is a direct descendant of a Taino chieftain.

Not only are the Taino alive and well, they are also wired! Via the Internet, Chief Peter told me that "barbecue" can be directly translated from Taino without the devious and dubious detour through Spanish.

Chief Peter translated **Taino barabicoa** to mean: "The sticks with four legs and many sticks of wood on top to place the cooking meat." And, translating **Ba** from **baba** (*father*); **ra** from **Yara** (*fire*); **bi** from **bibi** (*beginning*) and **cu** from **guacu** (*the sacred fire*), he said, "**Taino barabicu**" meant the "*sacred fire pit.*"

Chief Peter said the Timucua, Guacara and Calusa tribes of Florida and the Southeastern United States were Taino who migrated from the Caribbean with their culture. They gave us not only barbecue, but "hammock" and "hurricane" as

8

well. Familiar lithographs, from paintings by Jacques le Moyne, in 1564-65, depict Timucuans roasting game and fish on a rack of wood. That illustrates, says Chief Peter, the "Taino barabicoa."

Courtesy American Museum of Natural History

Taino *Barabicoa*

So, we now understand that *barabicoa* meant the rack and *barabicu* meant the fire pit. Although it is exciting to finally and unequivocally identify the origin of these words, both Chief Peter and I agree, that, no matter what they called what they were doing, the Taino pictured were not barbecuing.

Barbecue, whatever the origin of its name, means slow cooking in the dry heat of wood coals. The consummate barbecuer is one who makes the most pleasure during the long cooking period.

Like the technique of barbecuing, word variations, such as barbeque, bar-b-que and BBQ were a natural development. Literacy has never been high on the list of requirements for a barbecuer. Doubtless, languid Southern tongues dropped the "a" to call it barbicu. Even after learned lexicographers put an "e" on barbicu, many practitioners never saw the word written. As they took the technique north and westward, literate locals most likely spelled the word phonetically, rendering it barbeque or barbecue. BBQ and bar-b-q merely reflect our penchant for shortening words and creating acronyms.

One of the earliest recorded European's use of the word "barbecue" comes from the journal of Columbus' third voyage back to spain in 1496. He stopped to re-provision at the island of Guadeloupe, which was occupied by the Caribe Indians, deadly of the Taino, and cannibals to boot.

In *Conquest of Eden,* citing prior sources, Rinaldo Caddo and Charles Verlander, author Michael Paiewonsky, writes, "He reports that a human arm was seen being smoked on a barbecue."

The Birthplace of Barbecue
"Birth of the 'Cues"

Barbecue is the only American art form whose birthplace is even questioned. Bluegrass music sprang from the heart of the Appalachian Mountains; Delta Blues were born in the Mississippi delta and meandered along the Mississippi River up to Beale Street in Memphis, TN, and beyond. In New Orleans, jazz birthed from the same heritage as the blues before going up the river.

Barbecue also spread easily across the land, but its place of birth was a deeper mystery. That may have been because barbecue is so much older— more than 100 years older— than the United States. The special technique of cooking, **so different that it deserved a new name**, seemed to arise spontaneously wherever there were pioneering people and pigs.

According to H.L. Mencken, in *The American Language,* 1919, the word "barbecue," was in common usage in Virginia and the Carolinas by 1660. This was long before Alexander Pope, in *Second Satire of the Second Book of Homer*, ca 1735, wrote, " . . . Send me, Gods! A whole pig barbecued!" Pope, an important English author of the time, later defined barbecue as, "A West Indian term of gluttony; a hog roasted whole, stuffed with spices and basted with Madeira wine." Pope should have heeded his advice: "A little learning is a dangerous thing . . . ."

According to a lighthearted account by Charles Lamb, in *Dissertation Upon Roast Pig*, the method of cooking in dry heat, called roasting, was discovered in ancient China when an errant son, named Bo-bo, accidentally burned down a pig parlor and first tasted " . . . — cracklings!" Roasting, however, was as common in the new world as the old. But, whether performed on colonial hearths and spits, or Taino racks, it was no different from that method described by Homer at the battle of ancient Troy, thousands of years ago. There, according to Homer, Achilles and his friends, Patroclus and Automedon, entertained Ulysses and Ajax on the beach at Ilium.

"Patroclus did as his comrade bade him; he set the chopping block in front of the fire and on it he laid the loin of a sheep, the loin also of a goat and the chine of a fat hog. Automedon held the meat while Achilles chopped it; he sliced the pieces and put them on spits while the son of Monoetius made the fire burn high. When the flame had died down, he spread the embers, laid the spits on top of them, lifting them up and setting them upon the spit racks; he sprinkled them with salt. When the meat was roasted, he set it on platters and handed bread round the table in fair baskets, while Achilles dealt them their portions." **Book IX, Lines 205-224. The Iliad, Homer.**

Note that, even in those ancient times, competent cooks had learned to let the wood burn down to coals before presenting their meat to the heat.

While Francophiles, sycophants and ne'er-do-wells have tried to deny barbecue's American birthright, information collected in my years of research suggests otherwise. The preponderance of evidence points to North Carolina as the most likely "Birthplace of Barbecue."

A tract published in London in 1666, entitled *A Brief Description of the Province of Carolina*, stated "Hogs find so much mast (acorns and nuts) and other food in the woods that they want no other care than a swineherd to keep them from running wild."[2] William Byrd's daily journal kept during his survey of the boundary of North Carolina and Virginia, 1728-29, was published as *History of the Dividing Line.* In it, he observed, regarding the inhabitants of the region, "The only business here is raising of hogs, which is managed with the least of trouble and affords the diet they are most fond of. The truth of it is, the inhabitants of North Carolina devour so much of the swine's flesh that it fills them full of gross humors." He further noted, "For want, too, of a constant supply of salt, they are commonly obliged to eat it fresh and that begets the highest taint of scurvy." *Author's Note. Could have been the vapors.*

The conditions, therefore, were (1) Abundant hogs requiring no upkeep. (2) The necessity for cooking the whole hog, lest it spoil from insufficient salt for curing. (3) The threat of scurvy which is the result of lack of vitamin C. (4)

---

2 Source: Historical Collections of South Carolina, etc,. B.R. Carroll, ed. New York, 1816. Vol II, pp. 10-18.

Lastly, but not the least important, the long, slow cooking process aptly suited the North Carolinians' indolent life style, as described by Byrd.[3]

It is unlikely that barbecue sauce was developed as a prophylactic for scurvy, but some ingredients of the original basting/barbecue sauce are as healthy as they are complementary to pork. Peppers are several times richer in vitamin C than citrus, and acetic acid in vinegar is a natural bactericide. Both were cheap and readily available. The tartness of the vinegar contrasts pleasantly with pork's residual greasiness. Thus, water, vinegar, peppers and salt became the mother of all barbecue sauces. So prolific was she, that her myriad offsprings swiftly spread across the countryside in multiple evolutions.

Today, the Carolinas could aptly be called the *Balkans of Barbecue.* Only in eastern North Carolina do vinegar, water, salt and peppers still constitute the basic barbecue sauce. North Carolinians, west of the 80th parallel, added tomato catsup and brown sugar or molasses. South Carolinians added mustard to the baste for a finishing or table sauce. In this primordial cauldron of barbecue's beginnings, seasonings, sauces, cole slaws and, even hash, change from township to township, taking on almost religious fervor in the certitude of their righteousness.

As barbecue spread out from its birthplace, the sauce, **but not the technique**, began to change. North to Virginia, they follow the Lexington legacy, while Georgians, to the south, added mustard, like their South Carolina neighbors, to tomatoes. As barbecue moved westward, all manner of ingredients were added to sauces. More importantly, barbecue ceased to be synonymous with pork. While pork still reigns in the Southeast, beef is bigger in Texas and Missouri. Elsewhere, game, beef, poultry and, in Kentucky, even mutton, became fitting fare for the grill.

There are regional barbecue sauces, regional rubs, regional basting sauces and regional meat favorites, but, **there is no regional barbecue. Wherever it is barbecued, meat is cooked low and slow in the dry heat of wood coals.** Flavor it as you will.

---

[3] *William Byrd's Histories of the Dividing Line Between Virginia and North Carolina,* William K. Boyd, ed., Raleigh, 1929, pp. 52-86.

Barbecue easily gained widespread popularity along the eastern colonies and not just among the common folk. Presidents Washington, Jefferson and, later, Lincoln, attended barbecues. From an inauspicious birth and humble beginnings, its unique textures and flavors sped barbecue's spread, coast to coast and beyond. American-born barbecue is now an international force. On every continent, people are barbecuing — learning to enjoy the time as well as the food. The oldest American art form has been discovered by the world.

Transition

For many years, barbecue languished in the southern backwoods, practiced by a few diehards who had more time than ambition, hired done on special occasions by the wealthy or performed by those gifted few who barbecued for the public. Through the last century and up into the 1940's, the average family had neither the time nor the wherewithal to barbecue. It takes around 24 hours to barbecue a whole hog. Shoulders and pork butts take 12-15 hours; a brisket, about the same.

Middle-class Americans were working too many hours, with too little disposable income, to spend the time, and the money, required for barbecuing. They could only afford to throw a barbecue on special occasions. The 4th of July was always a favorite. Often they engaged the services of a local "old baster," who would come in and do the actual cooking. Politicians used barbecues as a way to get the populace near enough to their stump to hear their speeches. Farms, sawmills and ranches usually had a "hand" who was the resident expert on barbecuing. So the lore was passed along.

African-Americans, being lowest on the cultural totem, were often hired by the wealthy to do the actual barbecuing. Not getting to eat as high on the hog as his employers, the barbecuer got the less meaty and less desirable cuts, such as spare ribs and feet (trotters). As Blacks migrated to the North and Westward, they took their cooking skills to the cities and continued to turn the cheaper cuts of meat into savory succulence. It is no accident that Arthur Bryant and Ollie Gates introduced barbecued ribs and briskets to Kansas City and started a revolution which earned them international fame and fortune.

In Memphis, Tennessee, a first- generation American of German parents, returned to Memphis after serving as a cook aboard a ship in the U.S. Navy in WWII. His wife was a first- generation American of Italian parents. After working for a while at a pork packing house, he decided that he liked cooking and visiting with the public. He opened a barbecue "joint" with six stools. In a stroke of genius, he took a big bun and built on it a bed of cole slaw, made from his Italian mother-in-law's recipe, covered that with chopped barbecued pork, cooked by his Afro-American assistant, and topped it with a barbecue sauce from his Jewish landlady. This was the birth of the now famous All-American barbecue sandwich. Not finished with innovation, he began delivering them on bicycles. *Leonard's* is still serving barbecue.

In the 1940's, barbecue began to change with the rest of the world. Americans had more time, and more disposable income. Ex-GIs and shipyard welders began to cut up 55 gallon drums and fashion them into barbecue grills. It was no longer necessary to dig a hole in the ground, or to build a brick pit, for barbecuing. Bagged charcoal became more widely available. Charcoal braziers and sheet metal grills appeared overnight, like mushrooms.

In California, the Spanish heritage of roasting outdoors over hot coals, enjoyed a revival. This was invigorated, no doubt, by the influx of Southerners, migrating to better jobs and milder climates and, bringing with them the lore of barbecue. The mild climate inspired the patio culture of the postwar tract houses, and benevolence of prosperity encouraged outdoor entertaining. Small grills, which could fit on tiny patios, began replacing the traditional great stone and stucco pits.

While hamburgers and hotdogs were the most common fare, steak was becoming more affordable and undergoing a significant change. Instead of cattle being sent to slaughter straight from the range, they were penned up, and stuffed with grain, until they became plump and tender. This process caused fat to become interspersed within the muscles. This "marbling" changed broiled beef, from a jaw muscle exerciser, into a tender, tasty treat and parts, other than just the tenderloin, became favorable, flavorable fare for the grill.

While broiling steaks and 'burgers on grills was occurring across America, it was on the West Coast that a soon-to-be-famous food writer was misled into believing that this was barbecue. After his book on grilling, in which he totally confused barbecue with broiling, anything flung on a grill was mistakenly called barbecue. The sweet/tart flavor of the traditional Lexington (NC) barbecue finishing sauce was soon poured over simmering pot roasts and doused on chicken, baking in the oven— all in the well-meant, but misguided, search for the real flavor and texture of authentic barbecue.

In the past 30 years, there has been a resurrection of real barbecue, and a growing appreciation that barbecue is a distinctive cooking technique. Good Ol' boys with more time and funds began trying to duplicate, in modern steel pits, the tastes and textures that the ancient ones delivered up over holes in the ground. Gradually, challenges went out and contests began.

In Kansas City, a group of aficionados got together to form the Kansas City Barbeque Society and began to hold cook-offs. Now, they sanction and run contests in many states. Memphis, TN, introduced barbecue cooking competition into their May celebrations, called Memphis-In-May. The first contest was won by an elderly black lady cooking over coals in the bottom of a Number 3 wash tub. Now barbecue contests and cook-offs are held from Maine to California and from Miami to Seattle, and the fanciful portable grills may cost more than $50,000. Americans turnout in tremendous droves to sample true barbecue, view the plethora of pit designs and enjoy the spectacle.

During this period we have also seen a spectacular rise in the number of people cooking and entertaining on grills of all sorts. Gas grills now sell as well as charcoal and wood fueled grills, and a small percentage even use electric grills. While, barbecue has undergone an age of enlightenment, grilling is by far the most popular form of cooking outdoors. Even confirmed barbecue addicts grill at least ten times as often as they barbecue.

Grilling can turn ordinary food into sumptuous, savory fare in a family friendly atmosphere. It is not surprising that is the most popular form of entertaining at home.

Chapter Three

Barbecuing

Barbecue and Life have many similarities. As in life, *time* is the essence of barbecuing: without time, there is neither life nor barbecue. The successful life is not one spent solely engaged in toil, but one in which work and play are competently and enthusiastically accomplished in amiable balance. The successful barbecuer does not keep his nose to the grill, fretting, harrying the meat and hectoring the grill; he lets the grill do its job, while he takes maximum pleasure in the creative use of passing time. Those who excel in barbecuing are the ones who make most enjoyable use of their time.

Barbecuing is a leisure activity not to be engaged in haste. The *act* of barbecuing, unlike other cooking, is at least as important as the food. The cook is not isolated in a kitchen, but among the guests. The art, the skill, the husbandry of the food is openly exhibited, shared rather than secreted in the confines of a remote enclosure. Inclusion of the guests in the process increases their anticipation and heightens their pleasure and appreciation of the finished product.

Barbecue is delicious and succulent meat: a rare treat shared, but, as highly regarded as this bounty may be for itself alone, what makes barbecuing unique is the sharing of that most precious, irreplaceable gift: time. The barbecuer gives, shares with his guests, a generous portion of his most finite and valuable resource.

When you barbecue, approach the task with a clear acknowledgment of the investment of time, but with a keen awareness of the opportunities for its pleasurable uses and a devout commitment to its enjoyment. Otherwise, you may as well serve "take out."

Remember, also, that barbecuing is a cooking technique rather than a recipe. In covering the technique for barbecuing the various parts of different livestock, game, seafood and veggies, we will provide a Master Method which includes a recipe of seasonings. These seasonings represent only one option from the many listed in the Seasoning Chapter and are not intended to represent the only or even the "best" seasoning mixture. It is my sincere desire that, after reading this book and learning technique, you learn to mix your own seasonings from scratch.

Since barbecue began with pork, it is fitting that we do. It also began with cooking the whole hog; so will we. This doesn't mean that you should. I am frequently amazed that folk who have never before barbecued anything get the unaccountable urge to cook a whole hog. This is the equivalent of wanting to begin your singing career at the Metropolitan Opera. I recommend that you have a few hundred pounds of pork shoulders and butts under your belt before attempting a whole hog.

One of the five basic barbecuing positions.

Barbecuing a Whole Hog

While smaller hogs may be barbecued, the normal range is from 60 to 120 pounds, "dressed weight." There are several reasons for this. Smaller hogs will not normally have developed the fat structure which works its magic as it melts out of the mature carcass. Smaller hogs are much more likely to be roasted with exemplary results. If you are going to invest 24 hours cooking, you may as well get more than less for your time. Hogs larger than 120 pounds are normally just too much to handle with ease.

Unless a pet pot-bellied pig wandered through, the average supermarket hasn't seen a whole hog carcass in a quarter of a century; therefore, you must locate another source. Those who cook whole hogs regularly normally go to the producer (grower) to choose the size and style of hog that they prefer. They have it delivered to a slaughter house so that it can be cleaned and chilled before they need it. A local slaughter house is another typical source. Expect to pay more to have the hair scraped from the carcass, rather than skinned as normal. Some areas which are heavy into whole hogs, such as Memphis, TN, will have several potential suppliers. Since pork does not improve with aging, the sooner that the hog is cooked, once the carcass is fully chilled, the better. Before picking up the hog — which can be a pretty good chore — all preparations should be made to get it promptly to the grill, or, as an alternative, into proper refrigerated storage. The carcass should be maintained between 34 and 40°. Plan three days to a week ahead.

Quite obviously, one needs a grill adequate for the task. Not only must it support the weight, but it must allow ready replenishment of the coals over the long cooking period — without a lot of hassle. At 3 o'clock in the morning, wrestling with an ill-conceived pit can put a severe damper on enthusiasm. Perhaps, more important, irregular heat levels can cause unwelcome vermin to multiply. The grill must be able to maintain a steady output of heat at the appropriate temperature— despite the weather. It is rash to try to barbecue a whole hog without some sort of covering — tent or shed — over the pit and the firewood. Any moisture, fog, dew, rain or snow will suck the heat like an overzealous tax collector.

Collect an ample supply of charcoal and/or dry hardwood — oak, hickory, pecan, apple, etc., and fire up the grill to bring it up to at least 300° with exhaust vent damper fully open. It will cool down while you are loading the hog. After you load the hog, use the air entrance vent opening to control the temperature in the pit at hog level at around 200°.

The hog will not require much preparation. If your butcher didn't, you may want to take an axe and split the backbone just enough to allow the carcass to open and lay flat. Those who intend to cook their hog in a belly down, supine position, avoid this step. This method is normally reserved for hogs at the smaller end of the range. However, where the proof is in the pickin' rather than the presentation, the first method is preferred by those who regularly barbecue a whole hog. Having the hog cut in half down the spine reduces the strain of handling and does not detract from the cooking or the final flavor. Those who are more interested in tradition than flavor would consider a half hog desecration.

It is traditional to insert a wood block into the hog's mouth to keep the jaws from closing and allow an apple, or such, to be inserted before serving. Later, at some point when the need becomes evident, the snout, ears and tail are normally covered with aluminum foil, cheese cloth, or the like to prevent these appendages from burning. Some even like to remove the feet. That is an unimportant consideration. A minority has the skin removed from the hog. However, unless you intend to baste, this has little effect on the taste and the skin's function as a serving tray is lost.

Which brings up another fork in the road — "To baste, or not to baste?" I am of the basting persuasion, although I concede that whole hog is where basting has its least effect. Where in smaller segments of meat, the basting sauce can penetrate and flavor most parts, in the massive whole carcass, a much smaller proportion of surface area is exposed to the salutary basting solution. Therefore, while I consider basting essential for shoulders and butts, I feel that it is optional on the whole hog. Seasoning can be easily added when the meat is picked, pulled and chopped.

Of Time, Temperatures and Techniques

Cooking time is a function of temperature, and those who provide charts proclaiming "x" minutes per pound are the equivalent of weather forecasts by "Farmer's Almanac" folk. The beginning temperature of the interior of the meat can significantly increase or decrease the time required to cook. Barbecuing at 170° will take much longer than cooking at 225°. If the temperature in your grill or on your pit varies from 160 to 250, you just have to make certain that you have allowed adequate time for such vagaries of life. The only certainty is when you stick the probe of your just tested bimetal thermometer into the thickest part of the ham. I advocate planning on 24 hours for a 100 lb. hog. If it gets done an hour or three ahead of time, shut down the grill and let it improve with time.

When the grill is at the proper temperature, place the hog face down, seasoned or unseasoned, as you like, close the lid and record the time. The schedule will depend, to a degree, upon the capacity and characteristics of your grill. The appropriate time table for your grill will be developed over a period of time as you cook more on it.

Another consideration in barbecuing a whole hog, pork shoulders and beef briskets is that the optimum internal temperature is about 25 degrees higher than is needed to cook the meet "done". Roast pork is at its peak of tenderness and succulence at 160 degrees - or less - and a beef roast is prime at 145°. Barbecuing the fatty pork and beef cuts, in low temperatures, up to an internal temperature of 180°+, allows the fat to render the meat more tender. Of course at roasting temperatures, the outside part of the meat would be rendered tough and inedible, but at barbecuing temperatures the exterior does not dry out as much.

Take time to restore your body's liquid level; then start another fire of wood or charcoal to produce embers for replenishing the grill. This fire pit can be a shallow hole in the ground, another grill/pit or a 30/55 gallon metal drum with a coal removal slot cut out at the bottom of one side. In warm weather, put this far enough away that you don't get overheated while tending the grill. In cool weather, keep it close enough for comfort. Tend this fire first. It is food for your grill.

After about six hours, turn the carcass to lie on its back where it will rest until done. The real reason that you turn at about that time is that is about the last point at which the carcass is firm enough to turn without wanting to tear. The rest is a matter of time.

If you are barbecuing on a version of the original grill, a shallow hole in the ground with a rack above, the auxiliary pit is even more important and active. However, whatever your grill design, placement of the replenishing coals is important. More coals are required under the ham section, for instance, because the meat is thicker. Proper placement of the coals is a learning experience that you will continue to refine.

Unless you have planned for relief, fatigue will become a constant companion, an unwelcome visitor, which can ruin all your plans. If you are working the pit alone, use a timer with an alarm to arouse you at 30 minute intervals to tend the coals. This time period really depends upon your individual grill. A well made, heavy grill may run for four hours without attention, so you must learn the characteristics of your grill before starting to do a whole hog or pay the price in lost sleep. It is better if at least two people attend the pit at night. This measurably reduces the opportunity for error.

When the hog is done— at least 160 ° in the thickest part of the ham, the hog may be removed or allowed to cook until all the fat is rendered - about 185°. At this point the carcass is too tender to be moved intact without support. Many serve the pork from the grill, pulling or inviting guests to pull their own portions. An option is to remove the whole meat grate to a table. The long cooking period allows all the accompaniments to be ready for the main course — including a variety of finishing sauces, accurately labeled, so that guests can experience several.

Barbecued Pork Butts and Shoulders

When, in the course of human events, it became acceptable to barbecue less than a whole hog, the preferred cut among the cognoscenti was the front shoulder. Apparently, this daring deviation from the norm first occurred after barbecue had moved westward from its birthing place, up the foothills across the 80th parallel. Lexington, NC, is reputed to be the place where this heresy was hatched. For economic and other reasons, this deviation gained mainstream acceptance.

Shoulders, pork butts and picnic hams are part and parcel of the same front leg and shoulder of a hog. When the top of the shoulder is separated, it becomes a butt or a Boston butt. What remains is called a picnic or a picnic shoulder.

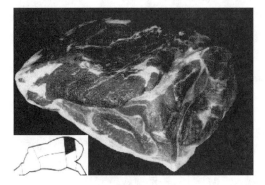

Butt

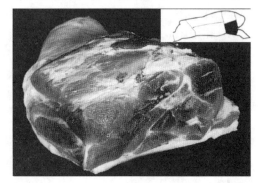

Picnic

The pork butt is to pork cookers what the beef brisket is to a Texan. Both cuts have layers of fat interspersed within the meat. When cooked low and slow, the fat melts while basting the meat to keep it moist until it gets done.

This is what creates that soft, savory succulence that cannot be had any other way. When this uncommon alchemy is performed in the dry heat of wood coals, the meat becomes barbecue. The misinformed, who equate barbecue with pork and vinegar, would mistakenly call it smoking. The unfortunate choice and misuse of this word have led to ruin of many good pieces of meat. Meat cooked in the dry heat of wood embers for 10-12 hours can easily absorb too much smoke. Meat cooked in the smoke and gasses of burning wood will become distasteful to the discerning palate within a very short time.

The best barbecue — and roasted meat — is probably cooked over wood coals in an open pit. The juices dripping onto the coals atomize and return as flavor bombs that embed themselves into the meat and later explode in your mouth. It takes more fuel and more time but, for those who can afford the time, the results unmistakably superior. Since we don't all have the time to dig pits and burn down all the wood it takes to cook in the open, man invented the covered grill.

Useful grills have certain basic functions designed into their form. Barbecue grills must consistently deliver heat at low temperatures over a period of several hours. Therefore, barbecue grills/pits must allow replenishing the coals without disturbing the meat allow the meat to cook at temperatures between 200 and 225° without burning on the outside, allow temperature control by controlling the draft and the distance of the meat grill from the fire grate. In such a grill, one with a mere modicum of mastery of the methodology can convert the lowly priced lump of meat into a prized presentation.

Barbecued Pork Shoulder

Select and trim a couple of Boston butts. Look for interspersed fat, but avoid large fat deposits. You may as well do two while you are at it. Trim loose debris an bring to room temperature. If you are into rubs, now is the time to apply the rub. Start the fire with 10-15 lbs. of 80% oak, 20% hickory. When the wood is fully flaming, add 5 lbs. good hardwood char coal briquettes. Open the grill's air inlet fully. Leave the exhaust vent fully open except to put out a fire.

Basting is little known, nor its efficacy understood, by many recent discovers of barbecue technique. However, from barbecue's birth, basting has been an essential element of the technique. This is not a mere happenstance. Basting moistens and protects the meat's surface while adding seasonings. Any competent barbecuer who has not experienced the benefits of basting will be amazed at the improvement his product will gain from basting with an appropriate sauce.

Smoky's Pretty Good Basting Sauce

Make a basting sauce as follows:

2 C.	apple juice or water
1 C.	apple cider or vinegar
1/2 C.	peanut oil or fresh lard
1/2 C.	Worcestershire sauce
2 cloves	garlic, crushed
1 large	onion, chopped
3 ribs	celery, broken or chopped coarsely
2	carrots, chopped
1	bell Pepper, chopped
1	bay leaf
1 T.	thyme
1 t.	paprika
3 T.	salt

Simmer 20-30 minutes. Baste the meat well with basting sauce and let it dry; then baste again before putting it on the grill. Thereafter, baste about every 20 minutes.

Note that this contains very little oil. A basting sauce should fit the meat. This particular cut of meat needs less oil. For loins and ribs, use 1cup oil. Before the current crop of leaner pigs, little or no oil was needed for pork.

When the wood is reduced to embers and the charcoal is gray, put the meat on and close the grill. Shut down the air intake until the temperature inside the grill drops to about 210Þ F. Check until you are certain that you have stabilized the temp around 210Þ F., then, relax.

All things considered, allow about 45 minutes per pound. The center temperature should be at least 160°. If you want softer, less fatty meat, continue cooking until the meat reaches 180-185° or begins to dry out— whichever comes first. When it is about done, lower the temperature of the grill and start basting with the finishing sauce. Initially, it may be thinned with the remainder of the basting sauce. Understand that many competition cooks and backyard chefs do not apply a finishing sauce at the grill but reserve it for the table.

Pretty Good Pork Barbecue Finishing Sauce

2 C.	water (substitute apple juice)
2 - 6 oz. cans	tomato paste
3 T.	mustard powder mixed with water
1 medium	onion, chopped
2 cloves	garlic, mashed
1/2 C.	Worcestershire
1/2 C.	apple cider vinegar
1/4 C.	brown sugar
1 t.	ground cloves
1/2 t.	ground mace

Combine and simmer 30-40 minutes. Adjust sweet/tart taste.

Remember to reduce the temperature when the finishing sauce is applied to prevent burning. Let the roast set after removing from the grill. Slice or pull meat from the bones. Serve sauce at the table. Ought to be a prize winner anywhere except eastern North Carolina. There, anything but vinegar, salt and peppers is sacrilege.

After you have perfected the technique, choose any of the rubs, basting sauces and finishing sauces from their respective chapters — or what the heck — create your own.

Barbecued Pork Ribs

Cities, like humans, develop characteristics that uniquely define their charms and faults. There are many facets to a city's soul and Ph.Ds may have formulae for divining its depths. But a better way to judge a city is by looking at what its people like to eat.

Take, for instance, ribs. Immediately three cities come to mind— Tuscaloosa, AL, Memphis, TN, Kansas City, MO. All are located on river banks and, except for Memphians' love of pulled- pork sandwiches, praise ribs above all other barbecue. St. Louis, Chicago and Detroit all have pretensions toward prominence as rib cities, but pale in comparison, although St. Louis does have the distinction of having a particularly trimmed rack of ribs called the "St. Louis Style."

There is a pattern that emerges in the passion for ribs. Ribs are usually the first commercially available barbecue in areas outside that nursery of barbecue— the Southeastern United States. An Ol' baster comes into town and opens up a barbecue pit. Bye and bye, folks will smell the smoke and come in to check things out. The tender, tasty ribs are in many cases the first exposure to barbecue and the experience is like a religious awakening.

Each of these cities has almost as many barbecue restaurants per capita as hamburger joints. Almost. And some of them produce edible barbecue. These are the ones that produce profuse paeans of prose from peripatetic Eastern journalists. Their mushy myths mean that they as gullibly swallow the barbecuer's tales as eagerly as they consume the ribs. The cook who cannot concoct a story as spicy as his sauce is doomed to failure as a barbecuer.

As eager innocents try to duplicate the flavors and textures of barbecue in their own back yards, they are sometimes misled by the earnest errors of the beguiled journalists. They may also be confused by the various names given to ribs from different areas of the hog. Loin back ribs from the loin section — nearer the backbone than the spareribs— are very tender, and those from small carcasses and weighing less than two pounds are called baby back ribs by fanciful merchandisers. Country style ribs are cut from the top ("high on the hog") and contain part of the pork loin section. They are, therefore, very meaty but the meat is loin rather than rib.

27

The classic barbecued ribs are the spareribs— the lower section of rib cage remaining after the pork chop has been removed. If the chine bone and the brisket bones are removed from the bottom of the rib rack, then the rib section is called St. Louis style.

PORK BONE STRUCTURE CHART & RIB GUIDE

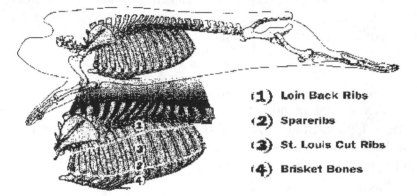

(1) Loin Back Ribs

(2) Spareribs

(3) St. Louis Cut Ribs

(4) Brisket Bones

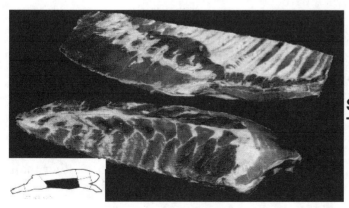

Spareribs — Before Trimming

**After Trimming —
St. Louis Style**

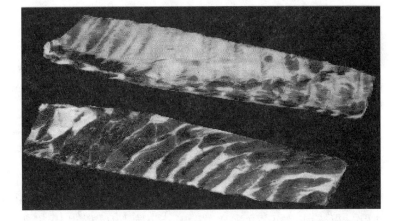

The choicest spareribs weigh in at less than three pounds — called "three and under" by those who get serious about such things. Larger ribs will be tougher and may require more magic to render them tender. Personally, I avoid the small imported "Danish" ribs because of lack of taste and texture.

As discussed in the "**Meat**" section, pork ribs can be broiled, roasted or barbecued. Those who want a quick fix and don't mind that the texture of the ribs is crunchy rather than tenderly succulent will be happy with broiling. Some of the more errant may even try to capture the tenderness of barbecued ribs by using meat tenderizers. Those completely lost in the wilderness may even commit the taste robbing travesty of parboiling ribs in a vain attempt to make them tender. If you want to broil, the so-called baby backs, being much more tender, perform better broiled than do spareribs. Country style ribs broil like a pork chop— which is exactly what they are.

Those who cook ribs in the roasting range, between 250° and 350°, get to eat earlier, but at what a price of taste and texture. These are most likely the folk who were introduced to ribs by restauranteurs who cooked them fast at roasting temperatures in gas ovens and burnt some ends in their haste. Suffering a lifelong aversion to charred and burned food, I have never learned to appreciate burnt ends.

When it comes to barbecued ribs, beginners may try the faddish, more forgiving loin back; those wanting more meat may cook the country style; but those connoisseurs whose palates can appreciate the taste and texture will insist on the incomparable sparerib — the prize that inspired the rib revolution.

29

You can produce barbecued spareribs as tender and delicious as any in the ribber cities by following the tried and true techniques of the barbecuing—cooking them low and slow in the benevolent, beneficent heat of wood coals serendipitously soaking up the seasonings, smoke and sauces. You only need a few details about selection, preparation, seasoning and cooking to turn out "killer" barbecued spareribs.

Selection

Choose sparerib sections weighing 3 pounds or less, that are bright pink, moist and not overly laden with fat. Look for the St. Louis cut because the brisket bone and chine are mostly waste. Expect to pay a little more for that reason. If the St. Louis Style is not available, you can cut or have the butcher cut the chine and brisket bones. Cook them for sampling. Keep the ribs chilled to around 40° until you are ready to prepare them. Buy the maximum that your grill can handle because you can always freeze any leftovers — an illusion, in most cases— and ten racks of ribs cook as quickly as one. Reconstituted barbecue is probably better than hot off the grill.

Preparation

Most skilled barbecuers agree on the necessity of removing the thick inner membrane lining the rib section. Some even advocate removing the thin membrane covering each rib. I find that unnecessary and a little much. Removing the inner membrane is really very simple. First step is to insert, somewhere toward the center of the rack, a rather blunt ended instrument— a Phillips screw driver, an oyster knife, even a wooden dowel— beneath the membrane and raise it slightly. Next step is, using a paper towel or cloth for friction, grasp the raised membrane and pull. It should come off in one piece. If you have catfish skinning pliers, they work wonders.

Trim off any extraneous fat and slivers of meat; then prepare to season. Here is where things get spicy. A serious controversy rages among the various purveyors of pork as well as among some adamant amateurs about the proper seasoning of ribs. Some swear by the dry rub, others by the wet basting sauce. Personally, I do both, have no problems with either and many times do both on the same rack of ribs. Barbecue is always spiced by controversy as well as herbs and spices, but those who learn to use an appropriate basting sauce will never again doubt its value.

I recommend that you do a dry rub and a basting sauce, thereby illustrating the simplicity of both and allow you to experience the effectiveness of basting. From the "**Basting Sauce**" section, select a basting sauce that seems interesting. Do the same with a rub from the "**Rub**"section. As an option, you can use part of the dry ingredients of the basting sauce recipe as a rub.

I suggest that you start with a rub of the type that your palate is likely to be familiar with. That is, if you are from the Kansas City, MO, area, start with the Generic KC Style. Texans and those from Western Louisiana might want to start with the Generic Texas Style, and those from South Louisiana will, naturally, be more likely to have tasted a Generic Cajun Style. Initially, it is more important to develop the technique. Once you have perfected the technique, the seasoning will provide a great range of variations for your experimentation and delight.

Apply the rub — as you would salt — from 5 to 10 minutes before putting the ribs on the grill. Sprinkle it on and rub it in. If basting, apply one coat of the basting sauce and let it dry, then apply another generous coat just before putting the meat on the grill. If you use a rub and a basting sauce on the same rack of ribs, make certain that they use the same set of seasonings and do not contradict each other.

Preparing the Grill

Barbecuing spareribs will require 5-8 hours of consistent heat from wood or charcoal coals at around 200-215°. Therefore, a generous bed of coals should be built in the grill. Depending upon the capacity of the grill/fire box, the coals will need to be replenished periodically — a period which only you and your grill know. Maybe at this point, only the grill knows. But that is something you must learn for each grill. So begin by keeping a regular diary in which to record not only dates, times and temperatures, but also the ambient temperature, humidity and wind conditions. Record your results, as well. This will be very important to you in learning to perfect your ribs.

Refer to **Burning Wood and Blowing Smoke** Chapter for wood selection, fire starting and maintaining a replenishment pit.

Gas grill users can approximate the barbecue flavor by putting green wood or dampened sawdust or wood chips in a commercially produced container or wrapping in aluminum foil and punching a few holes in it. Place the container

31

close to the flames and allow the smoke to build up before putting the ribs in. Do not do this more than once or risk over smoking. Smoke flavor is really absorbed in the early stages of cooking. Afterward, additional smoke residue is deposited on the exterior to the detriment of the flavor. Electric grillers follow suit.

Barbecuing, The Act

Place the ribs on the grill without their touching. Although some folk hang them vertically, turn them on their sides or creatively roll them up for small grills, I like to lay them flat. I want the juices, seasonings and rendered fat to stay in intimate contact with the meat as long as possible— more flavor is absorbed and surface stays moist longer. A moist surface means that meat can still absorb flavors and heat is transmitted faster and more efficiently through moist tissue.

Close the lid, and adjust the air intake— to reduce the air flow, and check back in about 15 minutes to assure that the temperature at meat level is around 200°. Baste while you are there. Once you have stabilized the grill temperature, go away and play for at least 30 minutes. Check the grill again, and baste and turn if you are using a baste. Check at about 30 minute intervals until you can establish the proper interval for your grill. Even if you are not basting, you may need to turn the ribs and rearrange them because of temperature variances within the grill. Try to get equal heat to all ribs by moving them, if necessary. Do not let any part of them dry out or burn.

Barbecuing ribs, like any other barbecuing, allows lots of time for doing other things than standing around a grill worrying the meat. The total time will be about 5-8 hours, depending upon temperature and weather. Find something fun to do and go do it — checking back occasionally as needed. This is the time to practice becoming a real barbecuer by learning how to enjoy the time spent outdoors with friends and family.

By and by, the rib meat will begin to withdraw from the ends of the bones. This is your signal that they are about ready to eat. It is also the time, if you choose, to reduce the heat and begin basting with the finishing sauce.

Do not expect the rib meat to fall off the bones. Mushiness is not why our teeth crave the sensation of meat: texture is. Mashed potatoes are tender, inexpensive and don't require a lot of time or effort to cook. If you want tender, eat mashed potatoes. Meat ought to offer some resistance to the teeth — we pay extra for that. When the ribs are ready, the meat pulls from the bone with minimal effort, but it should still offer some resistance.

By this time, I will have been basting with my finishing sauce of the moment, thinned by a little of the basting sauce. It won't be a garish, brash, ostentatious sauce calling attention to itself, but a mellow sauce, blending like a relaxed barbecuer at a social gathering, melding, mixing, complementing the meat by adding another level of flavors and textures.

The consummate host will slice the ribs individually and serve them warm to table accompanied by a couple of versions of warm finishing sauces.

After your appetite is sated, carefully taste a rib and record the taste and texture as well as any other pertinent information. If possible, wrap a couple of representative ribs in two layers of aluminum foil, label with date and put into the freezer for comparison later with future

---

Barbecued Pork Ribs

Ala Super Swine Sizzlers

The team of the Super Swine Sizzlers, led by Jim Turner of West Memphis, AR., has won the Grand Championship at the World Champion Barbecue Cooking Contest at Memphis-in-May and many other trophies and has, also, been named "Cooking Team of the Year."

Select your favorite slab of ribs— with the assistance of the butcher if required. Trim all excess fat and the inner membrane. Prepare the grill for barbecuing - 200º. Rub the ribs with the Super Swine Sizzler dry rub made as follows:

Super Swine Sizzler Dry Rub

2 t.	paprika
1 T.	onion powder
1 T.	garlic powder
1 T.	ground basil
1 1/2 T.	lemon pepper
1 T.	red pepper
1 1/2 T.	black pepper

Allow the ribs to come to room temperature while the coals are getting ready. Place the ribs on the grill, close the lid and baste at 30 minute intervals with 1 qt. vinegar, 1 qt. water, 8 oz. above mixture.

When the ribs are about done, baste with the,

Super Swine Sizzler Finishing Sauce

8 oz.	vinegar
1 gal.	commercial barbecue sauce
4 oz.	prepared mustard
8 oz.	lemon juice
1-12 oz.	beer
8 oz.	Worcestershire sauce
1 stick	butter
	brown sugar as desired

Simmer for one hour

With your natural talent, they should taste like grand champion ribs.

If you'd like to know more about memphis style barbecue, check out barbecue greats - Memphis Style, Carolyn Wells, Pig Out Publications, 4245 Walnut St., Kansas City, MO 64111.

Country Style Barbecued Ribs

Spring is the season of the year when budding magazine food editors and blooming food stylists (yes, dear friends) conspire to create flights of fanciful dishes and colorful misrepresentations and proudly proclaim them barbecue.

Food stylists are a relatively new arty-crafty group on the food scene. Maneuvering between the cook and the photographer, they started out as spritzers of water drops, shiners of oily surfaces and glisteners with glycerine. Then they expanded like an unpicked zucchini. I suspect that they are frustrated artists who, as children, expressed their talents by painting food upon the wall.

They are the people who blatantly show us steaks consumed in flames and expect us to be so ignorant as not to know that meat cooked in flames smells like the smoldering remains of a burned boot. They are those who think that blackened chicken is stylish while those of us who have suffered to consume it as a valid price of friendship would undertake a jail sentence rather than present it to a guest.

They are the curious folk who could not frame a photo of a hot dog at a children's backyard party without including roses carved of radishes, embraced in fronds of fennel and roquette. (Let us not forget the fleetingly fashionable roquette, which was never so popular by its English spelling, rocket.)

Presentation of food is important. Pretentious and contrived, artificial arrangements, no matter how arty, are distasteful. Outdoor cooking is fun first — good folks, good food and good fun. The old engineer's adage, "Keep it Simple, Stupid" is most appropriate for outdoor cooking.

To show how simple good barbecue can be try barbecuing "CountryStyle" ribs.

I have no idea how this name came about, but it certainly shows that folk in the country know a good thing when they taste it. Country-style ribs come from "high on the hog" and consist of a generous portion of the tender pork loin. They are, for all practical purposes a thick pork chop sliced open to expose the center of the loin muscle and the rib section is the same as that of the faddish loin back ribs

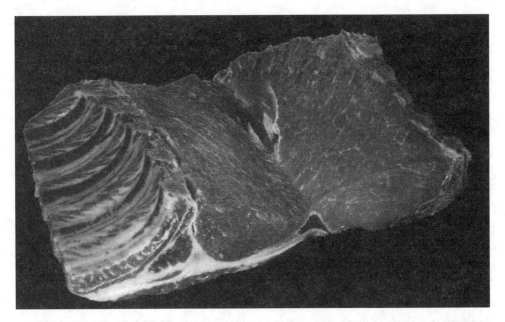

According to the North American Meat Processors Association, country-style ribs "shall be prepared from the blade end of a bone-in pork loin and shall include not less than three or more than six ribs. The chine bone shall be excluded by a cut which exposes the lean meat between the feather bones and the ribs."

Since the country style ribs are not as fashionable, at the moment, they often sell for less than the trendy loin back ribs — and loin backs are just country style with the loin meat removed. Makes you wonder why anyone would choose loin back over country style. The loin meat of the country style rib is so tender that it is almost a waste of time to barbecue. I personally like to broil this rib for a very short time and eat the tender, juicy meat while I am barbecuing a tougher cut.

But, if you want to barbecue country style ribs, here's how.

Barbecued Country Style Ribs

If you are generous, allow 3-4 ribs per person. Trim off excess fat and extraneous meat and wipe dry.

Dry Seasoning

Sprinkle generously with garlic powder, onion powder and paprika. Come back lightly with thyme, black pepper and salt and allow to come to room temperature.

Prepare the grill for barbecuing - temperature about 210 ° - and lay in enough coals for 3-4 hours of cooking. Control the temperature with the draft (air) inlet. Good all- hardwood charcoal is all that is required. Add white oak or hickory for additional smoke flavor, if desired.

Basting Sauce

Prepare a basting sauce of 1/3 cup each of oil, water and Worcestershire with 1 T. each of garlic powder, onion powder and 1 t. each of mustard, thyme, ground bay and celery seed.

When the coals are ready, baste the ribs and place on the grill opposite the coals. Close the grill and play. Baste and turn ribs about every half hour.

Finishing Sauce

Prepare a finishing sauce of 1 cup apple butter and 1/2 cup Worcestershire sauce and 2 T. prepared mustard simmered slightly. Baste when the ribs are done (begin checking after about 3 hours) and serve sauce on the side at the table.

You don't need fancy fixins to make good gobblins.

Barbecued Loin Back Ribs

I'm sorry, I just can't bring myself to call them "Baby Backs!"

Loin back ribs have the meat of the muscles accompanying the loin muscle and are more tender than that attached to spare ribs because the muscles get less use. Therefore the loin back ribs so lend themselves to the quicker cooking temperatures of roasting and broiling, that I, personally, rarely barbecue them. However, if you are compelled, the chore is really simple.

Select meaty ribs without excess fat and remove the inner membrane – if it has not already been done. Prepare the grill for barbecuing – 210°. Sprinkle with a dry rub from the "Dry Rub" selection, place on the grill and close the lid. In about 20 minutes, confirm the proper temperature or make corrections in the draft.

Go play. Turn about every 30 minutes until done. Basting with a basting sauce selection will improve their taste and texture – but that is optional.

Optional, also, is a finishing sauce. If you are into "Baby Backs," you will probably call it a glaze anyhow. So pick out a glaze and apply when the ribs are done and the temperature is lowered.

These are fine until you learn how to cook real ribs.

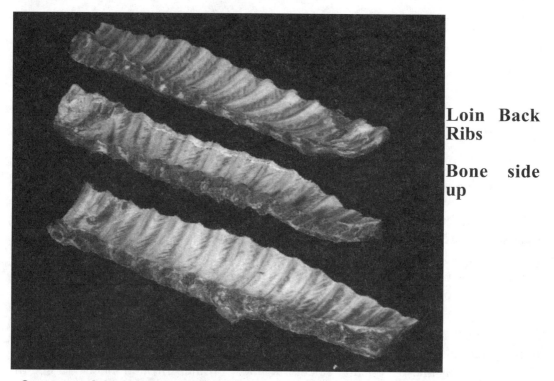

Loin Back Ribs

Bone side up

From the illustration of pork bones on page 28, one can observe that the loin back comes from the part of the rib bone nearest the back bone. The adjoining meat is the loin from which the pork chop is cut. When the loin section is separated from the rib bone to become a boneless pork loin, loin back ribs remain. Then the trendy loin ribs are merchandised as "baby backs," often at prices higher than than of the tender, delicious, versatile boneless, pork loin.

Whole pork loins, with the bone-in **almost always** sell for less than the loin back rib bone! So with a little effort one can buy the whole, separate out the bones to serve those into faddish foods and have the tender loin as a bonus.

Barbecued Pig Feet

Only the more adventurous, or those interested the experiencing some of the historical dishes of barbecue, are likely to barbecue pig feet, and this is unfortunate. Pig feet and the tough spare rib were most often those parts of the hog which were apportioned to black folk who often did the actual barbecuing.

Spare ribs, taken northward by those who had learned to transform these throw- away parts into tender and delicious barbecue, became an instant success wherever they were presented. Pig feet, somehow, just didn't get the same respect. That doesn't mean that they are not still rendered tender and delicious in back yards across northern urban America as well as in the South. And, among those who know, gnawing on a barbecued pig knuckle is at least rewarding as nibbling on a rib.

For the bold of spirit, the pork trotter offers an interesting, and cheaper, alternative to the barbecued spare rib. To experience them, try the following:

Barbecued Pork Trotters

Select 5-10 lbs. of split pig feet. They should require no trimming or preparation – they have already had their feet washed.

Sprinkle with a rub from the "Rub" section and choose a basting sauce that will agree with the rub.

Fire the grill for barbecuing – around 200-210 °. When the grill is ready, baste with the basting sauce and put on the grill. Turn and baste until tender — about 3 hours. Reduce the temperature and baste with the finishing sauce which you have chosen from the sauce section.

Enjoy a bit of history while tasting good barbecue.

Barbecued Pork Ham

True hams and ham steaks, cured or fresh, from the hind quarter, are not preferred candidates for barbecuing for a couple of reasons. Barbecuing serves best as a cooking technique when it can be used to render out fat, which bastes as it melts or to cook tough cuts of meat long enough for the connective tissue to soften. Ham and ham parts, have very little interspersed fat within the muscles. The fat that they have is rather dense and located in ridges and seams between the muscles or on the exterior. Hams are much larger than the pork butt and shoulder and, therefore, take considerably longer to barbecue. Perhaps the most telling reason is that hams roast more quickly and, prepared that way, are tender and delicious.

If you choose to barbecue a ham or ham steaks, I recommend a basting sauce with oil content. The ham will take 12-18 hours to barbecue — about 50 % more time than a shoulder or butt.

I heartily recommend taking a cured ham, water injected and all, and cooking it in a smoky atmosphere at hot smoking temperature (170-190° maximum) for a couple of days to turn it into a delectable dish, by itself or as a flavoring meat. This is covered in more detail in the **Hot Smoking** Chapter.

This simple, economical pit constructed of concrete blocks can easily handle a whole hog or a dozen butts and racks of ribs. The cover is cheap but practical. The hinge allows half the pit to be opened.

If the blocks are not cemented, the pit can be constructed and removed within a short period of work.

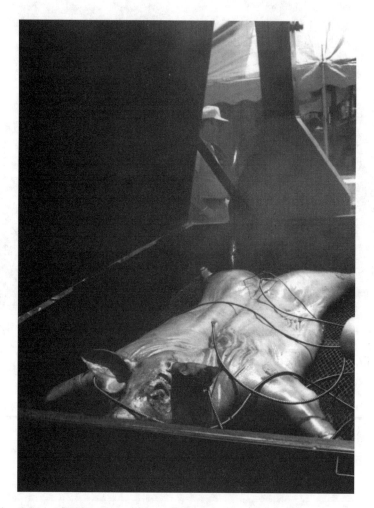

A wired hog! With the price of thermometers with remote probing drop-ping into the reasonable price range, using several will provide accurate informa-tion of temperature differences. This allow the barbecuer to move hot coals around as needed. The hams will cook slowest with the shoulders next. The trick is to get both ends done without drying out the loins and ribs.

Barbecued Chicken

Or "Bye, Bye Blackbird . . . !"

In popularity on the grill, chicken closely follows hotdogs and hamburgers. Unfortunately, there have been more chickens blackened, in the name of barbecue, than all the red fish in the world. Then there are those that produce chicken so greasy that you could lubricate a fleet of Volkswagens for a year on the excess oil. The problem, of course, has been bad information put out by magazine food editors and promoted by advertisements for barbecue finishing sauces.

Anytime I see a television commercial where meat is being cooked in flames, I know it is a product of flaming fools. When they show chicken flung on a hot grill and quickly covered in catsup confection, it is obvious that they are completely ignorant of grilling. Therefore, I never buy any product whose producers are so ignorant of its purpose. If they don't know how to use it, how in the dickens can they expect to create a useful, desirable product.

Looking back, it was the "if's" that did it. *If* he hadn't been so sincerely, god-awfully incompetent, I would probably never have been aroused to help. *If* he had not been such a close and longtime friend, I would never have even looked past the first couple of book stores. *If* there had just been one semi-competent book on the subject....

As it was, my good friend and boyhood buddy, drug the frigid fowl fresh from the 'fridge and fervently flung it on his flaming gas grill. He promptly soused it with one of the 457 varieties of commercial confections of catsupy "barbecue sauces"— pasteurized, homogenized, Bowdlerized, bastardized and advertised.

Naturally it came off the grill with all the taste, texture and appearance of a generic charcoal briquette, catalyzed and cauterized with caramelized sugary tomato paste. The inside was barely warm enough to support normal bacterial life. It was "Black on the outside, red in the middle"— the traditional American burnt offering to the false gods of advertising.

While I fortunately had the experience to ignore the Machiavellian machinations of the malevolent misanthropes merchandising their mess by misinformation and misleading television advertisements, I could see that my Ol' buddy, and millions like him, had been hoodwinked. His recipe and technique came directly from the television commercials.

Determined to help him out of this catacomb of cremated carcasses, I sought to buy a competent book of the subject of barbecuing. Surprise turned to dismay and then to disgust as I vainly searched for any competent coverage of the subject. Books were either the soothless, self-serving sentiments of manufacturers or the garrulous, egregious gushing of juvenile journalists glorifying any melange mismanaged on a grill.

Except for these "if's," I probably would never have written *The Great American Barbeque Instruction Book* and, therefore, might be gainfully employed in some more traditional occupation, with neat and regular hours — and paychecks.

Anyhow, that's why I rarely ever barbecue chicken. That and the fact that there is still so much badly barbecued chicken that, if we stopped cooking now, piled it all in one place and set it on fire, it would burn longer than the sun. But, I suppose as long as there are chickens and would- be barbecuers, there will be barbecued chicken.

Barbecuing chicken is about as easy as making instant coffee. You have to work harder to mess it up than to do it right. It could be downright boring if you let it. But the difference between a pretty good and a master barbecuer is how he enjoys his spare time. Barbecuing chicken allows real opportunities for fun time.

Several misconceptions about cooking on a grill congregate and combine at chicken- cooking time. Chicken can be roasted, broiled, barbecued or smoked on a grill — if the grill is suitable and the temperature is right for each activity. Broiling requires constant attention, frequent turning and no sweet sauces until it is done. Most beginners try to barbecue at broiling temperatures and, like my Ol' buddy, put the finishing sauce on too soon.

Barbecuing takes a longer time, but much less attention at the grill. Properly done, it is so easy that your brow should never moisten on even the hottest day. And, without some other entertaining activity, it is so boring it will put you to sleep.

Because chicken parts are quite different in coloration, tenderness and inherent fat, it behooves us to discuss poultry parts a bit. Meat of the thigh and legs of the chicken is darker than the meat of the breast and wings. The reason is that the leg and thigh muscles are used much more than the breast and wing muscles of domestic fowl and, therefore, contain more hemoglobin. Leg and thigh meat also contains much more fat than breasts and wings, so they take a little longer to cook, but are less likely to dry out quickly like the leaner white meat.

Because of the characteristics of the meat, I prefer to barbecue the thighs and legs and broil the breast meat. That, however, is a matter of choice. Just be aware of the differences. First, let's do the whole bird.

Barbecued Chicken

Choose about three fresh, plump, tender fryers. If you don't know how, ask your butcher to cut them into quarters. (My video shows how to do the chore in less than a half minute per chicken.) Trim the fat and remove the skin. On a chicken, the skin has most of the fat. Skin gets in the way of the flavoring and slips off with all the seasoning and sauce when you are trying to eat it. However, if you remove the skin, you must baste in order to keep the chicken from drying out. This is not like roasting when the crisp, crunchy skin rendered of fat is a delicacy not to be missed.

Basting Sauce

Throw the skin, fat and trimmings into a pot, add

1	large, chopped onion
2	cloves garlic
2	stalks chopped celery
1	chopped carrot
1 t.	thyme
1	bay leaf
	salt and pepper

Cover with water and simmer 20-30 minutes as a minimum.

Dip off some of the fat (let your heart be your guide) and pour up the liquid — about 2 cups. Make up any shortage with apple juice and add:

1/2 C.	Worcestershire
1/2 C.	apple cider vinegar

Or you can just follow the directions on the container of "Smoky's Legendary Basting Seasoning." Baste the chicken quarters and let them dry.

Baste again when the grill is ready. Put them on and close the grill. Use a mild smoke, if any. Maintain the temperature between 200 and 225º ; baste and turn every 20-30 minutes. Keep the basting sauce warm.

Finishing Sauce

1- 6 oz. can	tomato paste
1 1/2 C	water
1/2 C.	Worcestershire sauce
1/2 C.	vinegar
4 T.	unsalted butter or mild olive oil

Mix well and simmer until desired consistency. Then add

2T.	brown sugar
1/4t.	ground cloves

Adjust sweet/tart taste. Salt if desired.

After about 3 1/2 hours, the chicken should be approaching done. The breast quarters will cook faster than the thigh quarters and, therefore, may need to be moved to a cooler part of the grill to prevent overcooking. Check the interior of the largest thigh with your handy thermometer. When it registers about 150°, reduce the heat and begin basting with the finishing sauce thinned with a little of the basting sauce. Pour the finishing sauce into the remaining basting sauce — rather than adding some of the basting sauce to the finishing sauce. This eliminates any possibility of transferring any unbarbecued bacteria into the final sauce. Continue to baste as long as you are enjoying it and the troops can stand it.

Serve the warm finishing sauce on the side at the table for those who feel the urge.

Now you know why burnt offerings went out of style.

Winging It

It always amazes me how a fad like the *Hula Hoop* or *Pet Rock* can sweep the nation faster than the jet stream— but, what do I know? Chicken wings have been around at least as long as chickens, but just lay there on the plate until they were christened "Buffalo Wings!" Then chicken wings flew out of the closet.

Fact is, at least 98% of chicken wings cooked on a grill are broiled or roasted. That's fine. They are tender, covered by an oily skin and can be prepared deliciously at either temperature. The only rational reason to barbecue chicken (or turkey) wings for the longer period at lower temperature is because you are going to be cooking that long anyhow.

Wings, like sausage, will cook more quickly than larger pieces of meat and can be used to furnish a sort of continuous grazing for the guests— keep up the cook's strength as well. Since, wings have such a definite place in the scheme of things, I've included a couple of variations for barbecuing. Remember that you can pick up the tempo and cook them at higher temperatures if the situation warrants. And, if you are going to take the time to do wings, do lots of them. Left overs can be frozen and rewarmed for quick snacks that even the little finicky eaters will devour.

Icarus Wings

5-8 lbs. of chicken wings — look them over carefully to make certain that they are not bruised, discolored. If the tips are still attached, clip for the stock pot.

16oz.	Kraft Zesty Italian Salad Dressing
2 C.	water
1 t.	Tabasco sauce or Louisiana hot pepper sauce. Double if children and other tender mouths aren't present and add a dash or two of ground cayenne.

salt and pepper

Mix well and pour 1/4 of the mixture into a stainless bowl. Dip the wings into the sauce on their way to the grill. Warm the remainder and baste the wings as needed.

Tend the wings as you husband the other food on the grill, moving them out of heat's way as needed. When the meat begins to separate and slide from the bone, they are done. You may have to sample a few of them to make certain. When they are, it's time to apply the finishing sauce.

Winging It Finishing Sauce

1 C.	catsup
1 C.	prepared Mustard
2 T.	Worcestershire Sauce
1 T.	Louisiana hot sauce

apple juice to thin to desired consistency

Simmer and mix well.

If these don't fly to your fancy, pick out another sauce from the seasonings section and take another spin.

Mark Haggitt's Chili Lime Wings

5 lbs.	chicken wings, top joint only.
1 C.	lime juice
1	small (4oz) can of peeled and diced green chilies
2 T.	granulated garlic or 2 cloves minced
2 1/2 T.	paprika
2 T.	salt
1 T.	sugar
1 T.	lemon-pepper
1 T.	soy sauce
1/4 C.	vegetable oil

Puree the chilies in a food processor or blender. Mix all ingredients in a bowl. Marinate for 2 to 3 hours only. Grill wings, basting with left over marinade.

"Like 'em spicy? Add a tablespoon of cayenne, although I generally add only a teaspoon to allow for differences in the love of heat."

Mark, of Nashville, TN, is a good friend and a serious contender on the barbecue contest circuit.

Building a Better Barbecued Brisket

Julius Caesar is credited with writing, during his foray into Gaul, *"Boves est omnis divisa in partes tres."* Translated, that reads, "The cow (as a whole) is divided into three parts."

While he did not elucidate, anyone reasonably familiar with a cow carcass will understand clearly that the front end of a cow is made for roping, the hind end is for branding and the middle part is for cooking on a grill.

The brisket comes from the roping part.

Brisket, corned, cured, simmered with proper seasonings and sliced thinly across the grain is magnificent as the essential basis for a Reuben sandwich and, thus prepared, has also brought comfort and sustenance to multitudes as the prime constituent of corned beef hash. But, only those severely challenged would *twice* cook a brisket on a grill.

Inherent kindness precludes my further characterizing "challenged." The discerning will note that I did not modify challenged with "intellectually" or "gastronomically." However challenged, Texans seem to consider barbecuing brisket over mesquite weed as a test of manhood.

Many have wondered how, in the bastion of beefdom, this tough, stringy candidate for the corning crock came to be so revered. My personal opinion is that, in the distant past, creative Texans, looking to find some use for two eminently discardable items, started trying to sell tenderfeet and pilgrims on the idea of cooking the unmarketable brisket with the noxious weed mesquite, thereby ridding the state of two undesirables. Gullible Yankees, reared on boiled dinners and lacking a basis for comparison, considered it edible and began to call for it when they came to town. Texans, therefore, were forced into actually using the dubious duo. Then, like a "horse that couldn't be rode," the challenge of cooking a chewable brisket found many takers. Thus, as the pits were passed to new generations, rendering a brisket edible became a rite of passage: a challenge that could not be refused.

53

In any case, since this doubtful dish has become almost as widespread as kudzu, I am compelled to discuss how to make the most out of a bad situation. I barbecued my first whole beef about 50 years ago. As I recall, then, even the short ribs were gnawed clean before the brisket was attacked.

Bob Lyon, Sage of the Sasquatch, retired from teaching English and reclaimed his youth in outdoor cooking. Debuting in a chili contest in Terlingua, TX, he discovered barbecue. He went back home to Seattle and co-founded the Pacific Northwest Barbecue Association, which he serves as executive secretary and, among other activities, is the Pacific Northwest correspondent for the Kansas City Barbeque Society publication, *The Bull Sheet,* and for the *National Barbecue News*.

He became intrigued, fixated even, on the ritual of the brisket. In a rash moment, he even challenged the Commissioner of the International Barbecue Society, Texas hill country resident, John Raven, to a brisket barbecue, *mano a mano*, near Terlingua, TX, in the town of Welfare. Many briskets later, Bob says, "Every brisket is an adventure."

Bob's cooking team, Beaver Castors, has competed and won in national and international cooking contests. Jim Erickson, chief cook of the Beaver Castors, has won first place in several prestigious state and international contests in brisket— even when handicapped by using borrowed grills. He attributes his successes to choosing the brisket, using good technique and, in competitions, cooking several to choose from.

Choosing the Better Brisket

The brisket comes from the chest/breast area of a cow— the roping end. It is two alternating layers of muscle and fat. The two layers of meat are separate, but not equal: one is thicker and wider. When the brisket is observed with the fat layer on the bottom, the upper layer of meat is interspersed with strings of fat which do not render out during cooking. In restaurants, this layer is normally chopped with a little of the trimmings of the lower layer for chopped brisket sandwiches. The lower layer, although less fatty, also has streaks of fat— the size and shape of which offer some indication of how it will cook. Thick, ropy strands of marbling will probably yield a tougher product from a cut already fabled for toughness. Choose, instead, briskets with more slender, consistent streaks of marbling fat.

There seems to be a consensus that, all things being equal, flexibility is an indication of potential for tenderness. The exercise goes this way: Pick up the brisket, grasping it in the center. The more the ends droop, the more tender it is likely to be. Remember that tenderness, in the case of brisket, is a relative term. Do not for one moment, delude yourself into thinking that a limber brisket is a tender brisket. Compare briskets of similar size and temperature for the closest approximation of accuracy. Don't bet the ranch on any of them.

Jim Erickson rightfully points out, "Don't pay extra for prime grade." Prime only means that there is more fat marbled in. The brisket is already overly endowed with interspersed fat. Jim does advocate using a "certified" beef and his success lends credence to that belief. Charlie McMurrey, Jr., pitmaster as well as web master of *Barbecue'n on the Internet,* believes that buying at a butcher shop rather than a supermarket gives him an edge in finding a less tough brisket.

The brisket is a big triangular piece of meat, thicker at the apex. This end is called the *point cut* or the *nose* by those who get pumped up by using jargon. The straight, thinner, flatter end is called the *flat cut.* If you want to one-up them, point out that the deckle has been removed. The deckle is a slab of hard fat and tough meat on the inside of the brisket which should be removed to qualify as a "Beef Brisket, Deckle Off, Boneless" by the North American Meat Processors Association (NAMP). The point cut and the flat cut are two muscles seperated by a layer of fat. Briskets can bought whole, which includes the point and flat, of the muscles can be bought seperately as point cut or flat cut.

If you are serious, which is in itself a fault and likely to make the meat tougher, get more than one brisket. After they are done, choose the most tender for contests and guests whom you wish to impress. You can chop the other for sand-wiches or grease the axles on the chuck wagon.

The shape of the brisket is more an indicator of cooking time than weight is. A chunky 8 lb. brisket 5" thick will take longer to cook than a long, slender 10 pounder. Select a 10-12 pounder with a good 1/2" minimum layer of fat on the bottom side.

Preparation

Remember, "Every brisket is an adventure." After you have selected what appears to be the best available, it's trimming time. Trim the hump of fat from the pointy, nose end. This side will be on the bottom during cooking; the external fat will not do any basting and may actually interfere with seasoning. Don't bother with the fat layer on the other side. Tidy up by trimming off the thinnest parts and trim the fat off the sides.

Bring to meat to room temperature, regardless of what the beef people's representatives say or what the safe- food freaks cry. Warmed, the meat will absorb flavor more readily and that will reduce the cooking time. Check the internal tem-perature and record it in the rare chance that you may want to do this again.

"Aye, there's the rub..."

There is much ado about rubs. (It's hard to get away from Billy Bob Shake-speare when you write about grilling.) A rub is just a mixture of seasonings and has much less influence on the final result than rub club rooters would admit — even if they knew

Seasoning for any meat should complement the meat's natural flavor, not overpower it. We value meat, as the price reflects, for its taste and texture as well as a prime source of protein. It is illogical, therefore, to over- season, over- smoke and over- cook. Of course, it is difficult to over-cook the brisket.

I am amazed at the range of ingredients considered to be proper for a brisket rub. Salt is an essential ingredient because it serves as a conductor of flavors. Salt enters the meat by osmosis and can carry along certain flavors, but no externally administered flavors will penetrate very far into the meat — especially through that layer of fat. Chili powder, cumin and oregano are, in my opinion, more aptly used in chili and other Tex-Mex dishes. Sugar belongs in the dessert course and only a sissy would use a tenderizer.

Over the years, I have found a simple mixture that seems to bring out the best in beef without any off notes of taste and it doesn't over power the beef flavor.

Basic Brisket Rub

Mix thoroughly:

1 C.	salt,
1/4 C. each	garlic and onion powder
2 T. each	ground thyme, ground bay, black pepper, celery seed and Hungarian paprika.

Using this as you would for proper saltiness, rubbing it into the brisket a few minutes before it goes on the grill. Use this as a starter and build your own to suit your taste.

When a rub with salt as a significant ingredient is put on meat, the salt begins to draw moisture from it. That's why salt is used in curing processes. Moisture is very important in the cooking mechanism. Water conducts heat much more readily than dry tissue. It follows, therefore, that the longer you can retain moisture in the meat, the quicker the heat will be conducted from the exterior to the interior. Therefore, get the meat on the grill rather soon after salting. Getting the inside done before the outside is burnt to a brick-like texture is the secret to successful barbecuing.

ACT III

Cooking a brisket is a long-term relationship— longer than some marriages. Producing a better brisket requires 8-18 hours at consistent temperature with minimal smoke exposure. You can roast a brisket at 350° in a couple of hours, but the result would challenge a pit bull's jaw muscles. Cooking temperatures in the 200-215° range are most likely to bring a brisket to its optimum potential. This traditional temperature range for barbecuing is a result of centuries of trial and error. Brisket would actually be more tender if cooked at below 200°, but the time on the grill goes up drastically.

Smoke blowers need to comprehend that a little smoke applied over 10-12 hours accumulates to an excess. There are only two fuels for properly barbequing a brisket: wood coals and charcoal. Flaming wood produces tars, phenols, cresols and other noxious products. For a century, until EPA banned it, cresol was the active ingredient in sheep dip. It is my studied opinion that anyone who can tolerate to eat over-smoked meat probably has some sheep herder in his ancestory. Only confirmed Lysol freaks would enjoy the phenol flavor. Both cresols and phenols are known carcinogens.

Those who have cooked, burning wood in an offset firebox, may have, unwittingly, been saved by the placement of the exhaust vent. Where the vent exits from the top of the cooking chamber, the hottest gasses go out first. The meat, resting on the grill below, doesn't get as contaminated with the vile products of combustion.

Don't sweat the "smoke ring." The ring of color grading from dark on the outside to a pale pink deeper into the meat is not really a smoke ring at all. It is a chemical reaction of the meat's constituents. The depth of color depends more upon the moisture of the meat than upon the density of smoke. It has no bearing on flavor and is only important to smoke blowers. Next time you eat Chinese, check the "smoke" ring in the roast pork, which has never even had a passing flirtation with real smoke.

Build a proper bed of coals by burning down sufficient wood or charcoal to bring the whole grill up to 350°; then shut down the air intake to reduce the temperature down to 225°. Put on the briskets, fat side up and close the lid. Check in 20 minutes to see if the temperature has stabilized around 210° — if it hasn't, make adjustments in the air intake. If it has, go find something interesting to do.

How often you need to check the grill depends on the grill. If you are working with a small kettle grill, you may need to replenish the coals and move the brisket frequently. If you have properly heated and stoked a massive iron sidewinder, it may maintain its temperature for four hours and will require less frequent, if any, turning.

"What about the water pan?" Tell me that you are joking! A water pan in a closed grill is, at minimum, a gross waste of fuel. It takes more heat to boil a gallon of water than it does to cook a 10lb. roast to 180 degrees. And what do you get in return? "Nothing of value." The water pan was introduced by manufacturers of dinky little tin can cookers, without air flow control, as a means of controlling the temperature. As long as there is water in the pan, the temperature will not exceed the boiling point of water. It is only useful for those who cannot control the temperature of their grill. Barbecuing is cooking meat in dry heat. Water has no place in grilling until wash up time.

We may as well discuss that other grilling abomination, aluminum foil. Anybody who cooks his brisket wrapped in aluminum foil, probably puts catsup on his steak— after he has cooked it "well done!" At barbecue cook-offs in parts of the country, aluminum foil is known as the "Texas crutch." Aluminum foil is a crutch for those who over-smoke and over-cook at excessive temperatures. After hermetically sealing the damaged goods in aluminum foil, the abused brisket is *braised* (cooked enclosed with moisture) to try to retain moisture and tenderness. Is this barbecue? Absolutely not! Is this grilling? Certainly not! What, other than the thickness of the container, is the difference in heavy duty aluminum foil and a pressure cooker? Pot roast— pure and simple!!

This bit of chicanery is now euphemized among its practitioners as "steeping." Maybe they should call it "Texas tea" and bring out the doilies and crumpets! To the experienced taster, braised brisket has the same texture as pot roast, which it is, and loses much of its natural flavor. I find nothing wrong, however, with a back yard barbecuer wrapping his completely cooked brisket in aluminum foil to hold it until serving time.

After about 8 hours, check the internal temperature of the briskets with a bimetal thermometer. Most beef is edible after 125°— for a fine steak— but the troublesome brisket needs to get as close to 185° as you can stand. At that temperature, most of the interspersed fat has melted and mellowed the surrounding tissue into a reasonable facsimile of tenderness. Paul Kirk, Baron of Barbeque, teaches grilling around the countryside. He says that he tests for tenderness by inserting his thermometer probe laterally into the brisket. If it enters and exits easily, he considers it ready to remove.

The Finale

Even after the extra effort in selection, the trimming and seasoning and the long- term cooking process, the brisket demands still more than any rational fare for the grill. It still must be sliced in a particularly peculiar fashion in order to be rendered edible.

I am no slouch with a blade, but when I watched Texas native, Charlie McMurrey, Jr., dissect a brisket at a cook-off in Cookeville, TN, I recognized immediately that I was in the presence of a master brisketeer.

First, he removes the fat from the top side— that is the side that was on top during cooking. Then, starting on the flat end of the opposite side, he starts through that layer of meat, continuing slicing toward the nose end until reaching the internal layer of fat. He removes the fat separating the two layers of meat, separates and sets the top meat layer aside. The grain in this layer runs differently from the bottom layer and brisket needs to be cut across the grain to be chewable. It is instructive, at this point, to look closely at the directions of the grain.

He continues trimming and scraping away the fat. Then he places the top layer on the bottom— with the grains of both aligned. He is able, then, to slice both layers thinly across the grain.

Brisket begins to dry quickly, so have everything else ready to serve and serve it quickly.

At this point, the meat is ready for the finishing sauce — if you choose to use one.

Finishing Sauce

A finishing sauce is optional, but a simple one for a starting place is:

1Qt.	**catsup**
6 oz.	**prepared mustard**
3 T.	**apple cider vinegar**
1/3 C.	**Worcestershire sauce**
3 T.	**brown sugar**
1	**lemon, juice of**
1/2 lb.	**butter, unsalted**
1/2 t.	**salt**
1/2 t.	**black pepper**
1/4t.	**ground cloves**

Simmer until well blended.

Serve with ice cold Lone Star or a hefty Burgundy.

The absolute treasure of this whole exercise is that, once you have done it, you have nothing left to prove and you never, ever have to cook a brisket on the grill again! On, now, to the good and tender stuff! Hmm. . . . Rib roasts, sirloin roasts, pork loins . . . !!!

Barbecued Beef Chuck

The beef chuck— front shoulder— is tasty, tender, versatile and economical. It is one of the few cuts of meat that is equally desirable for cooking in moist heat— pot roasting— and in dry heat— grilling. It is tender enough for shish ka-babs, tasty enough for fajitas, the prime source of ground meat for burgers and it is my favorite cut of beef for barbecuing. Once you have barbecued a chuck, or tasted barbecued chuck, you will wonder why anyone having a choice would choose to barbecue brisket instead.

On the West Coast, especially California, where meat is butchered in the Mediterranean style— separated by musculature— the chuck, also called the *clod* or *shoulder clod*, and the parts thereof are shaped and named differently than they would be in the rest of the U.S. Elsewhere, the English style of butchering dominates, and the chuck (shoulder) is separated *square* cut. You sort of need to know that to know what to look for in your locale.

By either style of butchering, the beef chuck contains the first five ribs and therefore contains the same loin muscle which forms the rib roast, rib steak, T-bone, Porterhouse and Sirloin steaks. Called the loin or backstrap, the *longis-simus dorsi* (longest muscle) is a prized part of the beef carcass. It is even more delicious when you buy it boneless at $1.29 a pound when rib steak is $6.99.

In California, the Boneless Cross Rib roast is comprised mostly of the loin and other tender muscles. In the rest of the country, the Chuck Eye Roast is almost all loin and the Boneless Chuck Roast can have the loin muscle as its centerpiece — the closer to the rib section, the larger this muscle will be. The farther from the rib section, the smaller the loin muscle and the tougher the chuck comes. Some other muscles are beautiful but firm. Not quite tender enough for broiling, but a fine piece of meat for barbecuing.

Selection

This is a time when your knowledge of the muscle structure of a beef is really handy. If you are sort of lacking in this area, call the meat market manager or an assistant out for some advice. Most are pleased and flattered that you consult them. If this one isn't, find another place to buy your meat. (Regardless of what you may have heard, my close relationship with my meat market manager has nothing to do with the fact that she is an attractive young woman.) Get the meat person to help you choose a large chuck roast, or if there is not an 8-12 pounder that you like the looks of, ask them to cut one for you. The roast should be at least 3" thick – although you can barbecue a 2-2 1/2" by keeping the temperature low and paying attention so as not to overcook.

Preparation

Trim any exposed membrane, muscle covering, (fell), clumps of fat. Everything exposed that isn't desirable to eat should be cut away. Then, if you are into rubs, rub it with one that you select from the "**Seasonings**" Chapter. Don't do it too long before putting the meat on the grill or it will begin to draw moisture out. If you intend to baste, choose a basting sauce and baste once and let it dry; then baste again before putting it on the grill.

At the Grill

Fire the grill to maintain 200-220° for 5-8 hours. Burn down as much wood and charcoal as your fire box will hold; then reduce the air intake to lower the temperature to the desired range. Plan a fire pit for replenishing the coals. If you are using a gas or electric grill for *faux* barbecue, add wood, wood chips or sawdust in either a smoker box or wrapped in aluminum foil pierced with a few holes. Wait until the smoke starts billowing before adding the meat. One load of wood ought to provide adequate smoke flavor— don't be guilty of over smoking.

If basting, and I recommend that you do, keep the surface moist with the basting sauce. Move swiftly, understanding the open pit will lose heat very quickly.

After about 3 hours, test the internal temperature of the roast with a thermometer probe. The fact is that, anytime after the internal temperature has reached 145°, the chuck roast is imminently edible. It will be a little pink in the middle, juicy and tender. However, you can continue cooking until it reaches 180° at which point it will be thoroughly barbecued to maximum doneness. If you have not dried it out, the texture will be very soft and the taste will be quite different from a medium- rare piece of beef.

As you approach the last half hour of cooking, apply a finishing sauce of your choice that joins well with the rub or basting sauce.

When the roast is ready, remove to a cutting board, slice it thinly and serve on a warm plate. A couple of finishing sauces at the table will allow everyone who wants to experiment.

Visit with the meat markets in your area and talk with knowledgeable meat market personnel to see the variety of cuts available from the beef shoulder. Experiment and experience really good flavors and textures at economical prices.

Beef carcass showing shoulder and chuck at the upper left

Barbecued Goat

"There is no accounting for taste," somebody said. And except for tradition, habit and availability, people's choice and/or exclusion of certain foods are amazing.

Granted that Eskimos enjoy whale blubber because "it's there," and it provides a heavy-duty calorie count. The Masai of Kenya take delight, not only in the taste, of their dish of fresh cow's blood and curdled milk but, also, in the extreme convenience of a movable four-footed, fast-food factory. Neither of these delicate dishes are likely to enjoy the phenomenally popular appeal of pizza.

On the other hand, there are certain foods which, for religious and other irrational reasons, are taboo. Pork ribs will never please the palate of the Orthodox Jew nor the true-believing Muslim. Hindus are horrified by a hindquarter of beef and vegetarians view even veal verboten.

Some things we don't normally eat because they are not readily available. Some are a little strange to the provincial palate. I can understand a natural reticence to eat the first raw oyster or savor the first snail, but I really don't understand America's aversion to the thought of a tender goat as a savory source of sustenance.

Lamb, mutton, calf and veal are no strangers to the average supermarket meat coolers. Recipes are readily available and widely used. In other cultures, the goat is a highly prized piece of protein. Nowhere is he forbidden food. Suddenly goat is rapidly gaining popularity in the U.S. and not only among those newly arrived.

The goat can flourish on fodder that would starve a sheep, that could not support one cow per square mile. The goat is a more efficient converter of food to protein than is the beef. Like venison and other game, the goat has little fat and is, therefore, healthier for our plump population.

But by far the most important consideration is that goat tastes good. Properly prepared and cooked, it is tender and delicious with a mild flavor that favorably compares with venison and grass-fed beef.

Barbecued goat on the 4th of July has been an old favorite in my family long enough to be a hallowed tradition. Unsuspecting guests of narrow minds and delicate constitutions have devoured it with gusto and subsequently denied their actions to the snickering cognoscenti.

In the Southwest and in Mexico, roast kid (young goat), called cabrito, is a favored festival food, and we have included a recipe for cabrito in the Roasting section. Goat makes fantastic jerky and chili and constitutes the basis for many a delicious dish.

The two main obstacles to good goat are mental hangups and lack of a conveniently available supply except in areas of the U. S. which have a substantial Latino population. If you can overcome the first, the second is an insignificant hill to climb. Goat is becoming much more widely available and almost any full-fledged meat market can fill your request for a young goat. Kids should weigh in, dressed, at 7-10 pounds each; young goat will weigh 25-35 pounds. Both are tender enough for roasting. Full-grown goats on the grill should be barbecued to assure tenderness, but young goats make fine barbecue, as well. If you live in a rural area, and are up to the chore, you can butcher your own goat— just follow the instructions for venison in the **Game** section of the **Meat** chapter— or have it done by the supplier.

Having settled the question of supply, when you acquire the goat meat bring it to room temperature while you inspect and give a final cleaning. I prefer to separate the carcass by removing the two front shoulders and the rear hams, then splitting the back bone and cutting each side into manageable chunks. Remove the skirt and separate out the spare ribs. Those parts will cook faster than the rest. Now we are all set to put it on the grill.

But first, some considerations of the meat. Goat meat is lean, like venison and other game. Therefore, it needs oil, along with the slow cooking to render it tender. I recommend an appropriate basting sauce to help the process along. Let's get started.

Barbecued Goat

Basting Sauce

1	large onion, chopped
2	cloves garlic, peeled and crushed
1 pt.	water
1 pt.	corn oil – substitute as you like
1 pt.	apple cider vinegar
8 oz.	beef stock or bouillon
8 oz.	Worcestershire sauce
4 T.	salt
1 T.	black pepper
1 t.	red pepper

Saute onion, add garlic and cook until clear. Add other ingredients and bring to a boil, then remove and allow to cool.

Mop down the meat with the sauce and let it dry. Just before putting the meat on the grill, give it a second coat. Continue basting at 15 minute intervals in the beginning and thereafter as needed to keep the surface moist.

Barbecuing at around 200º, the ribs will be done in about 4 hours, and all the goat should be done in less than 8 hours. The choice of a finishing sauce is up to you. You can serve the meat with or without. If you choose to use a finishing sauce, select one from the Finishing Sauce section and baste with it near the end of the cooking time.

If this is the first time that you have tried goat, I predict that you will be pleasantly amazed.

"Oh, Baloney!"

If I told you that you have been passing by a cheap meat that is boneless, nearly fat-free, no waste, put-it-on-the-grill-and-leave-it easy, adored by children, absolutely delicious and guaranteed to be a piece de conversation as well as a piece de resistance, you'd probably say, "Baloney!"

Well, you'd be phonetically correct. But, while baloney expresses a rejection of nonsense, bologna is surprisingly tasty on the grill.

I was introduced to barbecued bologna, several years ago, at the Big Pig Jig in Vienna, GA, by the team from Firehouse Number 5 of Tulsa, OK. Until that time, in my opinion, nothing more deserved the epithet that its homonym expressed. Beside that it always made me burp. So it was out of a selfless act of kindness and a keen sense of duty that I sacrificed my body and my taste upon the altar of goodwill.

Wow, did I get a pleasant surprise. It was delicious and as burpless as a Burpee cucumber. (I have always enjoyed the irony of the fact that a Burpee rather than a burper developed the burpless cuke.)

The following year, barbecued baloney showed up in several variations at the Royal American Barbecue in Kansas City. It turned out to be a very popular treat as those who were intrigued by the idea became entranced by the flavor. Still, one six-pack does not a cookout make.

I was yet unconvinced that the lowly bologna could really cut the mustard as an all-American outdoor cooking fare. True to the code of my calling, I decided to submit it close scrutiny and extreme dissection in the pits. I am pleased to pass along the results of bologna's passing of the tests.

In general, the smaller 2-3" diameter rolls perform better than the larger 4-5" tubes. Whether purely pork or permeated with poultry, the taste and texture were about the same. Any beef parts successfully retained anonymity. Best results were obtained with slow cooking and generous garlic. Bologna is enhanced by judicious smoking, but beware of over smoking or cooking. It should still be moist and juicy.

If you want to maintain secrecy and surprise, cut the barbecued baloney into cubes, wedges or anything but typical slices and serve it up with toothpicks and a little barbecue (finishing) sauce. For children, any swiftly served shape suffices.

Barbecued bologna is an excellent *hors d'oeuvre* to appease a mouthy, mutinous mob until the regular stuff is ready. The seasoning scenario is yet to be fully explored. Try the one below, then let your palate be your guide.

Barbecued Bologna

3-5 lbs. small bologna   whole - remove the rind.

Basting sauce:

1 C.	water
1/3 C.	apple cider vinegar
1/3 C.	Worcestershire sauce
1/8 C.	peanut oil
3 T.	granulated garlic or garlic powder
1 T.	onion powder
1 T.	Hungarian paprika
1 t.	powder thyme
1 t.	celery seed
1	bay leaf
1 t.	ground mustard seed mixed with 2 T. water
1 t.	fresh ground black pepper.

Mix and simmer gently for a couple of minutes.

Prepare the grill for barbecuing - temperature 200-225°. Use oak and hickory for smoke. Coat the baloney generously with the basting sauce and allow to dry before putting on the grill. When the coals are ready, baste again and place on the grill. Close the lid and leave for 15 to 20 minutes. Return, baste and turn and baste. Adjust temperature if required and leave again.

After about 20 minutes, return and baste. The bologna will have swelled from its original size. You may choose to make lengthwise slits about 1/4 inch deep to allow it to continue expansion and to expose more surface area to the smoke and seasonings. Baste and leave.

Continue basting and turning until done or it is required to quell a riot. Normally it is properly done in about 1 1/2 hours, but this can be contracted or expanded as you desire.

Remove, allow to cool slightly, slice to any shape you consider appropriate and serve with warmed finishing sauce of your choosing on the side.

You may find "Ah, bologna" replacing "Oh, baloney" in your vocabulary.

Barbecued Sausages

Many kinds of sausages are excellent barbecuing fare for several reasons. First and foremost, they are delicious when barbecued, but the fact that they cook so quickly, makes them doubly desirable. Cut into short links, they make handy, tasty tidbits for eager eaters and soothe the savage stomachs, growling while waiting on the big stuff.

There being almost as many different sausages as there are barbecue sauces, the choices are almost unlimited. I would exclude only summer sausages which are already dry and rather hard and those, such as boudin, which have lots of cereals in them. Even sausages, which are already smoked, benefit from slow cooking on the grill and being basted with a finishing sauce.

If you make your own sausages (See **Sausage** section), you can mix your favorite barbecue finishing sauce into the ground meat before it is stuffed. Injecting a favorite sauce into the sausage before placing on the grill is another way to get additional flavors and moisture inside. However, I've never seen turned down those just thrown on the grill and basted with an appropriate finishing sauce. Be aware, of course, that temperatures too high will char the sugars in the sauce.

The rules for successful barbecued sausages are: have enough and don't overcook and dry them out.

Chapter Four

Broiling

Broiling is what about 99% of the 84% of American families who own grills do about 98% of the time when they light up their grill. This is the technique where the grill, and the griller, excel. Not only does the high temperature sear the meat, giving it that special flavor and texture that we crave, but the drippings atomize on the coals and return to the meat as flavor bombs. When a gentle wood smoke flavor is added, the fantastic flavors meld into a comely comestible, as savory as ever graced a table. As the grill transforms mundane food into mouth-pleasing morsels, tantalizing odors assail the nostrils, exciting pleasure receptors into ecstatic anticipation, arousing jaundiced appetites to raging cravings.

In addition to the magical transmutation, broiling is so quick and easy that even a clumsy, kitchen-klutz can perform like a celebrity chef on the patio. Time in attendance is minimal— almost too short for the full enjoyment of the pleasure. A lighting of the grill, whether gas, charcoal or electric; an intriguing interlude of preparation; a swift, intense rendezvous with the torrid coals and Presto! Magic is performed.

Broiling is the youngest method of meat preparation to become popular, with good reasons. First, the meat had to be developed to a point that it would be tender enough to eat when cooked for a short time at high temperatures. Until we started penning young beeves and allowing them to stuff themselves with all the high carbohydrate and protein that they could eat in a low-activity environment, few parts of the carcass had the tenderness to be suitable for broiling. The sirloin section from a grass-fed animal is like rawhide compared to the tender succulence of a grain-fed specimen.

Tenderness, in meat, depends upon a few conditions.

Age. The younger the animal, the more tender its meat. Selective breeding and pen-feeding bring modern cattle to slaughter at a much younger age than a short time ago.

Marbling. Fat interspersed among the muscle tissues melts away, basting the meat and creating a tender and tasty meal. Wild game lacks the marbling of domestic critters, bred for generations to plump up fast on a rich diet.

Muscle. Some muscles get used more than others and, therefore, are tougher. The short tenderloin muscles are the most tender. The long, loin section, running from shoulder to hip bone, is the second tenderest muscle.

Aging of the meat. Beef is coming to the market heavier at a younger age, but the search for speed has reduced the aging period for beef. This is unfortunate because proper aging not only makes the meat more tender, but gives it a flavor that cannot be found in fresher beef. If you are serious about serving the best steaks and roasts, either find a source for aged beef or learn how to age it for another 10 - 15 days yourself. Pork gains no appreciable improvement by aging. Lamb, goat, venison and other game, however, do.

Because they are tender and benefit from swift, short cooking, fish, shell-fish and vegetables are excellent subjects for broiling on the grill.

In broiling, the object is to cook tender morsels quickly in very high temperatures to brown the crust, but leave the inside less than completely done. Broiling is best accomplished in the 450-900° range, but 1000-1200° is not too much for a fine beef or tuna steak. I am aware of no benefits from mythical temperatures in the 1800° range.

For proper broiling, it is important that the surface of the meat be dry of water and mixtures thereof. When a wet steak hits the grill, instead of searing at 500° +, it boils at 212° until the moisture is evaporated. The surface will never regain the texture and taste of a dry surface properly presented to the grill.

Some meats, and especially seafood and vegetables, need some form of an oil coating. Chicken breasts and fillets of fish will dry too quickly unless their surface is oiled. Beef, on the other hand, is denied the opportunity to reach its maximum potential flavor if oiled before broiling. The oil is a barrier, however fragile, and must be heated to transfer the heat to the meat.

A few simple precautions insure effortless success.

1. Make certain that the grill is hot enough. Most food sticks because the meat grates are not hot enough to sear the meat. You will learn from the Heat chapter that broiling depends upon radiated heat and that a small change in distance between the food and the heat makes a great difference.

2. Give the food time to release from the grate before trying to turn it. Food will let you know when it is ready to turn.

3. Fat and oils will flame when they drip into the hot coals. Be prepared to move the food out of the flames. This is much preferred to trying to spray water on the flames. So, leave enough space on the grates to move the food if necessary.

4. Put whatever wood/sawdust you intend to use for smoke flavoring on and allow it to reach full bloom before putting the food on. Expect to get most smoke flavor into the food before each side is seared.

5. Avoid sauces, seasonings, glazes, etc., which have sugars. These will burn to carbon, char at the high temperatures and produce a hard, bitter shell.

6. Don't worry the meat or yourself. Put it down and leave it alone until it is time to turn. Then, turn it and don't mess with it until it is time to turn again.

7. Don't overcook! You can always return food to the grill for more cooking. You can't uncook it! Learn how to use your thermometer, fingers and eyes to know when food is cooked enough.

8. Have everything else ready so that when the food comes off the grill, it can be served at once.

9. Pay attention. Broiling is like making love. If you can't give it all your undivided attention, let somebody else do it.

10. Relax.

In Pursuit of the Perfect Steak

The old political promise, "A chicken in every pot," is as passe' as belief in politicians' pronouncements. But one who promised "a steak on every grill" would be certain to get a hearing. Regardless of the shrieks of the dietetic set, steak continues to be one of America's favorite foods. Steak represents more than just good taste and protein. Steak is a prize, a celebration, a just reward for a job well done.

Unfortunately, the symbolism must be as important as the taste, else good meat would not be so readily overwhelmed with premature exhortations of potent seasonings, burned like a pagan offering, then doused with the likes of catsup and "steak" sauce, in a vain attempt to recapture the taste and tenderness just destroyed. The virtue of a steak is in the steak itself, not as a platform for dubious sauces.

The **less** you do to a good steak, the better it tastes. Spend your time selecting, trimming and preparing the meat rather than on condiments. My complete rules for a perfect steak are brief and simple. **1. Get a good piece of meat. 2. Don't mess it up.**

Getting the good piece of meat requires a little knowledge of what to look for and experience in where to find it. All other things being equal, beef is graded according the amount of fat interspersed within the muscle tissue. Called "marbling" because it appears like the white spots and streaks in marble stone, this interlaced fat determines the grade and tenderness, with prime being the best, having the most marbling. Most prime goes to restaurants, so you are not likely to find it in your local market. Prime is followed, in order, by "choice" and "select," each having noticeably less marbling. We will only concern ourselves with prime and choice cuts.

Even when penned up, grain fed and plumped up, only certain parts of the bovine carcass are suitable for broiling. A 1000 lb. beef will yield only about 75 lbs. of meat suitable for broiling. Only those little used, large muscles are tender enough to become suitable candidates for broiling. Although two or three more cuts may be broiled, under the right circumstances, we list only the most desirable. The rib eye or rib steak comes from the rib section. All the other cuts come from the short loin or sirloin sections, which are located between the ribs and the rump. The tenderloin is located on the interior of the loin bones, and the *longissimus dorsi* (loin muscle) lies on the exterior of the loin or rib bones.

The **rib steak**, with the rib, or the **rib eye**, less the bone, is tender and flavorful. The major muscle is the long loin muscle that continues through the short loin and sirloin sections.

Next to the rib steaks – heading toward the hind quarter — is the **strip loin steak** sometimes called **club steak**, and it lacks any part of the tenderloin. It can be bought with or without the bone.

The **T-bone,** with the obvious bone shape for which it is named must have a minimum 1/2" of the tenderloin, measured parallel to the bone, opposite from the loin.

Next to the T-bone is the **Porterhouse**, which must have at least 1.25" of tenderloin, measured parallel to the bone.

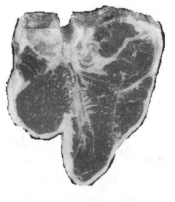

Beware of long tails on these steaks. They are fat and tough flank muscle. Not worth the price

When the tenderloin side of a porterhouse is removed, the remainder becomes a **club steak**. When meat remaining on the other side of the "T" is deboned, it becomes a **shell steak**, sometimes called a **strip steak**, with various prefixes -, i.e., **KC strip**, **NY strip**.

Most tender, and least flavorful, is the **tenderloin** from which come the filet mignon (the small end) **tenderloin steaks** and the basis of the famed dish, Chateaubriand. It has little fat interspersed and benefits from basting — after the initial searing — with butter or other oil. In some meat markets, you may see small tenderloin steaks wrapped with bacon. I wonder why one would pay $9.00 per pound for filet that tastes like $2.29 bacon.

Not quite as tender as those from the short loin, **sirloin steaks,** from the sirloin section, are large and have varying sizes and amounts and even different bones but are tender and very tasty in all shapes. The **pin bone sirloin** sits next to the porterhouse and has a piece of the tenderloin. Progressively farther away are the **flat bone sirloin**, **round bone sirloin** and **wedge bone sirloin.** One 3" thick steak can serve a crowd. **Sirloin tip** steaks are boneless, less tender but very tasty. This is where that cut most revered in Marin County, CA, the **tri-tip** comes from. The tri-tip is the *tensor fasciae latae* muscle, which is a triangular portion of the bottom sirloin butt.

All of these cuts are tender and delicious. The cuts most commonly available are tenderloin, sirloin, T-bone, rib eye and rib steak. None of these are fit for broiling, however, cut less than 1" thick. Cut 1 1/2 to 3" thick is even better. It is better to broil one large, thick steak and carve it after cooking than to portion it out into thinner pieces before grilling.

Having narrowed down the cuts, we focus on selection of the individual steak or steaks, to identify the meat with the best features. Unless vacuum-packed, the meat should be a consistent bright, light red color. Vacuum-packed meat will have a dark color with "bluish" tinge, but will turn red when exposed to air. The white marbling should be generously distributed throughout, and the flecks and lines should be fine, rather than thick. Thick, heavy marbling will produce a tougher steak, with a fatty taste, because the marbling will not properly melt out. The finer the marbling, the more tender the steak.

Get acquainted with the meat market manager, the butcher, or whoever is in charge. Let them know that you are a griller/ barbecuer, and intend to buy greater than normal quantities of good meat, and that you would like for him to have your business. Solicit his help, "Do you have any T-bones with a little finer marbling?" Bring him samples of your finished product, a bottle of wine for the holidays or other suitable gifts in recognition of his efforts.

Get to know those who stock the display cases. Speak to them— compliment their efforts. Then, when you look thoroughly throughout the case and do not find a suitable piece of meat, feel free to ask if they have any not yet displayed. Don't accept what is available unless it meets your criteria and, should the necessity arise, ask when they receive the next shipment, or politely advise them that you will come back another day. Do not hesitate to have them cut, after your inspection and approval, steaks to your desired thickness.

For adults with normal appetites, allow 10-12 ounces each of store-trimmed steaks and 14-16 ounces of steak with bone. For serious eaters, provide 25% more. Bring home the steaks and store in the 'fridge. Remove all catsup, steak sauce, teriyaki sauce, etc., from the premises, lest they taint the meat.

Regardless of what the "Beef People's" representatives and the USDA say, beef should be brought to room temperature before placing on the grill. Should there be any external bacteria, they will not survive the searing heat. So, at least a couple of hours before you plan to cook, take the steaks out of the 'fridge, and trim all the excess fat. (I render this down for various uses, one of which being fire starter.) Placing the meat on a thick aluminum, copper pan or cookie sheet will speed up the warming process by conducting the cold away more speedily. Cover lightly with plastic wrap but do not make an air tight seal— it needs to breathe.

For my palate, the pristine flavor of pure steak, properly grilled, is hard to improve upon. I prefer to put no seasonings on steak before it is cooked. However, for those who would like to baste or add flavors, a recipe is included at the end.

Whether broiling on a gas grill or over charcoal, the grill must be heated to the proper temperature. There are many theories on the proper grilling of a steak. Mine has been developed over years of experimentation, practice and tasting. My technique calls for very high temperatures 700°+. Those who test the temperature by holding their hand close to the grill and counting, at 700°, you should be able to count to only 1 in Roman numerals, "I!"

In order to properly broil a good steak, gas grills must produce at least 30M British Thermal Units (BTUs) and have adequate mass to absorb heat over an extended period and give it up suddenly to the steak. Fire up the gas grill on the maximum setting and close the lid. It will normally take from 10-20 minutes to reach proper temperature. Charcoalers, fire up 20-25 minutes with 2-5 lbs. of good quality, hardwood charcoal. When covered with gray ash or glowing red, spread the coals evenly. When the coals are spread, the meat grill should be not more than 3" above the coals. You will learn from the **Heat** chapter that radiant heat declines with the *square of the distance.*

Allow the meat grate to heat up. When the grill is right, wipe the steaks dry and place the steaks carefully and firmly upon the grill. Then leave them alone! Do not touch them, talk to them or worry them in any way! Steaks know when they need to be turned and will show you— if you let them. When a ready steak meets the heated grill, they seize each other with the intensity of newlyweds. At the proper time, they will turn loose. Flip them over with a spatula, not a fork. They will grab again. When they turn loose the second time, the honeymoon is over and it's time to get on with business.

Depending upon the thickness of the steak, its temperature before reaching the grill, and the mass and intensity of the coals or, in the case of gas grills, heat-collecting plates, the steak is well on its way. You may test for doneness with your finger. Press firmly into the center of a steak. Soft is very rare - 125°, barely discernible resistance is rare - 130°, definite resistance is medium rare -140°, firming up is medium -150°. I do not know how to test for well done.

Steaks thicker than 1 1/2" may require another flip or two. A 3 incher will require several turns. Do not let it burn. Move it aside or raise the grill if required. A thick steak will continue to cook after removed from the heat. Do not over cook. You can always put it back on the grill to cook it more. You can never uncook it.

If it was properly trimmed of fat, the steak will not cause flame ups. If flames appear, move the steak out of the flames until they subside or close the lid and shut off the incoming air. A properly cooked steak has dark brown stripes where it was in contact with the grill. It will have no part charred or blackened.

Immediately remove to a warm, not hot, plate and allow to sit for 3-5 minutes. All the other food should be ready and waiting for the steak. To serve at the table, transfer to a cutting board. Slice diagonal across the steak and at a slight angle from vertical and serve. Guests may add salt and freshly ground black pepper as desired.

A classic broiled steak! Plump baked potatoes with sour cream and chives, steamed broccoli and carrots, a crisp mixed green salad with vinaigrette and a solid, homemade bread need only a robust wine to complete accompaniments. Savor your reward.

Simple Steak Sauce

For those who wish to add additional flavors to the steak, the following is a simple, elegant sauce.

4-6 T.	**virgin olive oil, peanut oil or (what the heck) unsalted butter.**
6 T.	**minced shallots or 3 T. each mild garlic and onion**
6 T.	**shiitake mushrooms, sliced thinly**
2	**lemons or limes, juiced**
1/2 t.	**ground bay**
1/4 t.	**ground thyme**
1/2 C.	**red wine**

Saute the shallots in the oil until they are clear; then add mushrooms and saute until tender. Pour oil into metal bowl suitable for taking to the grill, add lemon/lime juice and mix well. Baste the steaks on all surfaces and set aside, covered, while preparing the fire.

When the grill is fully heated, drain and reserve the oil-juice baste. Place the steaks on the grill. Baste and turn when the steak tells you.

After steaks are removed, return remaining oil to veggies, add ground bay leaf and thyme and 1/2 cup red wine. Heat, deglaze and reduce by half. Serve over the steak at the table.

Party Steak

Many years ago when I was a young engineer my boss, Jeff Larrimore, would grill a monstrous steak for the quarterly plant staff night-out-with-the-boys. The memory of that meat was so indelibly imprinted on my palate that I chased him down across the ages to get the recipe.

The steak was a humongous cut of sirloin 2 to 3 1/2 inches thick which had to satisfy the healthy appetites of 20-25 guys who were rowdy, relaxed and hungry. It never failed.

Like most exceptional recipes, this one is very simple. He selected the right cut of meat, applied a simple marinade and basted it while it cooked. I am happy to share with you:

Steak Larrimore

Meat: Allow a minimum of 1/2 lb. of meat per person — a pound will put you on the safe side. The Pin-Bone Sirloin is the preferred cut. You may have to order it special, ahead of time. Get a full cross-section cut. I recommend that you deal with a meat market with which you have an established relationship.

Marinade:

16 oz.	soy sauce — get a premium sauce
4 oz.	Worcestershire sauce — buy the best
2 oz.	garlic powder

Mix well and pour over the steak – use a non- reactive container. Add water, up to 4 oz., to cover. Refrigerate and marinate up to 2 hours.

Basting Sauce:

1/2 lb.	unsalted butter
1/2 C.	lemon juice
1 t.	garlic powder

Build a hefty bed of wood coals for broiling. Remove the meat from the 'fridge, dry it off and let it come to room temperature— at least 3 hours.

Place the steak on the grill and leave it alone until it turns loose. Then turn it. Baste the first side and wait until the second side releases. Continue to baste and turn until the steak reaches about 125° in the center. After it sets and rests, there will be degrees of doneness from very rare to medium.

Slice it thinly, diagonally at about a 45-degree angle. Save the juices. This may be just the excuse you have needed to throw a big party.

Tri-Tip

Unbeknownst to vast majority of who most praise the tri-tip, this tender cut is best broiled or roasted rather than barbecued. Follow the directions in "Pursuit of the Perfect Steak" or any other steak- broiling recipe, or check the roasting recipes. Here's how Kathy Murphy, who caters large affairs, from her California base, produces her prized tri-tip.

"I start with at least a choice tri tip and trim most of the fat (but not all) off. I sprinkle it with a seasoning made up of salt, pepper, paprika, and garlic powder and let it sit for a while. We use big chunk mesquite char-wood and put the tri tip on a real hot fire fat side down. That really gets it going!

We just keep flipping it for about 45 minutes for an average piece, — about 2 1/2 pounds. We can tell by feel when it's done. We then slice it against the grain (important), and serve a nice salsa on the side. Pretty easy! Kathy"

Broiled Brisket

I met John Hughes over the Internet and he related this recipe and its history to me. I asked, and he agreed, to include it , along with the story of how it came to him. John B. Hughes first met Col. Beeson, in Germany, as a classmate of Beeson'sdaughter. Later, as a young USMC Lieutenant in Quantico, VA, John and his wife "adopted" by the Colonel and Mrs. Beeson who then lived nearby. Colonel Beeson was, obviously, as skilled on the grill as in the field.

Beeson Brisket Broil

As related by John B. Hughes

"Among the many ways in which US Military families make virtues of necessity, a surprising number learn how to eat well and entertain well using ad hoc, and not necessarily USDA "Prime" grade, ingredients.

You won't confuse the texture of brisket with that of Filet Mignon, but it's easy enough to cope with if you've sliced it right and haven't cooked it past pink, and the flavor is wonderful. On their best days, filets and strips don't begin to have flavor like this does.

The eponym for this one is in honor of a wonderfully crusty old retired USA colonel, who presumably invented it, and taught it to me.

Ingredients:
(Serves 4-6)

One beef brisket "flat"   **If you have to buy a whole brisket just split off the fattier layer and use that for some thing else. What's left is virtually fat-free...it is SO lean that it needs this treatment.**

One package powdered meat tenderizer Heinz, Adolph's, etc. The "Original Flavor" versions work best in this recipe.   (Ed note: MSG)

Procedure:

Mix marinade according to package directions, but marinate the meat several hours, as opposed to the fifteen minutes the package will recommend.

Grill over hot charcoal (you can skip the wood chips for this one) to **NO FURTHER THAN** medium-rare— about 5 minutes per side, depending on your fire. Baste occasionally with a little reserved marinade. It's best about halfway between rare and medium-rare, inside a fairly dark crust.

Allow brisket to "rest" off the fire for 5-10 minutes to "set" juices and facilitate carving. Warm marinade and collect any meat juices which accumulate as the meat rests (and as you carve it).

Carve in very thin slices (you may also want to learn how to sharpen a knife BEFORE you get to this point) across the grain and on the bias, so you get elongated oval slices, not a direct vertical slice.

Serve 2-3 slices per (initial!) serving, sopping cut surfaces in the marinade/juice which accumulates on the carving board/platter. Pass around reserved juices/marinade as a generous sauce. You won't need salt or pepper.

Serve with green salad, hearty, warm sourdough or French bread (to sop up the juices), and a mighty Petite Sirah, if you can still find any. If you can't, a good Cabernet or Zinfandel will also stand up to it.

Works well with flank or top round steak as well, but those usually cost more than brisket, and may NOT be as flavorful!"

"Col. Robert A. Beeson, USA (ret) was a West Pointer who survived the Bataan Death March, but still had to spend the rest of WW II in one of those health spas run by the Japanese in the Philippines in those days. He later ran an Infantry Battalion in Korea during *that* war. He picked up a few baubles like a DSC, Silver Star, some Oak Leaves on his Purple Heart, the CIB, and so forth, along the way. He later served in Paris with NATO, and in Germany with the Seventh Army, retiring in the late sixties." **John B. Hughes**

Fajitas and the Works

From Ron Vallery

The Meat:

3 - 4 lbs.	lean beef skirt steaks.

Meat Preparations:

Prep skirts by cross cutting the striated membrane, removing the "excess" parts as much as possible or they will be rubbery and tough.

Set meat aside in large bowl and let come to room temperature while you make the marinade.

Marinade

1 or 2 bottles	Lea & Perrins Worcestershire Sauce
2 sections	crushed, fresh, garlic (Mexican if you have it)
2 or 3	limes, quartered
1 t.	thyme
1/2 t.	cumin (optional if you like it or have none in the beans)
1/4 C.	brown sugar
1 sprig	fresh cilantro

In 2 quart bowl combine crushed garlic (you can save 1 crushed section and smear it over the steaks if you like it more "garlicky" or you cook your fajitas well done). Pour in the Lea & Perrins, add brown sugar, thyme, (and cumin if you're going to use it). Squeeze in the limes (thoroughly include some of the rind oils) and throw the sections in the liquid, crush a few sprigs of the cilantro (less the stems) on the edge of the bowl and grind the rest of the leaves; 2 t. total, into the liquid through your fingers to get the "taste" in.

Pour the liquid over the skirts and make sure the meat is ALL covered. (You can add some water but don't get carried away.) Cover with plastic wrap and let chill overnight if possible. An hour or 2 before you cook the fajitas, bring the meat and the marinade up to room temperature. (I've been known to put it in the sun for 1/2 hr. just before I cook it, but this will BUG the ladies!!)

Start charcoal fire and wait till glowing (use mesquite charcoal if you can get it, try REAL wood charcoal not briquettes— although everyone doesn't live on the border with Mexico).

Soak some 1/2 " dry mesquite wood strips 6" long in warm water for 20 minutes before cooking. When fire is hottest place 3 or 4 mesquite strips on fire and begin grilling the fajitas, keep covered to "smoke" them well and keep spray ing the strips to keep them from burning and to continue smoking.

Baste the fajitas once on each side before turning in the marinade to keep up the flavor. To me fajitas are best medium with a good "char" on the surface. If you smoke 'em right they'll be blue1/8" into the surface of the meat!!

Don't forget to keep adding strips, as they burn (you can't stop em' so don't try, just use water, and DON'T SPRAY THE MEAT, GUYS— or the fire— good luck on that task When the fajitas are done, quickly chop them up with a chef's knife (across grain) into 1/2 " sections and serve with salsa and beans in tortillas (recipes below).

Recipe for Salsa

6-8	tomatoes, Italian or regular, ripe but firm.
2-3	green serrano peppers. Take out MOST or all of the seeds or you'll be sorry tomorrow!!
2	sweet yellow onions
1/4 C.	fresh cilantro
2-3	limes
1/2 C.	Mexican or excellent Italian olive oil

Chop onions, tomatoes, peppers in equal amounts and 1 T. cilantro

Mix together without mashing or bruising tomatoes; make as much as needed but, to every pint, add 2T. olive oil and then squeeze 1 lime over the top, and as the lime rind fractures produce oil (it works like a salad dressing), carefully stir, cover and immediately refrigerate until used. Let come near room temperature before eating.

Recipe for Beans

pinto beans	(if dry soak, if canned don't)
garlic	
onion	
cumin	
cilantro leaves	

Sauté in pork fat (lard) in sauce pan until tender, add cumin powder and fresh cilantro leaves (to taste) with water and simmer ALL day— adding water as needed. You can add a smidgin' of chili powder or fresh chopped green pepper after the sauté, but don't make chili, guys.

The Dish!

Mix them all, FRESH steamed flour tortillas, or ones expertly made by a sweet lady who knows how to do it by frying them in an iron skillet and steam em' when ready.

Lay out the tortilla flat and put in

1/2 C.	fajita meat
2 T.	beans
1/2 T.	salsa

Roll it up and pig-out big-time. Tres Equis Beer with a lime squeezed in goes great with 'em.

"I'm a WASP from Denver & Boulder, Colorado, and I owe it all to the Mexican and Mexican American Folks who patiently walked me through it dish by dish." Ron

Easy Fajitas

Tasty, as well as trendy, fajitas are simple, easy and economical. They have risen mightily from humble origins. In the beginning, down in the Southwestern U.S. and Northern Mexico, fajitas were invariably made of skirt or flank steak which is about the toughest piece of cow meat South of the brisket. Therefore, it was a cheap piece of meat which was rescued from the meat grinder by the magic of the grill.

Then capitalism reared its ugly head and the law of supply and demand kicked in. This lowly castaway candidate now commands prices that would make a rib eye blush. When that began to happen, I just switched to cheaper, more tender cuts of meat, without feeling the least bit deprived. When chuck roast is $.97 per pound, it makes **great** fajitas! So do sirloin tip, round and rump roasts.

What makes fajitas distinctive is the marinade, and the marinade is also what rendered the tough flank steak chewable. It is simple and effective, and once you have eaten properly grilled with fresh ingredients, you'll never be satisfied with the paltry substitutes served to the public.

Fajitas for Four

2 lbs.	lean beef
3	limes (or lemons) juiced
4-5	cloves garlic, crushed
1/4 C.	mild olive oil

Slice the beef, across the grain, into 1/4" strips. Squeeze the limes/lemons into anon-reactive container and moisten both sides of each piece of meat. Heat the crushed garlic in the olive oil to arouse it from slumber, and, after it cools, pour over the meat slices.

Allow to set at room temperature for at least 30 minutes or overnight, refrigerated.

When I harvest the garlic, I blend the fresh garlic with olive oil and store in covered jars in the refrigerator for uses like this. It keeps its fresh taste, but must remain refrigerated. This is also commercially available

Fajitas wouldn't be fajitas without the accompaniment of salsa, and there are as many versions of salsa as there are chili recipes. This is a favorite of mine.

Fresh Salsa

1	large, sweet onion chopped very fine
2	small cloves garlic, chopped fine
1	large, meaty tomato or 4-5 plum tomatoes
1-4	green chilies, parched, peeled, seeded and chopped. Use serrano or jalapeno.
1 T.	fresh-chopped cilantro
1/2 t.	salt

Peel tomato and chop. Mix all ingredients and refrigerate for at least 30 minutes — overnight is better.

At the Grill

Fire the grill for broiling. This one of the rare occasions when I can recommend mesquite, but any hardwood will work. If the meat was refrigerated, bring it up to room temperature. Collect 8 flour tortillas, wrap in aluminum foil, and heat on the grill.

Broil the meat quickly, from rare to medium, and wrap in a tortilla, and store in the aluminum foil until all are done.

Serve with the salsa. Guacamole and a cold Cerveza are highly recommended.

Steak Buster

A cleaning chemical salesman cornered me the other day extolling the superior characteristics of his particular witches brew for cleaning grills. I explained the virtues of a good fire. Listening to his multitude of endorsers and unsolicited testimonials, reconfirmed the fact that Americans are phobic about *good, clean* dirt and grease.

In his early years, my son, himself now enjoying the perks of fatherhood, often approached the total immersion of Pigpen in the *Charlie Brown* comic strip. With teeth and eyes the only parts shining through layers of grime, his response to his mother's horrified exclamation was, "God made dirt and dirt don't hurt!"

While millions of dollars are spent on cleaning compounds and brushes, truth is that a good fire and a little wiping are all that is needed to keep the grill reasonably clean. After a good fire and wipe down, there remains only the small chore of re-seasoning the meat grill.

This small but very important detail is often omitted in my lengthy dissertations on proper care of grills. I was reminded of that fact the other night and am here to make amends.

The revelation occurred when my grilling buddy, and bone companion, Buster, and I were preparing to convert a common, ordinary piece of merely "choice" red meat into something wonderful.

After I had started the fire, under critical eyes, and allowed the coals to reach a friendly red glow, I replaced the grill over the coals— as is my usual practice. After the grill was burned clean, purified and sanctified by fire, I began the ritual that encompasses the greasing of the grill.

Conscious as we are of cholesterol, I always trim all the fat from any meat that I grill. After the artfully advertised "FULLY TRIMMED" state, only about 20% of the purchased weight is removable fat. I trim that. Not only because I want to save my allotment of saturated fat for other things but because Buster expects me to. I place this fat on the grill, and when it starts to melt, rub it back and forth across the grill, it cleans and seasons the grill and serves as Buster's appetizer.

Buster is not a calorie counter nor is he overly concerned with cholesterol. He does not discriminate between lipoproteins of different densities. Whether their station be high or low, he gives them equal treatment.Perhaps his only distinction is the thought that lipoproteins are not nearly as attractive as a mouth-o'-proteins.

So, after the fat has served its purpose in shining and seasoning the grill, it is served to Buster. Buster does not approach the tendered offerings rapaciously, like a couthless cur, but with the studied air of a consummate connoisseur.

He welcomes the aroma with his nostrils and savors the vision with solemn dignity. Only when he is fully satisfied with the visual and olfactory aspects will he expectantly take the first bite. Buster tastes no prime before its time. If the morsel meets expectations, he often turns to give an acknowledging nod to the chef.

Sometimes when lean steak is carefully trimmed of fat, it needs a little oil of lesser evil to soothe the palate primed for the flavorsome fat of pre-cholesterol counting days. If your palate pines for such, try the following oleaginous ointment.

Steak Buster with Baste

2-4 steaks	Sirloin, rib eye, T-bone or porterhouse. 1 1/2-2 inches thick. Trim the fat to wipe the grill.
5 T.	unsalted butter
1/2 C.	burgundy
2-4 T.	brandied pepper

Melt the butter in a sauce pan, add the burgundy and the brandied peppers, bring to a slow simmer, then remove. Cover the steaks on all surfaces and set aside, covered, while preparing the fire.

(If brandied peppers are not available, check the Seasonings chapter for a reasonable substitute.)

Load the grill for broiling - temperature 500-700°. White oak and hickory are recommended for smoke flavoring. Burn off the meat grill and rub it down with the fat trimmings. Do it as carefully as if Buster were watching.

When the grill is fully heated, place the steaks on the grill. Turn and baste after 3 minutes— depends upon temperature. Repeat twice. Steaks should be rare. Press the center with your fingers: Soft = rare, Soft with rebound = medium rare, Firming = get it off quick for medium.

Bring the remaining baste to a boil and serve over steaks

Buster would be proud of you.

BEEF OLE'

It lay there pulsating, throbbing and undulating like the nascent embryo of an alien creature. It was a peculiarly obscene green that seemed to verge on fluorescing. It was only a few inches from my hand and seemed likely to break out of its containment. What made it especially frightening was that it was in my refrigerator and I had no idea what it was.

While I have discovered some strange things before in my 'fridge, nothing in memory compared with the forgotten pasta dough. I had been experimenting with pasta as a container for good stuff to go on the grill. The little machine cranked out delicious fresh pasta for fettuccine, and I saved some dough for use on the grill when the rains stopped. The rains outlasted the dough.

I threw the creature, Ziplock and all, into the micro to zap the menagerie of microbes. It swelled to the size of a football and bounced as erratically when I threw it out for the dogs to puzzle over. Oh, well back to the laboratory.

One thing that didn't go awry was a South-of-the-border brochette. Chilies are fascinating. There are so many tastes and tempers that they continue to tempt and, occasionally, terrorize my tongue. Following the learning curve, I have bumped into some delicious combinations.

Beef Brochettes Ole`

For Four

2 lbs. tender beef	tenderloin, loin or sirloin cubed to 1inch.
2	med. bell peppers sliced into squares
1	med. red onion sliced into squares.
Olive oil to cover.	

Sauce

4	medium jalapeno or cascabel chilies
1/4 C.	oil

Fry for two minutes. Remove to soak for 20 minutes in 1 cup hot water. Remove from water, remove stems and seeds. Reserve water.

To peppers in the blender, add:

1/4 C.	white onion
2	whole cloves garlic
1/2 t.	cumin seeds, slightly parched in a dry pan
1	bay leaf
1 t.	fresh black pepper
1/4 C.	oil

Blend, add a little soaking water and re-blend. Pour sauce over the cubed meat and marinate for about 30 minutes.

Skewer beef cubes, alternating onion and pepper slices.

Grill over broiling temperature - 500-700 °, basting with olive oil and turning about every three minutes.

Return sauce to blender and add:

1 fresh tomato and 4-6 sprigs fresh cilantro.

Remove the brochettes when medium rare and serve with the sauce and fresh, warm tortillas.

Serve with cold bottles of Carta Blanca. You'll want to shout, "Ole'!"

Churrasco

Politics, economics, and other matters of state, have inspired many a cookout. Earliest writings about barbecue in this country refer to political events, where good food was used to put the audience in a more receptive mood. George Washington recorded a political barbecue in his journal. Kentuckians barbecued sheep for Tom Lincoln and Nancy Hanks in 1806. Although usually considered to be only a tool of the country politician, New York's Tammany Hall bosses were noted to be quick adapters of the effective technique.

Even in matters of war, the cookout was indispensable. At a cookout on the beach outside of Troy, Ulysses and Ajax came to persuade Achilles to rejoin the Greek's assault upon the city. The barbecue was used in this country to bring out potential recruits for militias.

Today, television, with all its pervasive power, has not replaced the barbecue and the fish fry. Food and feedback and feeling of the flesh are still essential ingredients of a successful campaign.

It should not be surprising then that politics and economics influence even the foods that we grill. Flank steak is as tough a cut of meat on a cow carcass. At one time, its price accurately reflected its status. Strangely enough, it is one of the few cuts of beef that can be imported into Japan; therefore, its price is abnormally high.

Unfortunately this has developed simultaneously with some recipes from Central and South America that utilize marinades to tenderize the tasty trim. However, in matters of war, politics and good food, ingenuity can save the day. When round steak and sirloin tip steak are selling at half the price of flank and are more tender— let them eat flank.

Churrasco was developed in either Brazil or Argentina, depending upon whom you ask. In its classic form, the tenderloin of grass- fed range cattle was spiral cut— like unwinding a jelly roll— then marinated and grilled. American beef, pen fed and marbled, is just too tender (and expensive) to cook in this fashion. It takes on the texture of mashed potatoes.

Churrasco is popular throughout Central and South America, and some early efforts importing the method into this country substituted flank steak. Personally, I find round or sirloin tips to be as superior in flavor as they are in texture. (Even though I consider "sirloin tip steak" to be creative marketing, rather than a bona fide steak)

Churrasco for Four

Cut about two pounds of round steak or sirloin tip steak about 3/8 inch thick. Trim all fat and membrane.

Marinade:

1	large onion
3	garlic cloves
1	jalapeno pepper, seeds and ribs removed
4 T.	olive oil

Blend until smooth, then add and mix:

1/2 C.	lime juice
1 t.	capers
1/4 t.	thyme
1/2 t.	salt
2 t.	fresh ground black pepper
Mix well	

Pour over the steaks, cover both sides well, and marinate, refrigerated, in covered glass or plastic container for a least two hours; overnight is fine. Turn the steaks a couple of times to insure contact with all surfaces.

Salsa:

1/2 C.	lime juice
3	garlic cloves
3	jalapeno peppers, seeds and veins removed

Blend slightly and refrigerate for a couple of hours.

Prepare the grill for broiling - 500-700°. Take the steaks and salsa out in time for them to reach room temperature before the meat goes on the grill. Now, bring out your grilling wok or screen and put it over the coals While the utensil is warming, assemble:

1	large bell pepper, sliced thinly lengthwise
1	large onion sliced into strips
6	medium tomatoes, coarsely diced.
2 T.	olive oil

Toss the veggies in the olive oil to provide a thorough coating. Grill the bell peppers and onions until clear then, return to the olive oil and put the tomatoes on the grill. Grill until softened; then add them to the peppers and onions and stir in 2 T. chopped cilantro and 1/2 t. cumin powder.

When the grill reaches proper temperature (you can't hold your hand two inches from the grill for more than two seconds), lay on the steaks. Give them about two minutes per side— not past medium.

Slice the steaks thinly on the diagonal. Serve the salsa and veggies at the table.

Ole' Simon Bolivar!

Sirloin Steaks

"The cobbler's children go without shoes," and a grown, college-trained daughter called me from Illinois, at day time rates, to question me about grilling steaks. It seems that the last one that she grilled was tough and not up to par in taste.

A little questioning on my part revealed that what she had broiled was round steak. Round steak can be made acceptable by broiling. But it requires more than just throwing it on the grill to make it tender. Round steak requires some marinade or other tenderizing treatment.

Lemon and lime, wine and beer, vinegar, pineapple and papaya, sweet and buttermilk all have acids or enzymes which attack the connective tissue and make meat more tender. How tender depends upon the strength of the solution and the time the meat is exposed to it. Of course, the meat itself is the controlling factor.

Meanwhile, back at the grill, other cuts of steak perform much better on the grill. Broiling works best on those cuts which can be cooked the quickest. The more tender the cut, the less time required to tenderize. Therefore, taste rather than tenderness can be the controlling factor.

Perhaps the tastiest of the tender cuts is the sirloin steak. This can be had in several forms, but in the average meat department of a supermarket the choice is limited. Sirloin strip, also known as the New York strip or the Kansas City strip, is the superior taste in steak. (In the East it is called K.C. strip; in the West, N.Y. strip) The texture is slightly tougher than rib-eyes and tenderloins, but it is still tender if not overcooked.

Bone-in sirloin steaks can still be found in butcher shops and meat specialty stores. They are excellent when cooked in a massive piece and sliced diagonally to serve a large party. Sirloin requires minimum effort on your part to become the centerpiece of a delicious meal.

Sirloin Strip for Two

Select a single steak of about 16 - 20 ounces. It should be well trimmed and show generous streaks of marbling. To prepare, trim all fat and membrane and allow to come to room temperature— at least two hours.

Prepare all other dishes and do all the other chores preparatory to eating. The steak will take 15 minutes, maximum, to cook and it should be served hot.

About 45 minutes before serving time, prepare the grill for broiling. Pile the coals generously for a broiling temperature - about 700°. White oak and hickory chips or wood burned to coals are recommended for flavoring. Use mesquite if you are from Texas or just have congenitally inferior palate.

When the coals are uniformly grey, level them out and place the meat grill 2-3 inches above them. Allow the grill to heat for 3-5 minutes and place the steak carefully and firmly directly over the coals.

In about 3 minutes the steak should release from the grill. Turn it promptly with a spatula - not a fork - and place it over a different but equally hot bed. About 2 minutes should give you a rare, 3 minutes a medium-rare. This of course depends upon several factors: the beginning temperature of the meat, its thickness, the heat mass of the coals and their proximity to the meat.

Here's the way to tell. Press the steak with finger or tongs. If it depresses softly and easily, it is rare. When it offers resistance, but still depresses, it is medium rare. When it is firm, it is done and ruined. **Don't do it.**

Remove to a cutting board and allow to sit for 3-5 minutes before slicing diagonally in 1/4 -1/2 inch slices. Salt, fresh ground pepper and butter are optional. Enjoy.

Tailgate Tyros

When dog days pass and dry winds stir the coloring leaves, purple-coated color analysts and silver-throated sportscasters begin their autumnal warbling. That signals: It's tailgate time across the land!

Round and raucous rowdies rumble into stadium parking lots in bright fall plumage and plunk down tailgates on pickup trucks. Slim and more subdued, the sports utility set slips in and slides out silver service on layered linen. The motor home mob moves in amidst amiable cocktail hours, munching finger foods as an intermezzo. Across the striped spaces, picnic baskets blossom into a Yogi Bear Heaven and draw crowds as quickly as the ticket scalpers.

Precooked fare fills serving boards from buckets of fast food chicken to acutely angled slivers of sulking, secretive sandwiches filled with mysterious mixtures of anonymous ointments and ornaments. Those with panache and elan, or similar attributes, set up the grill, accompanied by only a modest flourish of trumpets. The odor of charcoal starter assails the nostrils as a thousand swirls of smoke assault the atmosphere.

If you are weary of silly, sissy food sandwiches and flimsy firkins of fast food fowl, yet care not for the obnoxious odors of a pyre of petroleum products, fear not. Elegant eating and economy of effort can be synonymous, even in a parking lot.

The real reason for eating in a parking lot is to visit with friends and share good food. So preparations should not be so complicated or confining as to interfere with the main purpose. But, if you are hosting the gathering, care enough to serve the very best. That means something deliciously appropriate that you have done yourself.

The only valid reason for cranking up the grill is to produce a memorable, delicious meal. That doesn't exclude good bratwurst or knockwurst or other quickies. Whatever, the end result should be worth the effort required to do competent grilling, yet not unduly restrict the social activities.

The best time to plan your largesse is on the way home from the last game. Consider the things you saw that you didn't like: too much time, too much fuss, too much attention required.

Like all outdoor cooking, tailgating parties should be relaxed and relaxing occasions: minimal fuss, minimal effort— maximum pleasure. Since the real purpose of the gathering is to visit, food should be securely portable and easily assembled. Unnecessary chinaware, cutlery and condiments are out. Drippy is a No-no! Short time cooking is a must and minimal equipment is an imperative.

One of the neatest little edible envelopes is a gift from that troubled area of Earth we call the Middle East. It is pita bread. Made of unbleached flour and shaped like a small, flat pancake, but of tougher consistency, it has a slit on one edge that forms a generous pocket. To those who are familiar, it resembles a consumable canteen of pleasure. Stuffed with meat and vegetables, it is a sturdy, tasty envelope of food.

Tailgate Tyro

For 8 -10 hungry types.

6 pounds of well-trimmed sirloin steak cut about 1 1/2" thick. Slice into 1/4" thick strips and marinate overnight (or on the way) in:

1 C.	dry wine – sample it first to be sure it is good.
1/4 C.	extra virgin olive oil, virgin will do in a pinch
2	large onions sliced, or 1 T. onion powder
6	garlic cloves, crushed (substitute: 1 T. fresh garlic powder)
1	large bell pepper, cored and diced
4	lemons, juice of
3 T.	Worcestershire
2 t.	oregano
1 t.	thyme
1 t.	salt
1/2 t.	cayenne pepper
1/2 t.	fresh ground black pepper
1/4 t.	fresh ground anise seed, optional

Bring to a boil and let cool; then enclose meat and marinade in a plastic bag or covered container and refrigerate overnight or, if traveling to the stadium, eight hours or so at room temperature.

On-site, mix:

1/4 C.	olive oil or 1 stick unsalted butter
1 lb.	button mushrooms, sliced
1 can	marinated hearts of artichoke, chopped
1	8 oz. jar of olives

Salad makings — spinach, a couple of different lettuces, sliced tomatoes.

Start your trusty hibachi or other portable grill with shreds of dry oak under dense, hardwood charcoal or quick burning lump charcoal. (A starter chimney is a handy gadget). Warm the oil/butter mushroom/artichoke/olive mixture on the grill in a small pan. When the coals are bright red, add green trimmings of hickory/oak/fruit wood. Quickly sear the meat at high temperature— 500-700°— and remove to a covered container holding a little of the warm marinade. Don't overcook!

Line up the room temperature pita bread, spinach/lettuce and sliced tomato, in a spread formation with the meat and sauce. Then call the signals. Let each stuff the line at their pleasure.

Go on and make a touchdown. Don't sweat the extra points.

Beef Teriyaki

By the time one reaches my age, one has come to realize that time is our most precious asset. There is no restocking of the larder when the bottom gets close.

Having reared four children, I can still remember that the 24 hours allotted to a day are often inadequate for even young folk to finish all their "have-to's" and leave any time for their "want-to's." Therefore, I especially appreciate those things that transform chores into cheerfully chosen activities and call for less time and attention.

Whipping up a quick and healthy meal for rowdy troops, after a bad day at the sawmill, is rank and regular duty. Fortunately, there is a "transformer" nearby that is as versatile as any advertised with the Saturday morning cartoons.

Your little hibachi can save time, tune up taste and turn troublesome troops into teddy bears with tempting teriyaki. The ingredient list is short, steps are few, and total preparation time from 'fridge to the table can be less than ten minutes.

Teriyaki sauce can be purchased or you can mix your own. It only takes a few seconds and a few ingredients to make, and I guarantee that you will be better satisfied with your own.

Soy sauce, which is the main ingredient of teriyaki sauce and important in Oriental cooking, deserves more attention than it normally gets. While all soy sauce is a mixture of water, fermented soybean juice and salt, all soy sauce is not created equal. Since most Americans either don't know this or don't really give a Scarlet, grocery shelf space, in many areas, is dominated by only two domestic labels— both having more salt than is necessary.

If you enjoy cooking Oriental, take advantage of the many other varieties. Next time you chance upon an Oriental grocery or a well-stocked gourmet shop, take a look at the several different soy sauces available. Take home two or three and find the flavor that palpitates your palate.

Beside the meat, the other main ingredients are garlic and ginger. Grated fresh ginger and crushed fresh garlic blend into a surprising marriage that tempers both strong flavors. In the quick and dirty version, ground ginger and garlic powder are delicious, but do not soar.

Beef Teriyaki

To soothe six healthy appetites, select about 1 1/2 pounds sirloin steak or sirloin tip roast. Slice into strips about 1/2 inch thick, one inch wide and six inches long, or have your helpful butcher do it. Trim off all fat.

Quick and Dirty Version

In a proper size glass or plastic container, mix

1/2 C.	soy sauce
1 t..	garlic powder
1 1/2 t.	powdered ginger

Gourmet Version

2 cloves	crushed garlic
3 t.	fresh grated ginger
1/2 C.	dry sherry

Lay in the meat strips one at a time. Add:

2 T.	Teriyaki sauce and enough water to cover meat.

This can marinate from ten minutes to one hour or even overnight in the 'fridge.

If time is the controlling factor, fire up the hibachi or grill before mixing the sauce. However, if you start the fire after the meat is in the marinade, it will taste better and will not require any more time in attendance.

Put a dozen or so bamboo skewers in salt water to soak. Throw a couple of pots of water on the stove, one for noodles and one for tender green beans. About 10 minutes after the water comes to a boil the second time, both will be done *al dente*.

When the coals are ready, weave the strips back and forth onto the skewers and place on the grill. Dip into the marinade or baste as necessary. Meat will be done in about three minutes.

Serve up quickly with a little sauce on the noodles and lemon and butter on the crunchy green beans. You won't need a fortune cookie to tell you that this is your lucky day.

The Artful Hamburger

More affronts to good taste have been committed in the name of hamburger than in the name of art. "Hamburger" is as wantonly applied to the rubbery disk of misbegotten menagerie meat and adulterants served in fast food houses as is to an aptly appointed artwork of a master griller working with premium ingredients. A thick ration of heavy, aged ground beef, masterfully grilled and sheathed in generous slices of dense, fresh bread is magnificent, unadorned. With a little horseradish, piquant mustard and romaine lettuce, it can traumatize a rabid vegetarian.

When Leonardo set out to paint Mona, he didn't use wax crayons. Ground beef is pigment which can be used to create a Mona Lisa or an obscenity. If you plan to do a Mona, choose your pigment carefully. Select meat specifically for hamburgers. Proper meat for hamburger is freshly ground heavy, aged, lean beef. "Extra lean" lacks enough fat for flavor and texture and falls apart on the grill; "regular grind" fades away to become a mere memory of itself. It also causes flame-ups.

Select a nice chuck roast and, if you do not grind your own, have the butcher trim and grind it for you. Then you know the flavor, freshness and meat/fat ratio to expect. Several other cuts are tasty, but chuck is my favorite for hamburgers. Sirloin, rump and round will also work. If it has a bone, save it for stock. If the butcher is unable or unwilling to custom grind and time is short, choose the freshest (pale red) package of ground lean meat. Find another meat market before you buy again.

A meat grinder or grinding attachment on your mixer or food processor is a worthwhile investment for your kitchen. It puts you in control of quality, and, with ground meat, freshness is essential to quality. It also means that your ground meat is not going through a grinder which has just run a ton of meat of questionable character. Personally, I rarely ever buy ground meat. I choose to grind at home the meat I use. You can also trim roasts and grind the small pieces to save and cook later. The ability to grind other foods makes the grinder a handy kitchen implement. Get the sausage stuffer attachment, also. Think of bratts, Italian, kielbasa, chorizos and other tasty stuffed items. Among other uses, it stuffs manicotti.

If you don't make your own, find some good bread. The undercooked froth of bleached wheat flour posed as hamburger buns lacks flavor, nutrition and texture - unpalatable even to discerning bread mold. Suitable bread must, first of all, maintain its integrity while supporting a juicy hamburger. Bread should pleasure the eye like a plump Rubens nude and seduce the nose with promises, reveal sensual texture and give earthy sustenance. Choose any proper size, hefty rolls which tempt you or a loaf of hearty bread to be sliced into supporting roles. Later, I'll tell you how to make your own.

Choose greenery and condiments to complete the scene that your palate has envisioned. Pallid iceberg lettuce has only crunch and water; try a lettuce of substance, fresh spinach, cress or chard. Fresh, curly mustard leaves are a piquant surprise. Grated horseradish, mustard of choice, mayonnaise, sliced tomatoes and sweet onions, with perhaps grated cheese, sliced dill pickles and Greek peppers on the side, ought to do nicely. Remove catsup and "steak sauce" from the premises.

Now another flavoring opportunity presents itself. "To season or not to season?" is the question. Shoot them straight for a few times— no seasoning in the meat before broiling. (I never salt before broiling.) We will cover some seasoning variations in the future. Shape the meat into firm patties to fit your bread and about 3/4" thick and of even thickness. Allow to warm to room temperature. Fire up the grill.

When all the trimmings are prepared, the grill should be right, with charcoal glowing red and the heat so intense that you cannot hold your hand within two inches of the grill for more than a couple of seconds. If you are cooking with gas, turn to the highest setting and keep the lid closed until ready.

Gently place the meat on the grill. If the temperature is right, meat will seize the grill. Do not move or turn the patties until each releases. As soon as they release, turn them. When the second side releases, remove and serve. There should be no flame-up from the lean meat, but if flames appear, close the lid.

The meat will be uncharred on the outside and medium to medium rare on the inside. Juicy and delicious. Cover with condiments and bread and experience a real hamburger.

Maybe not quite a Mona, but even Leonardo did preliminary sketches.

Basic Broiled Chicken Breasts

Chicken is high on the list of favorite foods for grilling. Broiled chicken breasts make a delightfully delicious dish which can be dressed up or down with little effort. The variety of flavoring treatments is limited only by your imagination.

Unfortunately, broiling chicken breasts presents problems to many. A frequent complaint is that the meat sticks to the grill. This is solved by using a little oil on the relatively dry breast meat and **having the meat grate hot enough.** When the grate is properly heated, the meat will sear and seize. Then when ready, but not before, it will release. If you try to turn the meat before it is ready, parts of it may be left sticking to the grill. Be patient. Learn from the meat.

The most pervasive problem, however, is that the vast majority of chicken breasts are cooked well beyond their prime and turn out dry and tough. This is easily preventable. **Just don't over cook!** Every bacteria likely to be on a normal chicken — even a miserably mass-produced one— is dead and done by 160° even though some food fanatics keep recommending 180°. Almost all potentially harmful bacteria are deposited on the exterior by improper handling, not in the interior. Therefore, they quickly expire in the intense heat of the grill. As soon as chicken breasts are firm to the touch, take them off immediately. You'll be surprised and pleased at the moist and tender tasty morsels.

If boneless breasts aren't on sale, it's easy to buy whole chickens and debone the breasts. Some of you aren't heavily into deboning breasts, but it's your loss. It only takes about two minutes and a sharp knife.

Chicken breasts, whether you boned them yourself or bought them already deboned, offer a multitude of tastes, textures and treatments. We'll broil these on the grill and serve them bold and succulent, decorated only with branding of a properly heated grill.

Since grilled breasts are excellent leftovers with many uses, let's do eight.

Basic Broiled Breasts

8 breast halves of frying chickens. Trim off thin end or cut the breasts in half so that the thinner end won't be overcooked.

1/4 C.	olive oil
1	clove garlic, crushed
2	lemons, juiced
1 t.	white pepper

Heat oil and add crushed garlic and saute — do not brown garlic. Add the lemon juice.

Warming the lemons will increase the yield of juice.

Basic substitutions:

Butter or other oils may be substituted for olive.
Garlic powder may be subbed for fresh garlic.
Lemon concentrate may be substituted for lemon.

Seasoning variations:

Onion, thyme, sage and rosemary are traditional chicken seasonings.
Paprika or ground chilies add color.
Oregano, cumin and ground chili pepper create a Southwestern flavor.
Basil, oregano, thyme served create Italian flavors.
Ground coriander, cumin, curry powders create an Asian flavor.

Whether the grill uses charcoal, gas or electricity as a heat source, it must have time to reach the proper temperature. Charcoal or gas grills will require 20-30 minutes to reach broiling temperature. Fire them up and close the lid. The grates will almost self clean and require only a stroke or two with a wire brush or paper towel.

If the grates are not hot enough, meat will stick. Properly heated, it will seize, but turn loose when it is ready to turn.

Baste with sauce and allow to stand at least 10 minutes. The breasts will cook in about ten minutes after they hit the grill. Prepare everything else accordingly.

Baste again and place on the grill. Baste the top side and turn each piece quickly when it releases. If the grates did not create brown stripes, they are not hot enough. When the second side releases, rotate each piece 90° to form crossing a pattern of stripes. Allow only one or two minutes per side after the second turn. After a couple of minutes, press the center of the thickest part of each breast. If firm, remove at once. Don't overcook and dry out this succulent meat!

Remove from the grill to a warm plate and serve immediately. Should there be leftovers they will be outstanding in a chicken salad. Awesome, just warmed, sliced and served and openly susceptible to liaisons with any colorful sauce.

Deboning Chicken Breasts

The sharp edge is perhaps man's oldest discovery and is has been vital to civilization. Until the last generation, everyone understood the need for good knives, and everybody had at least one. But city living and mass marketing have brought us flashy jewels like the ginzu knives, which are best at cutting purses. But, unlike a good man, good knives these days are not hard to find.

You need a sharp knife with a blade from 4-6 inches long. If you are deboning the whole chicken, start from the back. If you just are just deboning the breasts, lay the bird on the back and make a long cut from top to bottom along the breast bone. If you are right-handed, do the left side first and rotate the bird before doing the other side.

Lift the flap beside the incision and make additional strokes from top to bottom, keeping the edge against the rib cage. Remove the first breast, rotate the bird and do the other. After two or three times, it's as easy as eating ice cream. Save the thighs and legs for your favorite use and throw the skin and carcass into a stock pot.

Keeping Abreast with Your Valentine

Some admire breasts more than others. I find them irresistible. They are beautiful and tender and deserve gently, loving attention — some say even adoration. Whether perfumed and coquettishly covered or presented bare and boldly in their natural beauty, they are delightful.

We'll broil these on the grill and serve them bold and succulent, decorated only with a fair complexion, tinged of pink. Perfect for a cozy, private dinner affair for two.

Valentine Breasts

Crush a small clove of garlic into 1 stick softened, unsalted butter. Add the juice of two lemons and keep warm. In 1/8 cup hot water, steep:

1/4 t.	thyme, ground,
1/4 t.	sage
1/4 t.	dry mustard
1/4 t.	rosemary (grind with mortar and pestle)
1/4 t.	onion powder
1 t.	fresh ginger, grated
Dash	cayenne pepper

After 10 minutes of steeping, add to butter mixture and mix well. Keep warm and allow to marry, or at least do some serious flirting, while you fire up the grill. Temperature should be "low broiling" about 400°F.

Press the breasts into rather uniform thickness. Baste with sauce and allow to soak at least 10 minutes. The breasts will cook in less than ten minutes after they hit the grill. Prepare everything else accordingly.

Baste again, sprinkle nicely with paprika and place on the grill. Baste the top side and turn quickly. Allow only one or two minutes per side. Baste frequently; turn often. Do not overcook or allow to brown.

Those of us who are properly attuned, observe that when breasts become firm, they are ready.

Remove from the grill to a warm plate. Serve to your valentine with veggies of your choice and a white wine with some character.

"A jug of wine, a pair of breasts and, thou beside me at the grill…."

Grilled Chicken Breast with Green Sauce

"The wedding guest, he beat his breast . . ."
These days there are better reasons for beating one's breast than listening to a delirious old sailor. This is especially true since boneless chicken breasts, so readily available and economical, can profit from a little beating.

The other day, while salivating in the meat market at the prospects of a good steak because whole rib eyes had just gone on sale, I was surprised by some attractive packages of veal-colored meat labeled "tenderloin." Terminally curious, especially about food, I gave it a closer look.

Chicken! Chicken breasts to be exact. I don't know what the FDA's opinion would be from a truth-in-labeling standpoint. Personally, I was a little miffed. Breasts are breasts and loins are loins and the twain rarely ever meet.

Notwithstanding the mislabeling, as an attorney would say, the boneless breasts were attractive and temptingly priced. About half the regular price of a rib eye. While I normally buy a whole chicken, debone the breasts, save the thighs and throw the bones in a stock pot, I picked up a package without a twinge of conscience.

Chicken breasts are easily flavored in so many styles and are so quick and easy to prepare that the fact that they are low in cholesterol and fat is almost immaterial and irrelevant. They require so little time on the grill that the major challenge to the master griller is creating a subterfuge that will allow him to enjoy a satisfactory period of pleasurable activity before he has to bring them in.

The accomplished griller needs no advice from me on how to extend his pleasure period at the grill, but few will spurn the opportunity to try a different taste.

Grilled Breasts with Green Sauce

Four boneless breasts — for four adults. Trim any cartilage, fat and extraneous bits. Place each breast on a sturdy, flat surface and pound flat with a cleaver or other suitable weapon. Tidiness suggests placing the breast between two layers of waxed paper before attacking it. Beat the breast until it is about 1/2 inch thick, or slightly less.

Coat both sides with a marinade/basting sauce of:

1/4 C.	virgin olive oil
1	clove garlic, crushed
1	lemon, juice of
1/2 t.	ground thyme
1/2 C.	dry white wine

Mix and cover while you build the fire for low roasting temperature — about 300°. A delicate smoke of fruit wood and white oak will be appropriate. While the coals are getting ready, prepare the green sauce.

Roast, skin and remove the seeds of one medium bell pepper and one (or more jalapenos). Chop fine.

5 heaping T.	chopped fresh parsley
5 heaping T.	chopped celery leaves
4 heaping T.	chopped cilantro
4 heaping T.	chopped green onions
2 tomatillos	finely chopped (use canned if fresh is not available) or green tomatoes
2	cloves garlic, crushed
1	small onion, chopped fine
1 T.	capers
2 T.	extra virgin olive oil
1/2 t.	ground cumin

Saute all, except cilantro, gently over low heat until onions are clear. Do not brown. Stir in chopped cilantro.

Place the breasts on the grill directly over the coals. Turn as quickly as they release. Baste. When the second side releases, move the breasts away from

114

the coals and add green (or soaked) wood to the coals. Continue to turn and baste until done - 160º. With skill, you may be able to prolong the fun for a half hour, but normally 10-15 minutes is more than ample.

Remove and serve quickly, with warm green sauce on the side. An avocado salad, boiled new potatoes, steamed baby carrots with a good white wine will make you want to do a Tarzan yell while beating your own breast.

Broiled Chicken Livers

Chicken livers are not everybody's favorite, but I enjoy them several ways— two of which involve the grill. I cannot resist making an occasional pate, and nothing adds distinction to my pates like using livers, gently grilled in a pleasant smoke, instead of being boiled. If you are into 'Cajun cooking, grilled livers will also spice up your "Dirty Rice" dishes. For both uses, I actually hot smoke the livers, at around 190º, until just done.

Grilled chicken livers can also deliver a delicious main course.

Skewered Livers and Vegetables

1lb.	chicken, turkey, or duck livers, inspected, trimmed, rinsed and drained
1/3C.	olive oil
1	medium onion, halved into top and bottom then quartered
12	cherry tomatoes, halved
1	medium bell pepper, cut into 1/2" pieces
1	lemon, juice of
1/2 t.	ground bay
1 T.	fresh chopped dill
1 T.	freshly mixed hot mustard (ground mustard and water)
1 t.	grated horseradish

Sprinkle livers with salt and pepper and skewer livers and vegetables alternately. Brush with oil, and grill until just done. Mix all other ingredients except dill. Unload the skewers to a warm plate, pour on the seasoning mixture and sprinkle on the dill.

Now that you know how easy and delicious they can be, try your own variations and don't forget the pates.

Staking My Claim on Pork Steaks

Odd, isn't it, that we broil so many beef steaks, treasure them, brag on them and present them as examples of our excellent culinary skills, but treat the same cuts of pork like a homely orphan with a history of behavioral problems. The fault, ". . .dear, Brutus," is not with the pork, but with ourselves. I'll take an oath on that

The real problem is the pork producers, USDA, professional food- safety freaks, and the legal profession. Nobody wants to get sued for undercooked pork. So, while the trichinae parasite is killed at 137°, all the worry-warts still recommend cooking pork to 185°, which renders it fit only for exercising massive mastication muscles. Properly grilled, pork rib steaks (a.k.a pork chops), pork loin steaks (a.k.a pork loin chops) are succulent, savory and softer than a baby's bottom.

There are three secrets to broiling pork steaks and chops.

1. **Thickness.** The meat should be at least 1" thick and 1 1/2" is even better.

2. **Oil.** Pork has been going through a reconstruction project to reduce fat that would put ordinary obese humans to shame. The result is a pork carcass so lean that it has no marbling. Meanwhile, the beef people have been packing the arteries of cattle with fat to increase the marbling. Therefore, when the lean pork meat meets the hot grill, it does not sear with lovely stripes like the beef steak, but tends to blacken. If you rub the pork with a little oil, this prevents the blackening.

3. **Doneness.** Don't overcook! Have an accurate bi-metal thermometer handy and after you have made the second flip, insert the probe into the center of the pork steak. It may not be ready yet but STAY ALERT! As soon as that reaches 140°, snatch it off. It will continue to cook up to 145-150°, depending upon the thickness. The texture will rival a fine beef steak and the taste will absolutely surprise you.

As when broiling beef, I do not normally put salt or other seasoning on pork before broiling. I do not pronounce that to do so is wrong, but I just usually don't. You may choose to marinate or season pork steaks before grilling. I prefer the pristine pork. After you try the following recipe, mostly to prove to yourself that broiled pork is tender and delicious, flavor it any way that you like. Check the mustard marinade for pork.

Broiled Pork Chops for Four

4 pork chops (with bone) or steaks (without bone) cut 1 1/4" thick and trimmed of extraneous fat. These will be about 12 oz. each.

Wipe dry with a paper towel and brush with olive oil, peanut oil or, BEHOLD! melted lard.

> **If you use lard, make sure that it is fresh. You can melt down pork fat and make your own. Reguardless of what the "Chicken Little" crowd says, you can bring the pork up to room temperature (about 70 degrees) without the sky falling or the bacteria eating your flesh.**

Build the coal bed for about 400-500° — slightly cooler than for steak. If you are using a gas or an electric grill, turn it on, close the lid and wait for it to reach about 400° — hopefully your grill is up to it.

Place the oiled steaks carefully on the grill and give them about 3 minutes — depending upon the temperature at the grate, then check one to make certain that they are not burning. You do not want to create a tough, dry skin and, since oiled, the meat will not seize the grill as an unoiled beef steak would do.

When there is some browning, flip them. Repeat the process for the second side. Shortly after you flip the second side, check for internal temperature. Let that reading be your guide. If they are above 100°, stand by. If you are below, the steaks may require another flip. But, steady on course! Pay attention! Once they touch the 140° mark, remove them to warm plates.

Have salt and freshly ground pepper ready at the table. Stand by for a shock.

Alternate seasonings:

(1) 1/3 C. oil and 1/3 C. prepared mustard. Apply and grill immediately or marinate up to 1/2 hour.

(2) 1/3 C. oil, 1/4 C. water, 1 t.. garlic powder, 1 t. onion powder, 1/2 t. thyme, 1/2 t. fresh ground black pepper. Simmer until the water has evaporated and the oil is infused with flavor. Apply and grill.

(3) 1/3 C. oil, 1/4C. water, juice of one lemon, 1/2 t. thyme, 1/2 dry mustard. Marinate up to 1 hour.

These are three great marinades for pork. Don't be piggish.

Unlike beef, pork can be reheated without the merest hint of rancidity. Beef fat seems to react with oxygen more readily to give that "warmed over" flavor. That is why left-over beef steak is best eaten without reheating.

Pork Shish KeBabs

Ever since Bo-bo burned down the pig parlor in that famous Chinese arson case, roasting and broiling have been a favored way to prepare pork. Fortunately, we no longer have to choose between "the whole hog or nothing," and we don't have to torch the pig parlor. Pork loins and tenderloins are plentiful and lend themselves to a variety of delicious treatments.

While fish and beef have joined lamb as a popular subject for the skewer, pork rarely gets that treatment. The main reason is that pork normally gets over-cooked and becomes tough.

That's a small puddle to a strong jumper. All we need is a proper marinade to loosen up the porker. This one is guaranteed to relax all concerned.

Soused Pork Kebabs

1 1/2 lbs. pork loin, trimmed and cut into 1 inch squares.

Marinate 30 minutes at room temperature or overnight, refrigerated, in a mixture of:

12 oz.	good beer (sample for quaility)
1/2 C.	orange marmalade
1/4 C.	lemon juice
1/2 C.	soy sauce
2	cloves garlic, minced

If refrigerated, remove the pork from the 'fridge to allow to come to room temperature.

Prepare the grill for low broiling temperatures about 450-500°. Soak bamboo skewers in salted water.

Prepare veggies as follows:

16	large mushrooms, remove stems
1	large bell pepper cut into 1 1/2 squares
16	pearl onions, peeled

Drop onions into boiling water for about 2 minutes; then rinse under cold water.

Impale pork and veggies alternately on skewers and place on the grill. Baste with marinade, turning and basting frequently, for about 10 minutes. As soon as the meat firms, take it off. Pork is fully cooked and safe at 140°.

Serve hot and think kind thoughts of Bo-bo.

Variations:

Pork kebabs can be prepared quickly without marinating with a variety of accompanying vegetables and seasonings. For some interesting variations, try these; then experiment with your own.

Intersperse combinations of onion slices, bell peppers, hot chilies, bok choy, celery, pearl onions, fennel slices, tomatoes, fresh ginger, limes/lemons/kumquats for delicious variations. **JUST DON'T OVER COOK!**

Lamb Brochette

Tender verses...

Mary had a little lamb,
bell peppers and tomatoes
skewered with an onion sliced
and broccoli with potatoes.

Since the majority of what most Americans know about lamb has come from one source, I have taken license to revise that most important reference—with apologies to its author, Sarah Hale.

This is the problem with lamb. Most folk tend to think of it as a cute little creature trailing Mary off to school. I think of it as tender, versatile meat that is as healthy as it is delicious. Being of extremely mild flavor, it joins easily with a variety of seasonings and treatments. Lamb pleasures the palate in plebeian pots or regal racks. It is economical and deserves to be included in your repertoire.

A quick way to prepare a healthy, delicious and beautiful main course on the grill is to skewer small pieces of meat or seafood with alternate slices of savory vegetables. The smaller pieces cook more quickly and provide more surface area for introducing flavors. The variations of flavors, textures and colors are limited only by your own imagination.

While skewers are usually shown loaded as in the above poem, I find it more practical to hoist the vegetables on their own skewers and use only small pieces of essential savory vegetables - peppers, onions, lemon or lime - with the meat. Veggies need a slower fire and different time than meat. Separation provides better control and allows for more variety.

To give six people *delirium nibblin's*, try this savory broiled

Lamb Shish Kebab

| 2 | cloves garlic crushed |
| 1/4 C. | extra-virgin* olive oil |

Stir garlic into oil and set aside.

Trim fat and membrane from a leg of lamb and cut about two pounds into 1 - 1 1/2 cubes. (Cut up and store the remainder for stew and save the bone for stock to use another day.) Spread cubes in a shallow pan or tray.

Mix the following in a small bowl:

1 t..	ground thyme
1/2 t.	ground bay leaf
1 t..	paprika
1 t..	fresh black pepper

Rub the seasoning mixture into the meat, brush all sides with garlic-oil, cover and let warm to room temperature while you assemble

2	limes (or lemons), thinly sliced
2	ribs fennel, sliced into 1" diagonals
1	large onion, quartered vertically; then separate sections by growth layers.

Assemble on skewers by alternating lime, fennel, and onion slices between meat cubes. Soak bamboo skewers in warm salt water before using.

Fill other skewers with your choice of vegetables such as sweet or hot pepper, onion, tomatoes, mushrooms, et cetera, and brush with garlic-oil.

The above steps may be done ahead and the food refrigerated for several hours. If you do this, remove the meat from the refrigerator in time for it to gain room temperature.

Fire up the grill in advance and bring it to broiling temperature - 500-700°. Place the meat on the grill, over the coals, and allow 3 to 5 minutes per side for medium rare. Place the vegetables where the heat is less intense (300-400°) and baste and turn as needed.

Serve at once with a little rice pilaf. Salt at the table if desired. This will make you review the *Child's Garden of Verses* in a completely different sense.

*Virgin olive oil is from olives that have never before been pressed. Extra virgin oil is from olives that never even thought about being pressed.

Cooking food on skewers, which seems to have originated in ancient Persia (now Iran) has many names around the world. Lamb grilled on skewers is shish kebab in the Mediterranean/Middle East, *shaslik in* Russia and *sate* in Indonesia. And, of course, *en brochette,* in France, *suyas* in Nigeria, *anticuchos* in South America, *carnitas* in Mexico. Sate is currently *very* trendy. What would merely have been seasoned and skewered beef shish kebab is now dipped in coconut milk and rubbed with peanut butter and transformed into chic cuisine.

The fact Is that you can skewer strips, slices, chunks of meat, fish, poultry, vegetables and fruits and combinations of them ground and shaped on a skewer for quick, tasty treats. And you can call them what you like.

Broiled Lamb Chops

Those who have never had a lamb chop properly broiled on a grill are truly gastronomically deprived. I don't know whether my letting the secret out will drive the already ridiculous prices up by increased demand or if increased demand will cause more production and, thus, lower prices. Either way, I could not in good conscience keep the knowledge from you.

Lamb, although practically anonymous in the U.S., is one of man's oldest domesticated meats and still the favorite in much of the world. Among this viand's many virtues is versatility. Lamb chops and steaks are amenable to many treatments, but they are delightfully delicious simply broiled on the grill.

My brother, Doug— who also cooked and photographed the food on the cover— is himself a "pretty good cook," (Those familiar with barbecue customs are aware that is high praise.) He served up some grilled lamb chops that could have been improved upon only by an encore. The recipe is so simple that, after you try it, you will be encouraged to create some of your own. Since his family nickname is "Buddy," I call this:

Buddy's Lamb Chops
(For four)

2	lamb chops per person, trimmed of extraneous fat
2 t.	granulated garlic
4 oz.	prepared mustard
1 t.	salt
1 t.	fresh ground pepper

Sprinkle chops with garlic, salt and pepper and cover with mustard. Allow to marinate for 30 minutes at room temperature.

Broil quickly until center temperature is about 145°: remove to warm plate and enjoy.

Variations for Marinade

Lemon juice, soft, unsalted butter, salt and pepper.
Olive oil, garlic, rosemary — heated and allowed to marry.
Olive oil, shallots, brandy — heated and allowed to marry.

Lamb is best eaten warm. The fat congeals quickly and is unpleasent to the palate. Warm the plates and serve directly from the grill.

SEAFOOD

"There's a whole lot of fish in the ocean . . . "

One reason for the immense popularity of blackened redfish, no doubt, is that it lends some legitimacy to all those other dishes that have been blackened by mistake in the past. The real reasons for its fantastic flavor are the herbs and spices whose instant cremation permeates the fish with their essence before the fish is overcooked.

There are many other excellent recipes in Chef Paul Prudhomme's repertoire and many other tasty fish in the sea. Their sudden notoriety has redfish now suffering severely from over-fishing. Do yourself and the redfish a favor by substituting one of the many other species that will taste as good and cost less.

Redfish is a member of the drum family whose characteristics include firm flesh and mild flavor. Some common species that are delicious broiled, blackened or bronzed are bass, billfish, cod, drum, grouper, halibut, ling, mullet, permit, pompano, salmon, snapper, spadefish, triggerfish, trout and turbot. Pond-raised Mississippi catfish are a special treat.

Like beginning vaudeville players, fish may have different name in different towns. Check out the names in your locale with a good reference— a book or a fish market manager. (Check out the manager too!)

The tastes generated by blackening and bronzing can be created on the grill as well as in the pan. Grilling fish allows almost infinite temperature variations. Low temperatures allow cooking with minimal change in the appearance or texture of the exterior and very high temperatures can form a crusty bronzed or blackened finish.

Select the freshest, firmest fish fillets not more than 3/4 inch thick. If the fish has any odor, marinate in the refrigerator at least one hour in the following. Otherwise, skip the marinade.

1/2 C.	yogurt
1/2 C.	water
1	lemon, juiced
1 T.	fresh chopped parsley

Fire the grill for medium broiling temperature. If you plan to use wood chips for smoke seasoning, soak chips and three bay leaves, broken into quarters, in water while the fish is marinating.

Bronzed Fish Fillets

Bronze Seasoning

1/4 lb.	unsalted butter in a shallow pan (substitute light olive or corn oil)
1 T.	salt
1/2 t.	thyme
1/2 t.	paprika
1/2 t.	onion powder
1/2 t.	garlic powder
1/2 t.	rosemary
1/4 t.	caraway seed, ground
1/4 t.	white pepper
1/4 t.	red pepper
1/4 t.	black pepper

If marinated, remove fillets from marinade and pat dry. Sprinkle seasoning mixture evenly and rub into the fish on both sides. At the grill, put 1/2 the chips and leaves on the coals.

Melt the butter and pour in a shallow pan. Dredge one side of the fillets in the warm melted butter and place buttered side down on the grill. After two to three minutes, add remainder of chips and leaves to coals, baste or pour remaining butter over the fillets and turn.

After two or three minutes, remove and serve on warm plates. Garnish with lemon and orange slices. Don't hurt yourself.

Grilled Bass

Upon first tasting fish properly grilled over good coals, most folks have been amazed at the fantastic flavors and textures. Many have even been inspired to fire up their own grills and fling on a few fish fillets. That fish may crumble and fall through the cracks if not handled properly has frightened off others.

A little information solves a lot of the problems of grilling fish. Choosing the right fish, right size and cut, using a little oil solves most of the problems. There are several handy accessories that make it unnecessary to ever consider sealing the tender morsels in two layers of heavy duty foil and calling it grilling.

Grilling is the best way to prepare oily fleshed fish. This method gives the oils a chance to cook out and improves the fish's flavor. Billfish, pompano, king mackerel, ocean perch, turbot and tuna are saltwater species that  improve with grilling. Buffalo and carp are freshwater species that change dramatically when grilled rather than fried. Although delicious when traditionally fried, catfish is outstanding when seasoned and broiled on the grill.

High oil content isn't the only criteria for choosing a fish to broil. Any firm-fleshed fish improves when flavored on the grill. Those who pass up the opportunity to taste broiled bass fillets or steaks are missing a treat.

The only fish not really suitable for grilling are those with very low oil content or soft flesh. Whitefish, for instance, aren't good even when grilled.

The real criterion for choosing fish is freshness. The fresher the better. Quick frozen, as are Mississippi catfish, and saltwater species taken by properly equipped commercial fishermen can retain excellent characteristics. I have not yet found any fish that was previously frozen, then thawed and displayed on ice as though it were fresh to be worth bringing home— except for the cat.

Except for catfish, I rarely ever use a commercially frozen fish. If you don't fish or have a generous friend that does, find a fresh fish market and get acquainted with its owner. He should also be able to advise you on the characteristics of each species to help you make a choice.

The potential problems at the grill can be avoided in several ways. The main problem, of course, is the possibility of fish sticking to the grill or coming apart when it is done. The problem of sticking is easily solved by rubbing the grill with a piece of fat pork or brushing it with oil just before adding the fish. My preferred method is to dredge the fish or fillet in unsalted butter or oil on its way to the grill.

The problem of crumbling can usually be avoided by turning the fish only once, if at all, or by using a large, thin spatula, with an opposing arm, or two spatulas when turning and removing.

Some grills, especially the cheaper ones with small wire grates set wide apart, are not suitable for grilling fish. Several accessories handle this very well. Baskets, having a top and a bottom, equipped with a long, sturdy handle, make the job of turning simpler than sopping syrup. Another alternative is laying a square of stainless steel mesh upon your grill.

If you choose to use a basket, make certain that it is sturdy and that it is adjustable to handle fish or fillets of different thickness. There are several styles to choose from. I like the one called a "steak basket" because of the reasons just mentioned. It can also handle other foods, such as veggies.

Bass, whether fresh or saltwater species, are lean, firm and delicious on the grill. Only saltwater species are available for sale. Unless you catch your own or have a friend who is a better fisherman than connoisseur, you'll have to settle for saltwater species.

Find your fish and bring it home. Keep it cool and moist. Don't leave fish uncovered in the 'fridge— that dries them, spoiling taste and texture. You may choose to soak them in a little milk and water with a few dill seeds or a small piece of fresh dill. Allow six to eight ounces of fillet per person.

Prepare the grill for slow broiling - about 400° and a gentle smoke. Use white,apple, citrus or a little bay wood. You may also throw on three or four whole bay leaves, just when you add the fish.

Grilled Bass

For two pounds of filets, prepare a mixture of

1t.	garlic powder
1t.	dry mustard
1t.	ground thyme
1t.	rosemary
1t.	cayenne pepper
2	lemons
1/4 lb.	unsalted butter

If you have used a marinade, remove the fillets, pat dry and lay out in a shallow pan. Squeeze the juice of two lemons over the filets, covering both sides. Sprinkle the first five ingredients on both sides and press it into the fish.

At the grill, melt 1/4 pound unsalted butter in a saute pan. Pour the warm butter over the filets and place them, oiled side down on the grill. Pour the remaining butter into the pan which contained the fish and place it where the butter and lemon juice will remain warm. After about 2-3 minutes, or when the fish is half done, brush or pour butter on the upper side and turn. Remove the fish when it becomes opaque but before it dries out. If you are using a fish basket, butter both sides of the filets before putting the basket on the grill.

Serve the fish immediately and try to restrain yourself.

Grilled Panfish with Batter

Cooking over coals is the second oldest form of cooking. It was a distinct improvement over the original method— cooking in flames. While flame-fouled food betters most raw meat, discerning palates continued to look for better flavor.

Coals were soon discovered to be eminently superior to flames. They have been preferred to flames ever since. Just about everybody except magazine food editors and television commercial producers know this.

What I am gradually closing in on is the fact that every time I get impressed with a discovery on the grill, I have to face the fact that it was probably common- place two or three million years ago.

Be that as it may, I tried something new to me, and it turned out well enough that it's worth sharing.

As superfine as broiled fish can be, we sometimes just crave crispy little critters with batter on them. That means frying. Right? Wrong!

Next time you have the opportunity to cook bream, bluegills, crappie or any other panfish, give your grill a try.

Battered and Grilled Panfish

Clean your fish as usual. You may leave the heads on if desired.

Wipe dry and salt and pepper. Any other seasonings that you choose may be added as well. Prepare the grill for broiling - temperature about 500°.

Make a batter as follows:

1 C.	flour, pancake mix or tempura
3/4 C.	peanut oil
1/2 t.	garlic powder
1/2 t.	onion powder
1 T.	lemon juice
1 T.	salt
1 T.	black pepper
Mix well.	

Dip the fish into the batter and lay it on the grill. Allow to brown— 2-3 minutes and turn. Brown second side and check for doneness. Fish is done when the flesh is flaky and translucent. Do not overcook nor over-brown. If you are worried about overcooking, lower the temperature or move the fish to a cooler area of the grill..

This batter may hit a home run.

Grilled Grouper

According to a recent survey, the most common complaint about outdoor cooking is "it is a lot of trouble to get started." Nothing could be farther from the truth. Therefore, I am always shocked at the surprise exhibited when people see how easy and trouble-free it is to cook on the grill.

There are three good reasons for cooking outdoors. 1. It tastes better. 2. It is easier, more convenient. 3. It presents an opportunity to have fun.

Everybody knows it tastes better. Once you learn how to make it easier and convenient, you can put more creativity into the "having fun" part. There are times when it may be more desirable to be engaged in fun-type activities indoors than outdoors. Especially when temperatures outside are hovering around 100°.

Don't sweat the temperature. It makes no difference what the temperature is outdoors. You need not spend any more time outside than you want to.

Gas or charcoal, it takes less than a minute to light up the grill. Go play for 20 - 30 minutes. Put your meat on the grill. If you are broiling, total time on the grill is about ten minutes. You need not be present all the time.

If you are roasting, come back in about an hour to look at at the meat. If barbecuing, check by to baste at about 1/2 hour intervals. Just to show how little time is required at the grill, try timing this dish. Use any watch, clock or timer. Place it near the grill. Accumulate the time that you spend at the grill. It will surprise you as much as:

Grilled Grouper

With Shrimp and Mushroom Sauce

For four: 4 six-ounce steaks (or fillets) about 3/4 inch thick, trimmed and dried.

Sauce:

1/4 lb.	unsalted butter
2 T.	onion
2 T.	celery
1/2 lb.	shrimp, peeled and chopped
1/2 lb.	mushrooms, sliced
2 T.	flour
1/2 t.	thyme
1	small bay leaf
1	lemon, juiced
1/2 t	white pepper

At the grill, melt butter in small sauce pan. Put onions and celery in sauce pan and saute until transparent. Stir in thyme, bay leaf and pepper. Add mushrooms and saute until tender. Mix flour and lemon juice with enough water to make a smooth paste and blend into the other ingredients. Quickly adjust water to make a light smooth consistency. Add shrimp and saute until pink.

Brush both sides of steaks and place on the grill. Turn steaks. Do not over cook. Remove steaks to warm plate. *

Add sauce and serve while hot.

Later check the amount of time at the grill.

*Fish is done when it becomes opaque and before it will separate into flakes. Do not overcook.

135

Grill Braised Snapper

"Curses. Foiled again!"

Just because I occasionally figuratively flog those who insist on sealing food in foil and flinging it on the grill to "smoke," does not mean there are no legitimate uses for foil in cooking outdoors. It's just that blowing smoke about great smoky flavor, then assuring that it can't happen is grossly misleading. Properly used, foil can further increase the versatility of the grill.

There are some dishes that require the food to be cooked in juices and sauces. These can also be prepared on the grill, and using aluminum foil is one of the ways to do it. Heavy-duty aluminum foil can be shaped into pans or trays or used to line pans. When the food is cooked uncovered, smoke is allowed to flavor.

Foil allows us to produce some fantastic flavors and delightful dishes. For instance, for a fish dish that a French chef might call "Rouget en Papillote," we simply and easily use the colorful and delicious red snapper and aluminum foil to produce.

Grill Braised Red Snapper

Select a 3-4 pound fresh red snapper cleaned and dressed with the head intact. Keep the fish cool and moist. Rinse and wipe dry before cooking.

Line a baking pan with a layer of heavy aluminum foil and allow the foil to stick up above the pan sides at least an inch.

Into the pan, put

1/4 C.	unsalted butter or peanut oil
1/4 C.	grated onion
1 T.	chopped, fresh parsley
1 T.	chopped chives
1 C.	chopped mushrooms, divided
1 T.	chopped fresh basil
1 T.	chopped fresh dill
1/2 t.	rosemary
1/2 C.	dry white wine

Salt and pepper the fish and place on the bed of herbs.

136

Reserve an additional 1/2 cup mushrooms and 1 teaspoon fresh parsley from the amount listed above..

Prepare the grill for baking. Start out at about 375° and a heavier than normal smoke - which may include a couple of fresh or soaked bay leaves.

Place the pan on the grill and allow to cook for 15 minutes — actual time will depend on temperature and proximity to the coals. When the fish is slightly browned, spoon the juices over the fish, place remaining mushrooms on top of the snapper and sprinkle on the parsley. Cover the pan with another piece of aluminum foil and fold the edges to seal.

After about 15 minutes, remove the cover and baste with the juices. Remove when the fish flakes easily when tested with a fork.

Pour up the juices. Carefully slide the snapper onto a suitable dish and spoon the mushrooms sauce over it. Garnish with lemon slices and fresh parsley.

Guaranteed to make you take up the foil, even if you have never fenced in your life.

Seafood Stuffed Salmon

Ala Paul Kirk

Several years ago, I had the awesome responsibility and tough task of serving as chief judge at the Great Lenexa Barbecue Battle in Lenexa, Kansas, where the Kansas State championship is decided. Besides enjoying the company of old and new friends, I had to sample and pass judgement on sixteen different servings of championship quality barbecue. It's a tough life.

Lenexa, which is just outside Kansas City, is high-level competion In order to win the Grand Champion honors, a contestant had to cook in several categories: beef, pork, brisket, ribs, lamb, whole animal and a wild card. The wild card can cover anything from armadillo to rattlesnake.

There were 140 teams entered from several states. Barbecue rigs made from 55 gallon drums and ancient refrigerators were in abundance. One was made from cast-off offset printing plates. Naturally, there were some custom-made honeys made of stainless steel and 100 dollar bills.

The best thing I tasted wasn't even barbecue, strictly speaking. My friend Paul Kirk, a professional chef, a passionate barbecuer, author and teacher, is known in the Kansas City area and beyond as the Baron of Barbecue. The dish he served up in the wild card category was certainly baronial, even if not barbecued.

He slowly smoked a whole salmon, stuffed with a shrimp and crab stuffing. It melted in the mouth and almost caused melt-down of the knee bones. It was also so pretty that it made the eyes water. For a fitting occasion, you may want to give it a try. This is my best re-creation.

Smoked Salmon with Seafood Stuffing

Choose a bright-eyed fresh salmon 20-24 inches long. Wipe carefully with a little vinegar and water. Keep the knife flatly parallel to and firmly on the backbone. With the sharp fillet knife, slit the underside from head to within an inch of the tail. Do not cut through the top of the fish, but cut closely enough that the fish can be fully opened up. Lift up the backbone and slip the blade under it. Carefully cut close to the bone all the way to your tail stop, then remove the bone.

Cut carefully on both sides of the back fin and remove. Remove rib bones with a pair of pliers. Handle the fish gently.

Stuffing:

1/2 lb.	lump crab meat
1/2 lb.	shrimp, peeled and chopped.
1/4 C.	chopped onion
1/4 C.	chopped celery and tops
1/4 C.	chopped green onions
1 C.	coarse bread crumbs
4 T.	chopped fresh parsley.
4 T.	chopped fresh basil
1	clove garlic, minced.
4 T.	Butter or olive oil
	black pepper
	cayenne pepper
	bay leaves

Saute veggies in oil until wilted. Add shrimp and stir until they turn pink. Stir in crabmeat, bread crumbs, basil, peppers and parsley. Mix gently but well. Bread crumbs should absorb all the juices.

Spoon the stuffing into the salmon cavity - really stuff it. Secure the edges with tooth picks or wrap in cheesecloth. Place carefully on the grill with the large end nearest the coals.

Prepare the grill for roasting temperatures - about 350º. No strong woods. Use white oak, apple, bay or citrus. Alternate previously soaked small bay leaves at three or four intervals during cooking. This should be done in about 30 minutes or when the thickest part pierces easily and cleanly.

Remove carefully to an appropriate serving dish. Garnish with lemon, limes, oranges, parsley and small potatoes. Carve after everybody has an opportunity to enjoy the visual feast.

Simple, Savory Grilled Shrimp

Americans consume about 600 million pounds of shrimp annually. I would guess that 500 million pounds are either boiled or fried. That's a pity because shrimp are so versatile. It's like playing the piano using only two notes— which, by the way, covers the range of my singing voice.

Most of the shrimp caught in U.S. waters and brought to market are either the brown shrimp or the white shrimp. Pink shrimp get lumped into the brown group and Caribbean whites fall in with whites. Shrimp imported frozen from other countries may be one of several other commercial species. Brown and white seasons don't coincide, so we have the opportunity to have fresh shrimp more months than if they did.

As you know, shrimp are sold by "count." The count, 21-25 or 16-20, indicates the number of shrimp of that size that it takes to weigh one pound. Depending upon where you buy them, shrimp may be called some rather indefinite names, such as "Jumbo," "Extra large" or "Medium." While one man's "Medium" may seem pretty small to you, there is an official scale.

The National Marine Fisheries Service has published a standard reference. The categories are for raw, headless shrimp. It gives you some idea why "Medium" looks so small. A 10-15 count is "Extra colossal." Can you believe it? It sounds like P.T. Barnum was a consultant. "Medium," meanwhile, is a 43-50 count. The middle of the chart looks like this

Size	Count
Jumbo	21-25
Extra large	26-30
Large	31-35
Medium large	36-42

If you really want to go petite, some species run as high as 160 per pound.

Selecting shrimp is just following your nose. Fresh shrimp have no odor and retain their natural color. If they smell like ammonia, pass them up. If they are beginning to look like they have already been boiled, look for something else. Don't worry about any iodine odor. It only means they are from deep water.

In addition to being succulent and savory, shrimp have several delicious attributes. They have more protein per ounce (20.5%) than beef, pork or chicken. They are a little rich on the cholesterol scale, but it is not the bad kind. And their fat content is unsaturated. Plus, they deliver enough iodine to make you goiter-proof for a year.

Pay a visit to your friendly fish monger while shrimp are in season. Go for "Large" (31-35) as minimum and try for at least "Jumbo" (21-25). If his selection doesn't suit you, ask him when his next shipment will arrive. Go ahead and place your order and schedule your event.

Invest in a shrimp-shucking tool to make the chore of peeling shrimp and de-veining much easier. Your local gourmet shop ought to have them. I recommend the metal model rather than the plastic. You simply insert the tip of the tool under the shell just behind the head and push. The shrimp pops out of his shell in prompt and pristine fashion.

Savory Broiled Shrimp

For four adults, rinse and shell (not the other way around) about 2 pounds of jumbo shrimp.

Marinade

3	limes or lemons, juice of
1 T.	grated horseradish
2 t.	dill seed (heated) or 2 T. fresh dill weed
1 C.	dry white wine
1 C.	Snappy Tom or V-8 juice with 1/2 jalapeno pepper
3 T.	light olive oil
3 T.	finely chopped onion
1	clove garlic, mashed

Mix well, stir in shrimp to coat well and refrigerate in a covered container or plastic bag. Marinade 30 minutes to 2 hours.

Prepare the grill for broiling - temperature about 500°. Break up three bay leaves and soak in water. When the grill is ready, brush the grill with butter or olive oil and lay on the shrimp. Drop about half the bay leaves on the coals and close the grill. Using tongs, turn shrimp in about 3 minutes and add remainder of bay leaves. Remove as soon as shrimp firms up - 2-3 minutes. Don't worry about under cooking, but don't overcook. Serve immediately.

It is best to precede this event with preliminary munchies and appetizing accompaniments or you will have to fight for your fair share. Enjoy.

Variations:

Broiled shrimp are delicious simply basted with butter and lemon juice, which is the way I grill them most. However, they can be easily flavored for any taste that you choose. If you have a favorite flavor that you have tasted in shrimp fried, boiled or baked, try to reproduce that on the grill.

To peel or not to peel? Both have appealing rationales. The peeling can add more flavor— unless allowed to burn. If marinated, I normally leave the shells on. But, most of the time, my shrimp shells go into the stock pot. Therefore, the shrimp usually arrive at my grill already shelled.

Zesty Shrimp KeBabs

While most dishes can be cooked on any grill, this one can even be cooked on a small hibachi. This can be served as a casual hors d'oeuvre, where each cooks his or her own; a fish course of a long meal or the main course. Suit yourself.

Smallest of the grills, the hibachi, is a bonsai version of a grill— a miniature. They perform beautifully for broiling teriyaki and small shish ka bobs. Even a couple of hamburgers, small steaks or seafood will fit the grill. Normally of cast iron, the sturdy grills are less than a foot tall with a surface area about 10 by 12 inches.Because the good ones are sturdy and well designed for draft, they can produce much more intense heat than some larger, but less efficient, grills. Prices range.from $7-$35. Very good ones can be had in mid range.

Zesty Shrimp KeBabs

For four

4 lbs.	Shrimp, medium or jumbo with heads and shells will yield about 2 lbs. of meat.

Marinade

1 C.	dry white wine
2 T.	lime or lemon juice
1 t.	Tabasco sauce
1 t.	mustard, ground
1/2 t.	onion powder
1/2 t.	garlic powder
1/8 t.	ground cloves
1	ground bay leaf
1 T.	finely chopped dill weed
1 t.	ground coriander

Blend mustard, in 1 T. warm water before adding to other ingredients. Add shrimp. Marinate in refrigerator 1-3 hours.

Skewer shrimp with alternating slices of sweet onion, thinly sliced, celery and Florence fennel and lime.

Skewer the shrimp (or fish: see note below) and return to the 'fridge while the coals are getting right. Let each person hoist his is own petard. Broil each about three minutes per side. Serve with finger-ready steamed vegetables, boiled small potatoes and fresh French bread.

This hibachi treat will give you a yen for more.

Substitute fillets of any firm fleshed fish - 6 - 8 oz. per person. Remove extraneous parts and cut into strips approximately 1 inch wide and 3 inches long. Just don't over cook.

In a simpler version, just baste the shrimp with a mixture of 1/2 melted butter and 1/2 butter and 1/2 lemon or lime juice. This is a quick, delicious treat.

Oysters on the Grill

Perhaps it is because it has so few things to recommend it that I think of February as an especially good oyster month. In the old days, a sack of oysters, bought or caught in February, would keep outdoors in an old oak barrel all month or until the last one was consumed.

If you truly enjoy the tasty bivalve in all its variety, buying oysters by the sack makes them convenient and economical, if such an option is available. Pour oysters from the sack into an intermediate container and rinse off all muck and mud. Discard any open or movable shells.

Place a suitable size, non-reactive container — a plastic garbage can will do — out of direct sunshine and fill with cold, fresh water to about 3/4 of capacity. Then add 1/4 lb. salt per gallon and stir. (I used to use ex-whiskey barrels, but the oysters got plumb silly.) Then place the *selects* into storage barrel and sprinkle in a half cup of cornmeal.

You may adjust the saltiness of the oysters by adding more salt or less to the water. If you keep the oysters more than a couple of weeks, exchange some of the water and add new salt and meal. If the weather turns warm, add enough ice to keep the temperature of the water around 65° F. Remove any oysters whose souls have obviously gone to that great oyster bed in the sky.

You will probably select the smaller oysters for eating raw on the half shell or for frying. Save the larger ones for soups, stews and gumbos. Medium size can go either way.

If shucking oysters is not one of your favorite pastimes, let me drop a hint. Give the oysters a 5 minute bath in carbonated water (club soda) just before you open them. They get so intoxicated from absorbing the carbon dioxide that they practically pop open for you.

The easiest way, of course, is to put them on the grill. They open up themselves with a big smile and invite flavoring in several different ways.

Grilled Oysters in the Shell

Select 40-50 medium to large oysters; scrub clean. Fire up the grill for low-medium - 250° and have a good supply of hardwood for smoking.

Place the oysters on the grill so that their bottom shell will parallel to the grate and will not spill any of the good juices when it opens.

Stuffing

1/4 C.	chopped green onions
1	clove garlic, minced
1/4 lb.	unsalted butter
1/4 C.	lemon juice

Saute garlic and onion until tender; then add lemon juice and stir well.

When the oyster shells open, remove the top shell and secure the bottom in a level position. Don't lose the juice. Add 1/4 t. of the sauteed mixture to each oyster.

Add oak or hickory wood for a rather heavy smoke for ten - fifteen minutes. Sample frequently. Do not overcook.

Try as many variations of seasonings as you desire. You may also want to just smoke some heavily, add a little olive oil and use for flavoring other dishes.

This can make a varied feast when you don't feel like going through all the fun of shucking oysters.

Variations: Oysters cooked on the grill add another level of flavors when used for Oysters Rockefeller and Oysters Bienville.

Soft Shell Crawfish

When the early awakening azalea bursts forth its first red-orange blossom, it reminds me that similarly colored crawfish are likely tasted soon. Well— that's what they remind me of anyhow.

Last year, I made a significant discovery in the delicious galaxy of craw fish cuisine. It was so new and unique in concept and so startling upon consumption that I thought it deserved a full-fledged investigation before being reported.

What I had tasted was soft-shell crawfish. Long have I taken delight in devouring the delicious, crusty crab, caught between changes of armor, and broiled to a careful combination of crunch and tender succulence - drenched extravagantly in lemon juice and butter and kissed by the subtle aroma of savory herbs and spices.

After years of wrestling the reluctant mud bug from his colorful carapace, the tantalizing thought of effortlessly eating the uncloaked crustacean added zest to my zeal.

Soft-shell crawfish, like soft-shell crabs, require a lot of human attention. The crustacean must leave his shell in order to grow. When he exits the old suit, he is very vulnerable, and must hide in the short period he is unsuited. He expands rapidly and his new shell begins to harden.

Experienced human eyes must detect the pubescent polypod, and experienced human hands must move him to a holding tank of many cells and flowing water. As the crustacean progresses toward nudity, he or she is moved into other compartments with others in a similar state of undress. This is because the belligerent bugs also enjoy the tempting taste of crawfish, and the hard shells attack the softies.

When the changelings are completely nude and swelled with pride, they are quick-frozen to keep them at their plump and tender best. Shell hardening may be delayed by severely lowering the temperature of the water in the tanks, but the only certain way to maintain the tender exterior is freezing - other than immediate consumption, of course.

When soft-shell production began, the price was pegged at $10.00 per pound. This made producers eager to burn the midnight watts to save the little softies. The prodigious profit potential also provided a proliferation of producers. However, disorganized marketing efforts caused the supply to outstrip demand (pardon) and put the whole process into chaos. I am convinced the problems of production and distribution will get worked out.

Therefore, I think it time to tell the soft-porn tale of born-soft tails so you can be prepared to seize a proffered portion should the opportunity present itself. The same cooking technique can be applied to Maine or Spiny Lobster.

A word of warning. A pound of soft-shell crawfish, properly prepared, are roughly the equivalent of 6-8 pounds of boiled crawfish in performance as well as price. One pound is amply adequate for two normal appetites.

Broiled Soft Shell Crawfish

Quickly thaw one pound fresh or frozen soft-shelled crawfish in running water or water that is frequently changed.

1/4 lb.	unsalted butter
2	lemons, juiced and 1 reserved
1/4 C.	dry white wine
3 T.	shallots, finely chopped
1/2 t.	ground bay
1/2 t.	ground thyme
1/2 t.	Hungarian paprika
1/4 t.	ground mustard
1/4 t.	ground cayenne
1/4 t.	fresh ground black pepper
1/2 t.	salt

Melt butter over medium heat and gently saute shallots until clear. Remove shallots. Deglaze with wine, bay leaf and thyme. Mix other ingredients, including shallots, and sprinkle on thawed crawfish.

Prepare the grill for low broiling - about 500°. That means that you can hold your hand two inches from the grill about a second. Fruit woods and citrus (or sassafras) mixed half and half with white oak are a good mixture for smoke. Without citrus or sassafras, use hickory up to 20 percent of the total.

When the grill is ready, baste the crawfish well and place directly over the coals. Make certain that there is plenty of butter on the underside. Baste the topside and turn quickly — within two minutes. Baste and turn again and then repeat. The crawfish should be done within 10 minutes after hitting the grill. Sample one to check. If they need more cooking, move them away from the coals and close the grill lid. Do not overcook.

Serve with boiled new potatoes and fresh asparagus or sweet peas and a good white wine. This will make you look for a crawfish nudist camp.

Soft-shelled crabs, Maine and spiny lobsters are even better when broiled on the grill. Select the smaller lobsters, remove from the shell and baste with fresh butter and lemon juice. Do not overcook – they get tough and tougher.

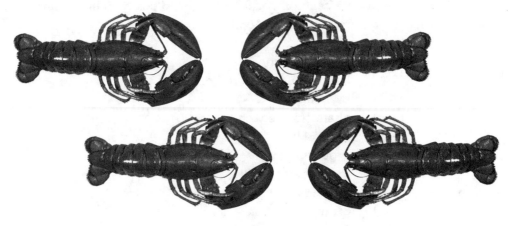

Mock Crab

Normally, if you like the taste of what you have to eat, there is no need to marinate seafood. Add seasonings before you put it on the grill and/or put them into the basting sauce to be absorbed while cooking.

Occasionally, you may marinate, to add more of a distinctive flavor to a food which will not be cooked but a few minutes. Be careful not to overpower the original flavor — unless that is your intent.

Broiled soft-shelled crabs are as delicious as they are rare and expensive. We can fake this fantastic flavor and texture with a masterful marinade.

Crab Masquerade Marinade

6-8 oz. fillets of fresh fish per person

Use any firm fleshed fish with low oil content. Sheepshead, grouper and drum are superior specimens as well as fresh-water bass, perch and bream. Slice the fillets about 1/4 inch thick and trim extraneous parts.

In a glass dish, mix

2 C.	water
2	lemons, juiced
2 T.	liquid crab boil

Layer the fillets into the marinade, cover and refrigerate for 2 to 24 hours. Remove fillets, pat dry and brush with a mixture of:

1/4 lb.	melted butter
1/4 t.	garlic powder
1/4 t	onion powder
1/4 t.	white pepper

Brush with butter mixture and broil to a golden tan, about two minutes per side. If you creatively invested the money that you saved by faking the crabs in a good white wine, earn double bonus points, otherwise just savor the flavor.

Frog Legs *al Fresco*

All summer they grew fat and sleek, lounging in the sun beside the water, eating all day, frolicking, and making music late into the night. Day after day, I ate my porridge and watched and waited and sorely fretted.

Long did I count their numbers— and their days. Then, the long wait was over and my summer of discontent ended. The agony of long-postponed pleasure had run its course. The first cool morning signaled the time of reckoning.

Actually, my pain of waiting was somewhat assuaged because the little darlin's were eating mosquitoes and other little six-legged varmints while they fattened up. But I had admired their long, plump legs from a distance long enough. So, I harvested about two thirds of the bull frog population before they went into hibernation.

A properly done frog leg is a neat, easy-to-eat, delicious little morsel. Six plump, tender legs will weigh around one pound and can form the centerpiece of a delectable meal.

Fortunately for the frogs— and unfortunately for humans— most folks are introduced to frog legs at the dinner table only in the battered and fried format. Most often, especially in restaurants, they are overcooked until tough and dry. It is not surprising, therefore, that folks whose acquaintance with frogs is limited to such short shrift are less than enthusiastic about the juicy little gams.

If they are of the foreign, frozen variety, they can make you think that frogs are only fit to sit on lily pads eating bugs or to enter a frog jumping contest. That is as far from the truth as Calaveras County, CA, is from Key West, FL.

Unless you participate in the sport of frog grabbing or have a friend who does, the freezer section of the food market is your most likely source of supply. My experience is that domestic frogs are superior to foreign frogs, French provincialism notwithstanding. But even most foreign frogs can be rendered tender and tasty with a tad of talented treatment.

The succulent saucy songsters from my pond required no special treatment to transform them into savory servings. But here is how you can fix your foreign affair.

152

Frog Legs *al Fresco*

Two dozen legs will amply feed four adults. Thaw the legs in sufficient water to cover with about 4 T. vinegar per quart of water. When almost thawed, rinse thoroughly under running water and place in a glass or plastic dish.

Cover with 1/3 water, 1/3 white wine and 1/3 milk and refrigerate for 30 minutes to 24 hours. Meanwhile mix a marinade/basting sauce as follows:

1 C.	white wine
1 T.	fresh lemon juice
1 clove	garlic, crushed
2 cloves	shallots, crushed
1 T.	chopped fresh parsley
1 t.	thyme
1	bay leaf
1 dash	grated nutmeg
1 stick	unsalted butter
1/2 lb.	sliced mushrooms

Saute garlic and shallots in 1/2 of the butter; then add all other ingredients, except mushrooms, and simmer gently for a few minutes. Saute the mushrooms in the rest of the butter.

When the sauce has cooled, drain and dry the legs and baste them with the sauce.

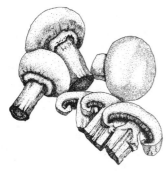

Prepare the grill for low broiling temperature - about 400º. Citrus, bay or fruitwood are the preferred woods for smoke.

When the coals are is ready, baste the legs again and place them on the grill. Continue to baste and turn frequently. Depending upon the temperature, the legs should be perfectly done and tender to the teeth in about 20 minutes. You may have to force yourself to sample a couple to determine their peak.

Strain the remaining marinade/basting sauce into the mushrooms, mix in a dollop of sour cream and bring it up to simmer temperature.

Remove the frog legs to a warm platter, spoon the sauce over them and garnish with fresh parsley and lemon slices.

You may begin to share my affliction of being unable to hear the chorus of a frog pond at night without salivating.

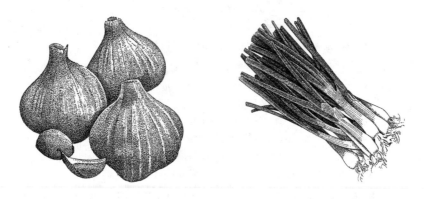

Sausages

The Wurst I Ever Had Was Wunderful

Charlie Brown and I have a perpetual fascination with redheads of the opposite gender. I even went so far as to marry one. I was more than pleased, therefore, to find a lovely, young member of the carrot-topped species cozying up to the wet bar early at the party.

Smooth-talking-devil that I am, it was not long before we had become right friendly. As the evening progressed, so did our relationship. Before long, it was apparent that we might wind up sharing more than just pleasant conversation. By the time the party was breaking up, we had a firm agreement on what the exchange would entail and when it would take place.

She had planned a visit of several days with her parents in Milwaukee which gave me plenty of time to enjoy the anticipation. Slyly savoring sensuous sentiments scintillated my senses on a soaring scale. Voluptuous visions tenderly tormented as time trudged tardily.

Sometimes, the joy of anticipation exceeds the pleasure of fruition and the act itself is anticlimactic. Ah, but this time, even my wildest fancies of imagination paled, and palled, beside the real thing. As I slowly unveiled the lush and lovely charms, I became ravenous with desire. Their beauty, and perfect form, exceeded all my previous experience.

Yes, Dear Readers, it was a night to remember. In my book of memories, the fresh bratwurst that the young lady brought to me from Milwaukee will always have a special place.

Bratwurst, for those who have not been fully exposed to the lovelies, are fresh sausages, about weenie length and a little larger in circumference. Not seasoned with sage and red pepper like Southern sausages, they have less fat and less seasoning than the traditional American breakfast sausage. These robust links, of German ancestry, are a serious sausage, meant to be a main course.

Nowhere is the art of making the best of the wurst situation more diversely and deliciously practiced than in Milwaukee, WI. The individual artist paints from the palette of his own palate. Each neighborhood seems to have its champion in a small-sausage stuffing operation. As with the boudin of Southern Louisiana, big commercial operations fail to survive the cut, in the wurst-case scenario.

Bratwurst's popularity continues to spread southward as the technique filters down. The Kansas City area has several producers of wonderful wursts and an expanding cadre of wurstheads. Commercial attempts occasionally show up in Deep South meat departments. But if you should ever find a little redheaded girl going home to Milwaukee, do whatever she asks to get her to bring you back a few. Properly grilled, they make a trip to the snowbelt seem attractive, even in January.

Grilled Bratwurst

Allow 2 bratts per person. Fire the grill for roasting — stemperature about 325°. Provide a nice medium smoke; I use white oak and apple. Place the bratts on the grill and close the lid. Cook for about 30-40 minutes, turning as required at 10-15 minute intervals. Bratts are done when they become firm. Do not overcook and dry them out.

Secure some hefty buns, even if you have to make them. The crummy, crumbly, cheap hotdog buns will not do. If you are unable to find buns, eat the bratts on a plate with good, heavy duty bread.

Proper accompaniments are a full-flavored mustard and real sauerkraut. I recommend the kind packaged in glass and normally available in the refrigerated storage area of the supermarket.

A few sliced onions, a few cold beers and a few good friends will round out a memorable meal.

Perchance a redhead?

"You Can't Teach an Old Dog New Tricks"

Right after marshmallows, most people learn how to cremate a wiener. The kid who has never burned a hot dog on a little fire outdoors is truly deprived. Hot dogs have the exceptional characteristic that no matter how bad or how burned or how gritty, one is always good to a kid. God knew what he was doing when he put hunger amongst us.

Hot dogs are reputed to be the item most often cooked on a grill. Somewhere around four billion pounds are consumed each year raw, boiled or roasted. Those of us in the know realize that those cooked on a grill aren't actually roasted; they are more likely broiled— and most likely burned.

Because they are so popular, I thought hot dogs deserved a decent dissertation. So I went down to the local commissary and checked out the offerings. Nothing is as simple as it used to be.

In addition to the traditional weenie of ground up pork and beef parts, there are a lot of strangers. Chicken, turkey and soybeans have joined the crowd, along with the beef people's representatives. In the interests of science, I got one of each. All except the soybean, that is. As far as I know, I eat soy beans in tofu and soy sauce - with emphasis on the soy sauce.

My fondest memories of hot dogs are associated with baseball games, where weenies were generally steamed or boiled. Therefore, as a bench mark, I ran the first batch through boiled. My all-time favorite hot dog is a fat weenie, generously slathered with mustard, chopped onions and sauerkraut and bedded down in a warm bun that stays together long enough to be consumed. This fond flavor was developed in the years when every town with more than two barber shops had a semi-pro baseball team that played on Thursday and Sunday afternoons. That hot dog remains the all-time-best fifteen-cent bargain. A nickel

 drink still left enough money from a quarter for a bag of peanuts. (That was after I had walked six miles, each way, to school— through the snow.)

With my bench mark newly polished on the palate, I carefully marked cryptic identification on each variety and invited some friends with sons of immense appetites and indiscriminate palates. I told the parents that I was grilling steaks, waiting until they arrived to clarify that they were "tube steaks."

As a matter of pure research, I also tested a theory that had come to me in the wee hours of the morning— whence come brilliant thoughts that need to be quickly written down and captured, before they escape forever. With the weight of weenie wonders weighing heavily, I had for some weeks entertained the idea of simmering weenies in one of my legendary basting sauces before putting it on the grill. I expected, thereby, to transform this close cousin to a road kill into an elegant example of gastronomic ecstasy. Had I not properly fortified myself I would, no doubt, have trembled in anticipation.

But, alas, another bolt of bedtime brilliance bit the boards. Smoky's First Law of Weenies is, "It is easier to grow pearls inside hickory nuts than to change the taste of weenies."

Not one to falter in the face of foul fortune, I prepared a superb assortment of green woods for subtle flavoring on the grill. Presenting statistically valid samples to carefully controlled conditions, I grilled each lot to perfection. True to tradition, I properly burned some. When done, I cut each weenie in half, to allow precise testing on a properly primed palate.

The results of the tests were clear and decisive. Those who like hot dogs, liked them. Smoky's Second Law of Weenies is, "It is easier to grow pearls inside hickory nuts than to change the taste of weenies."

The all-beef and the all-turkey varieties got highest marks. Price and promotional verbiage proved irrelevant. Everybody was surprised by the variety—proving the theory that most people just take a bite of whatever is in their hand and keep on talking.

In summary, hot dogs are still a viable victual that most kids and many adults enjoy. They are quick, easy and nutritious. Don't try to improve them.

Keep the temperature lower than for normal broiling. If you drop the temperature to around 300°, have patience, long skewers and a sturdy grill, you can let the kids do their own. Allow a few extra for the dogs, dirt and burnt offerings. Afterwards, stir up the coals, add more charcoal and relax until the grill is ready to cook whatever you intend to eat.

Philosophically, weenies aren't quite as good as I remembered nor nearly as bad as I expected. Gastronomically, they are not likely to change.

Chapter 5

Roasting

Roasting was, no doubt, man's earliest form of cooking. Meat must be marbled, or very young, in order for it to be tender enough for the quick, hot coals of broiling. Barbecuing requires several leisurely hours over the coals— not likely for the barely-man creature consumed by hunger and surrounded by others eager to consume him.

So a piece of meat impaled on a stick rested in the radiant and rising heat of wood coals as long as the eager eaters could wait. Most likely, "well done" was invented by the timid softies of future cities. Certainly a little pink would never turn off those who had, for generations, eaten their meat without benefit of fire.

Centuries before the oven was invented, meat was roasted or, after clay pots, boiled. Meat cooked enclosed in the oven is, to be accurate, baked. Therefore, roasts cooked in an enclosed grill are technically baked. I find the distinction rather meaningless, however, since in either case, the meat is cooked in dry heat by radiant and convective transmission. Enclosed in a grill or oven, meat may also receive heat by conduction (see the chapter on "**Heat**") but if mounted on a metal spit above hot embers, the spit would also conduct heat into the interior of the food. Cooking in an enclosure is much more fuel efficient and suffers in comparison to true roasting only in that the meat may not benefit from its juices dropping into coals below, being wafted back, and deposited, as flavoring upon the meat.

Cuts of meat a little too tough to broil benefit from the longer exposure to lower temperatures by becoming more tender and tasty. The time and temperature also provide opportunity for seasonings to serve their purpose. Fruits, vegetables, nuts and cheeses can also benefit from roasting temperatures. And, never forget, that the versatile grill can bake a cake, a loaf of bread or a pan of beans.

Rib Roasts and Bone Companions

Should the occasion arise when I must call witnesses to verify my competence at the grill, my first call will be for Buster. Actually, if he is in the neighborhood, I will not have to speak a sound.

Buster is 85 pounds of pussycat, except for garbage trucks, which he can hear long before the imperfect human aural organ registers a hint. And, except if a strange male enters the house and tries to close the door on Buster's head before he has satisfied himself that my red-headed wife is safe, he is a genial giant.

My wife and Buster formed a mutual admiration society when he was just a fuzzy pup. He took upon himself the task of protecting her, sticking his head in the door, like Marshall Dillon, just to make sure that everything was as it should be. It is a chore which he takes seriously, reserving for himself alone the decision when to remove his head from the door.

But that is not why I would value him as a witness in my defense. Buster likes my cooking.

The same keen sense that announces an approaching garbage truck, at radar range, brings him strolling, nonchalant but purposeful, at the first squeak of the opening of the grill. Since his taste has matured, Buster has never missed a firing of the grill.

Nor does his attention wander during all the puttering and preparations. He is more constant than the Dog Star. His is not given to whining, barking and jumping about. Such activity is beneath his dignity. He maintains a casual but constant surveillance. Only his big brown eyes give evidence that he follows every move. He gives all the appearance of believing that he is invisible.

Buster is the consummate connoisseur and behaves as though Miss Manners had used him for her model. Even though the eager twitching of his nostrils belies his calm, he never asks and no doubt would die before he would beg; Buster waits, intensely interested, studiously observant, but correctly calm until he is served.

Perhaps it is because he knows, beyond doubt, that he will be the first judge of the offering that he maintains his kingly calm. Maybe he also knows that what is served will be cooked to his desires. Buster prefers his beef medium rare. He correctly shuns over cooking and over smoking.

When he is served, he does not gulp and grovel. With proper, even majestic decorum, he savors the aromas; then, without fail, he turns to give an appreciative eye. When he has fully appreciated the aroma and appearance, and it has, incidentally, sufficiently cooled, he eats with slow, savoring bites with no less gravity than an embryonic oenophile at a wine tasting.

He has a voracious and therefore, plump female friend in the neighborhood with whom, in certain seasons, he will share his other food. Never, even at the absolute peak of her desirability, will he share his portion from the grill.

With such an honest admirer, it is not surprising that when I spied the rib roast in the meat cooler, I thought of how much Buster would enjoy the succulent meat closest to the bones. If pressed for comment, he would testify that we both enjoyed the

Buster's Grilled Rib Roast

Allowing one rib per person, select a section which has minimum surrounding fat and in which the rib eye is large and consolidated without fat or membranes interspersed.

Prepare the grill for broiling (700°), but have enough coals for cooking and additional 15 to 30 minutes at roasting temperatures (350°). A rib roast should be seared (browned) well on the outside, then moved to a lower temperature to allow the center to reach 140° (medium rare) without drying out the outside.

Bring the roast out of the 'fridge in time to allow it to reach room temperature before it goes on the grill. Beef does not spoil by becoming warm. Soak all sides thoroughly in lemon juice and coat heavily with fresh ground black pepper. Minced garlic in virgin olive oil is a taste you may want to try next time.

When the coals are right and the meat is warm and the cook is ready, place the roast firmly on the hot grill. In about 5 minutes the first side should turn loose the grill. Turn the roast — with tongs or your hand — do not pierce it with a fork. Let the second side sear and release.

Move the roast to quiet corner of the grill, or shut down the air intake, to about 350º for 15 to 30 minutes depending upon the size of the roast. Use a thermometer , looking for about 140 degrees , or press it with your fingers. Take the meat off when it still responds promptly and pleasingly to your fingertips.

Allow it to cool for 5-10 minutes before carving out the bones for Buster. Salt as desired at the table. Buster knows rib roasts.

" Prime rib" and "standing rib roasts" are really names for recipes than any real distinctions in meat. You are as likely to find a black pearl in an oyster as to find prime grade rib sections in the average meat market. Prime rib is merely a name for the rib eye or rib roast. So is the standing rib roast, which cooks just as well sitting or laying down, as it doies standing. Other excellent candidates for roasting on the grill are sirloin tip and some chuck roasts. Rump, although a little tougher than the sirloin tip can still be tender if not overcooked. The tri-tip is another fine cut, but, like the rib eye, almost demands broiling instead.

Meatloaf on the Grill

"There's gold in them thar grills!"

The idea of changing something of little value into something precious has seduced man for centuries. Alchemists labored long, in lonesome laboratories, secretly seeking to solve the mystery of how to turn lead into gold.

Magical black boxes have been used to create instant wealth, by turning ordinary paper into money, or to divinely detect oil deposits deep beneath the earth's surface. Except for the creators of the little black boxes, the only enrichment that anyone got was experience. Expensive, but valuable.

The only black box that I know of that really works magic is a good grill with a tight cover. Turning the mundane into the magnificent on a grill is almost as easy as waving a magic wand. Take, for instance, the lowly meatloaf, plebeian even at its tastiest, but placed in the magic box with proper incantations it is transformed into a royal treat.

Grilled Roasted Meatloaf

3 lbs.	ground chuck
1 C.	finely ground bread crumbs
2	eggs
1/2 C.	plain yogurt
1/2 C.	finely chopped onions
3	cloves, minced garlic
1/4 C.	bell pepper, blanched and finely chopped
1/4 C.	finely chopped tender celery tops
1/2 t.	thyme
1/2 t.	ground bay leaf
1/4 t.	cayenne pepper
1/2 t.	fresh ground black pepper
2 t.	salt

Dry real bread in oven or toaster until brittle and crumbly. It is okay to let it brown a little, but do not toast it. Break it into a blender or food processor and reduce to fine crumbs using the pulse button. A rolling pin rolled over crumbs in a plastic bag works very well . Measure and return one cup to blender. Add all herbs and spices except garlic, onion, bell pepper and celery and blend briefly but thoroughly.

Blend ground beef and bread crumb mixture and spread on waxed paper in a layer about 1/2 inch thick. Beat eggs, blend in yogurt, mix in onion, garlic, bell pepper and celery and spread evenly on meat.

Roll up the whole thing like a jelly roll. Shape into a roll 3 - 4 inches in diameter. Wrap the waxed paper around it to smooth the surface , then unwrap and and place on a shallow metal pan. Allow the loaf to sit for at least 10 minutes.

The grill should be prepared for roasting - about 350° and will need to maintain the temperature for about an hour and a half. Use moderate smoke. When the grill has reached 350°, place it gently on the grill end opposite the coals.

Close the grill lid and go away. Check back in about 30 minutes to adjust the temperature if necessary. If your grill can sustain the temperature, disappear for another hour. The loaf is done when the internal temperature reaches 155°.

Sauce

1- 6 oz. can	tomato puree or tomato paste
1 C.	water
1 T.	onion flakes
1/2 t.	garlic powder
1/4 t.	thyme
1/4 t.	ground bay leaf
	salt and pepper to taste

Simmer until thickened

When meatloaf is done— 155°, remove from the grill, drain juices and stir them into sauce. And allow meatloaf to sit for 10 minutes before slicing. If you don't have a long sharp knife, saw gently with a serrated bread knife. Salt individual servings, if desired.

After all those things that have gone up in a puff of smoke, here comes magic from the grill.

Variations on the theme.

Any recipe that you can cook in the oven improves when cooked on the grill. Take your grandmother's recipe and give it a try.

POULTRY

Cornish Hens

What to cook is rarely a problem around our house. We are still in the "hunter/gatherer" stage of development. We take advantage of whatever fortune turns our way. There was a whole lot of smiling the day the Cornish hens flew in.

We are normally too civilized and polite to openly discuss it— ashamed even— but, in our more honest moments, we must acknowledge it. There is something basic to our nature in the urge to tear into a whole carcass, ala *Tom Jones*. I think that is a large part of the attraction of Cornish hens.

Gone, if indeed they ever existed outside the movies, are the massive medieval meals where a whole chicken was merely one of the several meat courses consumed by each gourmand. Presently, propriety and personal health prevent our pandering to these prurient passions.

But, what the heck, anybody can decorously devour this diminutive doughty as a delicious diversion, demurely denying overdoing it. Besides that, they taste good, are simple to prepare and make a beautiful presentation.

"Cornish," applied to chickens, has only recently gained currency regarding their qualities as an edible. When they first came on the market, they were called "Cornish Game Hens" in recognition of their heritage. The breed developed in the Cornwall region of the British Isles as a compact, tightly feathered fowl with small combs. Endowed with these physical attributes and a bellicose nature, it was one of the first breeds use in cockfighting. Later bred with the wild game fowl from the East Indies, they became the parent stock of what is now called "game chickens."

But these tender little darlin's we are about to prepare have neither been sullied by harsh thought nor violent act. Their only flaw, in my estimation, is that they are inclined to be on the chubby side. Roasting them on the grill gets rid of all that excess fat and cholesterol.

167

Plan on a whole bird for each adult. There is not much opportunity to choose because, unlike common poultry, Cornish hens are shipped covered and frozen. Thaw for 12 hours, in the 'fridge or in cold water for about 2 or in the microwave according to directions.

Roasted Cornish Hens

Remove giblets, wash inside and out under running water. Wipe dry and rub with lemon juice inside and out. Sprinkle outside with a mixture (for 4 birds) of:

1 T.	Hungarian Paprika
1/2 t.	thyme, ground
1/2 t.	bay leaf, ground
1/2 t	sage, rubbed
1/2 t.	garlic powder
1/2 t.	onion powder
1/4 t.	ground cloves
1/4 t.	cayenne pepper

Allow to sit at room temperature while you prepare a stuffing.

2 C.	bread crumbs — of real bread or rolls
1 C.	apple sauce
1/4 C.	celery and tops, chopped fine
1	fresh, medium orange, peeled, seeded and chopped, with juice.
1/8 t.	ground cloves

Mix well and pack each bird tightly. The mixture should be rather dry with just enough moisture to hold it together. Add more bread crumbs if required. Pin the cavity closed.

Prepare the grill for low roasting - about 300°. Use fruit woods— apple, pear and citrus, if available, for smoke. Do not over smoke.

Place the hens on racks over a drip pan and close the grill. When the juices dripping into the pan begin to brown, add just enough water to the pan to prevent burning. Use these juices for basting, near the end.

168

Allow about 40-60 minutes for cooking. Test for doneness with the thermometer in the thickest part of the thigh without touching bone, then check the center of the stuffing. Remove at 155° or when the drumstick twists easily.

Allow to cool for 10 minutes. Serve with fresh asparagus, lightly steamed carrots and new potatoes in their red skins.

You may want to read a verse from Miss Manners before serving to assure proper decorum during dining.

Cold Duck

There are only three good reasons for cooking outdoors. 1. It is more fun. 2. Particular food tastes better when cooked on a grill. 3. It is easier to cook outdoors. There may be some other reasons— your spouse won't let you fry the chitlin's in the house, the gas/electricity is off, etc. But the good reasons are that it is easier, better and more fun.

When the wet winter winds whip in and whine at 30 knots, the particular food has to be a whole lot better when cooked outdoors to justify cranking up the grill. These are the times discretion and good planning are the warmer part of valor.

The real secret to maximum enjoyment from cooking on the grill, of course, is in letting the grill do its thing while we are occupied with activities more pleasant than hovering over the firebox. Some things, however, require more attention than others. Nasty weather is not the time to be barbequing chicken— unless you happen to get your jollies running in and out for 3 or 4 hours to baste. Personally, I get sort of picky about what I cook outdoors during excremental weather.

Foods that require a very short time on the grill, such as steaks and burgers, are a good choice. The other type of goodies that go good on the grill in grungy weather are those that require a long cooking time, but no attention between putting it on and taking it off. Roasts, whole poultry, meat loaves, etc., can be abandoned worse than a homely girl at a high school prom.

There are a couple of prerequisites, however. A grill of sufficient size to hold ample charcoal and wood for the cooking period is a must. The grill must also have an adjustable air intake that will allow controlled combustion over the long period. With adequate combustible material, temperature is dependent upon the amount of oxygen that the fire gets. So, a 20 pound pile of charcoal will produce no higher temperature than a 4 pound pile, given oxygen at the same rate— but it will burn 5 times as long.

Gas grills must be able to put out enough BTUs to overcome the heat loss from the weather, and pre-heated to around 350°.

Roast duck is a different delight this season of the year. I call this one

Cold Duck

1 duck - about 5 1/2 pounds

Trim excess fat, prick lower thighs and lower breast several times and score with a sharp knife. Salt and pepper inside and out.

Stuff the duck with

1/2	medium apple, sliced
1/2	small onion, sliced
2	stalks of celery and leaves

Basting Sauce

While the duck is coming to room temperature, baste several times, with a mixture of

1/4 C.	pepper vodka
1/4 C.	peach schnapps

Reserve half C. for deglazing

Fire up the grill to produce roasting temperature - 350° - for 2 1/2 - 3 hours. Remember that the cold outside temperature will require extra charcoal to produce the equivalent summertime BTUs. Citrus is the preferred wood for smoke flavoring this dish. Fruit woods are acceptable.

Place the duck, trussed if you are into bondage, on the grill over a pan with about 1/4 inch water. Close the grill and adjust the air intake. Check back in about 30 minutes to assure that the grill is maintaining the proper temperature.

Baste while you are there. Then go play for about and hour. Check and baste again.

Check for doneness at about 1 1/2 hours total cooking time. Temperature in the thickest part of the thigh should be 160 degrees and juices should run clear when done. Remove the duck, then pour the fat off the pan juices; deglaze pan with

1/2 C.   baste mixture

then add (this can be done inside)

1/2 C.   peach preserves

Blend and cook until thickened.

Keep sauce warm while you carve the duck. Serve the sauce on the side. Served with a light, slightly fruity wine. It should make you think of spring and fruit trees blossoming in the brilliant sunlight.

Turkey Time Anytime

How strange we are to ignore a tasty, economical source of protein ten months out of the year. Unlike chicken, which we consume year round, we reserve turkey for that period between Thanksgiving and Christmas. Surely our tradition drives the turkey producers up the wall.

Besides tradition, turkeys present a few differences from chicken that make some folks hesitate. Their large size puts off some people. Even if they have a large oven and time, not many enjoy turkey seven days in a row.

Then there are those who have a terminal case of "over cook" when it comes to turkeys. They consistently turn out turkey breast as dry as a dust devil's breath. To head off such disasters, they use elaborate schemes involving aluminum foil, roasting bags and even boiling. Here is another place where a good grill, and a little organized laziness, come to the rescue.

These days it is relatively easy to buy smaller turkeys or even turkey breasts or thighs year round. Therefore there is no need to cook so much that you get sick of it before it is gone. Surprise yourself several times a year with a tasty turkey dish. The cooking part is easier than taking a nap.

Select a turkey that fits your needs— fresh, if available. I find the cheaper brands as good as the premium. If it is frozen, carefully follow the directions for thawing. Trim excess fat and skin and pat dry.

Fire up the grill for roasting - about 300°. Build a good, large bed of coals and reduce the heat by closing down the air supply. Collect a small amount - 3-4 pounds of green fruit wood, white oak and hickory.

If using gas, preheat the grill to 300° with wood chips/sawdust before putting the turkey in.

Seasoning

Sprinkle the turkey inside and out with a mixture of

1 t.	garlic powder
1 t.	onion powder
1 t.	celery seed, ground
1 t.	ground sage
1 t.	ground thyme
	fresh ground black pepper
	salt

Place turkey on the grill, opposite the coals, breast up. Close the grill and go away for about an hour.

Check the temperature of the exhaust, look over the coals and put on a few pieces of green wood. If you must use chips or dried wood, soak in water for at least thirty minutes.

Maintain the temperature between 300 - 350° with a gentle smoke floating from the exhaust. Tidy up, close the grill and go rest from your labors.

Check back in about an hour later and insert your handy thermometer in the center of the thickest part of the bird. When it reads 160°, time is up. It is done. Remove and let it sit for about 20 minutes before carving.

It should be as juicy as fresh gossip and tender as a baby's sigh.

Roasted Quail

One day a friend of mine asked me about a different method of cooking quail. We both agreed that fried quail and grits form the standard of excellence against which all other recipes must be measured. This, of course, means that many Yankees have never enjoyed the ultimate quail dish.

The questioner's reputation, fortunately for him, rests more on his writing talents and exploration of the outdoors, rather than upon his skill as a hunter. Knowing of his prowess as a hunter, I feel comfortable in declaring that he acquired his quail twelve to a box at the local quail farm rather than off the point of a bird dog.

Quail hunting is, to me, the ultimate hunting sport. Walking through the brush, briars and kudzu that the crafty little creatures use for cover will burn more calories than a marathon race. Watching a pair of enthusiastic dogs working energetically across the woods in the crisp autumn air pleasures the soul to a degree that few scenes can match.

While the taste of quail needs no adornment, the challenge of finding the foxy fowl and bringing it home makes the delicious bird even more precious. The cost of keeping dogs year 'round, finding proper places to hunt and firing errant shots into the empty air make the price of pen-raised quail a bargain.

So expensive a fowl tempts many to anoint it with extravagant seasonings and sauces. This is a mistake. A bird of such a naturally delightful and delicate flavor, deserves to be prepared in a manner than enhances rather than overpowers its sweet succulence.

Quail is a light white meat but because of its healthy, robust living habits, quail is a little tougher than pen-raised chicken. Pen-raised quail are, of course, more tender than their wild brethren. The challenge is to prepare quail in a manner that does not increase its tendency toward toughness while retaining the pristine flavor. Roasting offers many auspicious options.

Roasted Quail

Allow at least two whole quail for each adult. Allow another for each person who has never tasted quail and one each for those who have.

Carefully clean each bird, removing pin feathers and damaged parts an wipe dry. Prepare the grill for low roasting temperature - about 300°. No hickory or mesquite smoke. Use fruit woods or a little white oak, if any, for smoke flavor.

Basting Sauce/Glaze

Prepare a basting sauce of

1 C.	orange juice, strained
1/2 C.	gin — use a decent brand, but not Bombay Sapphire
1 T.	lime juice
1/4 lb.	unsalted butter
1/2 t.	ground thyme
1/2 t.	cayenne pepper
6	juniper berries, bruised

Melt butter and add bruised juniper berries. Stir on low heat for two minutes; then mix with other ingredients.

Baste the birds inside and out and allow them to come to room temperature. When the grill is ready, baste again and place breast up on the grill. Close the grill. Baste every five minutes or so until done - about 30 minutes. Do not overcook.

When the thigh bone twists easily or the thermometer reads 150°, remove from grill. Serve surrounded with lightly steamed broccoli and carrots and new potatoes if you can find them..

French bread and a decent wine will make you want to whistle "Bob White."

PORK

Cajun Roast Pig

Cochon de lait

Certain meats have become a tradition for special occasions, such as turkey at Thanksgiving and the goose at Christmas. In many parts of the world Easter calls for lamb, but not in the generous and bountiful land settled by the displaced Arcadians. Easter Sunday in the bayou is the day for family gatherings and *Cochon de lait* — suckling pig.

I was recently privileged to share friendship and food with a Cajun family at their annual Easter gathering. The food was outstanding and was exceeded only by the hospitality.

The festivities began on Saturday with 500 pounds of crawfish from the family ponds, boiled to the perfect texture, and seasoned with the skill derived from a long practiced art form. Potatoes and corn-on-the-cob, introduced early into the spicy brew, assumed the special flavor of the crawfish boil. Lips and throat were, of course, cooled with the product of the choicest cereal grains, reduced to their essence.

Sunday morning, long before dawn, they fired up the Cajun microwave, and, beside it, hung the Easter pig with fore and after legs outstretched to catch its warmth.

Later brothers joined in to assist the tending of the coals and freely share their expertise. With his one eye sparkling more than most pairs, the octogenarian patriarch of the clan flavored the activities with peppery comments and sage advice.

The day was bright and warm. Mother Nature decorated earth's new-green cloak with sequins of bold colored flowers. It was a perfect example of what outdoor cooking is all about— sharing good times, preparing good food in the open.

Roasting a pig, dangling vertically, spread-eagle before a mound of glowing coals is an art long practiced in the land of the Arcadians. Early practitioners draped the pig on a length of chain from a tripod of green poles, his legs held asunder by green oak stakes. It was rotated, randomly by a sharp kick to the end of the oak stakes.

But ingenuity and technology replaced such ragged techniques. This pig hung from a metal bar and was constantly and evenly rotated by an electric rotisserie motor attached to a vertical shaft. The pig was held open, confined appropriately, in a sheath of, appropriately, "hog wire" fencing. Some practitioners use a steel drum to contain the coals with a vertical slot 8-10 inches wide cut down the side nearest the pig.

The carcass is begun head down, and as it cooks, the rendered fat drips to the ground. The skin begins to crisp into the delicious cracklings. Cracklings with taste and texture like those that so stirred the soul of Bo-bo, youngest son of a pig farmer in ancient China that he was moved to burn down his father's pig houses to satisfy his craving and thus, by this extravagance, brought the discovery of succulent roast pig to the world.

When the fat ceases dripping from the fore-end, the pig is rotated vertically so that the hams are on the bottom to receive the full effects of being closest to the coals. When all dripping stops, the pig is removed to a suitable table and released from his trappings. Eager hands dart in to sample the steaming succulence.

If you would like to experience cochon de lait, roast suckling pig, all you need are a pile of wood, a pig, a little ingenuity and a few hours that you can spare for fun.

Cochon De Lait
(In a Cajun Microwave)

One suckling pig, weighing fully dressed, (which means the opposite) 15-20 pounds, brought to room temperature and trussed open with green oak splints or encased in metal screening (that's where ingenuity comes in).

Build a large fire, a stack of wood 4'x4'x4'. Using a drum will contain the coals and reduce the amount of wood needed. A children's' outdoor swing frame

will make a nice support. A hook at the end of the chain will allow easy attachment and removal.

Sprinkle the pig generously with red and black pepper, garlic powder, onion powder. Lightly salt and sprinkle with thyme as an option.

When the coals are ready, hang up the pig. You should be roasting— temperature 350°. You can only hold your hand beside the pig for about 10 seconds.

Keep the pig rotating - do not let it burn. Plan fun-time activities to occupy about 25 minutes per pound. Keep the pig and the good times turning. When the fat stops dripping from the head end, take is down and reverse it. When it stops dripping from the ham end, remove it to the table. Let it cool enough to handle, if you can wait.

Remove the binding and carve it up. *Laissez les bons temps rouler* ! Let the good times roll!

Most pigs, of course, are roasted horizontally on a grill, rather than dangling vertically beside a pile of burning wood. This is just another example of the ingenuity of the outdoor chef.

Pork Loin Pinwheels

When rising sap makes the trees spring green, even jaded appetites can be brightened by a new twist on an old favorite. Pork loins are delightfully delicious and downright simple to convert into a sumptuous centerpiece that pleases the eye and pleasures the palate. In a burst of creativity, born of boredom and bedevilment, I stumbled upon a combination which bears repeating.

With company coming and a couple of pork loins thawing, I really didn't want to give them my usual, simple treatment of rubbing them down with my pork and poultry spice mixture and throwing them on the grill at about 350° in a little oak and hickory smoke until they reached 150°. Even with this basic treatment, they are always dependably delicious and leftovers, should there be any, make fine sandwich stuffing.

Cruising through the 'fridge, I spied and recovered celery, onion, carrots and bell peppers. Still not sure where this flight of fancy would take me, I cut them into thin strips while I pondered. Even while trimming the little fat there is from the top of the loins, I had not found the path. Suddenly, as a sharp knife slices though meat, my reverie was severed— asunder, even.

Grabbing my chef's knife, protruding Excalibur-like from its wooden block, I began slicing the loins lengthwise in a spiraling cut until each loin lay out as a flat bed about 3/4" thick, thus discovering

Spiral Stuffed Pork Loin

Ingredients

1/4	pork loin, trimmed and spiral cut
1/2 C.	celery, chopped fine
1/2C.	onion, chopped fine
1/2 C	carrots, julienned
1/4 C.	bell pepper, chopped fine
1/4 C.	olive oil

1 T.	ground bay
1 T.	thyme
1 T.	sage
1 T.	salt
1 T.	pepper

Saute the veggies in olive oil until they are clear. Sprinkle the openly inviting loins with a mixture of ground bay, thyme, sage, salt and pepper.

Spoon the veggies generously onto the meat, roll the loin back into its original configuration and secure with 3 bamboo skewers. Finally, baste generously with the oil left in the saute pan.

Fire up the grill for roasting at about 325°. Add a few green hickory or oak twigs. When the grill is ready, lay on the loin and close the lid. Pop a long cool one and relax.

Check the internal temperature in about an hour for the approach to the target temperature of 145°. At that point, take the loin off and let it grace the table for about 10 minutes while the juices set.

Slice across the grain in approximately 1" segments, and the pinwheels will virtually roll off the table. Don't plan on leftovers.

Spring Lamb

If March springs out like a lamb, is a "Spring Lamb" appropriate for the season? You bet. As a matter of fact, an earlier version called, appropriately, "Early Spring Lamb" is also known as "Easter Lamb" because of its connection with certain ceremonial meals of some religions.

Partially because of its reputation for purity, lamb is one of the few meats not excluded from the diet of any meat-eating religious sect or nationality. (The Cattlemen's Association does not qualify as a religious sect.)

So, with all the garlands, why do so many Americans turn up their noses? Therein, lies the problem.

Many people object to the odor of mutton. Include me. Mutton smells a lot like sheep and sheep scent is not one of my favorite fragrances. Many cooks, unfamiliar with lamb, have a tendency to produce lamb that smells like mutton, looks like mutton and tastes like mutton. Not a great idea.

Simple rules followed in the selection and preparation can make lamb one of the mildest and sweetest of meats. The lamb should be young. Look for light, pink colored, rather than brownish flesh, and small bones. The fat should be firm and pearly of color and sheen. Older animals have harder and more opaque fat.

In preparation for cooking, carefully trim all fat and membrane before cooking and skim all melted fat from juices, sauces or gravies. A dish that is as pretty as it is delicious and could truthfully be called "fit for a king" is a

Crown Roast of Lamb

The crown roast is made from loin and rib chops and usually weighs 8-10 pounds. Tell your butcher what you plan and when since he will most likely have to order it. A whole rack will have 8 ribs— a crown of two racks (16 ribs) will feed up to 8 people.

He will slice part way through the chops and cut the backbone so that the chops can be easily separated when done. He may scrape away some of the meat from the tip of the rib bone to expose a clean bone— called Frenching. Whether you do this or not, wrap the bone ends with aluminum foil or a little piece of bacon to keep them from burning.

Prepare the grill for roasting - about 350° degrees, light on the smoke.

Basting Sauce

1 C.	water
1/2 C.	olive oil
1	large bay leaf
1	dozen sprigs fresh parsley or 1 T. dried
3	celery stalk tops
1	sprig fresh or 1/2 t. ground thyme
1/4 C.	chopped onions
1/4 C.	chopped carrots
1/4 C.	chopped celery
1 t.	fresh ground black pepper
1 t.	salt

Simmer for ten minutes and rub plenty basting sauce into the roast. Let dry before placing on the grill . Place on the grill , over a drip pan. Baste and close the lid. Check the temperature. Maintain between 250° and 300°. Baste at 15-20 minute intervals.

The roast should be deliciously and beautifully done in 1 1/2 hours. It is rare at 135° and should not be cooked beyond an internal temperature of 150°.

Remove and allow to set for 5 minutes before carving. Serve on warm plates. Lamb cools quickly, but is much tastier warm.

Prepare yourself for a religious experience.

Variations

Because lamb has for centuries been favored in many countries and societies, there is an abundance of different sets of seasonings. The traditional combination of garlic and rosemary is popular on the northern shores of the Mediterranean. The southern shores and the Middle East use a variety of unusual seasonings.

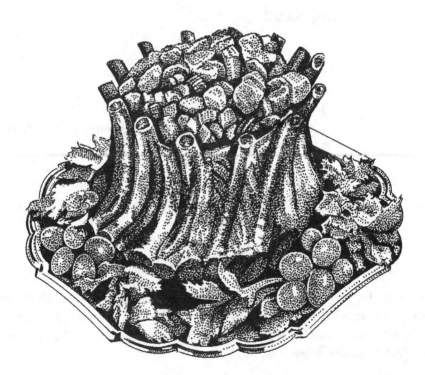

Eggplants on the Grill

Despite the ravages of weeds, worms and weather, the small garden delivers diverse and delicious delights. I long ago learned that a small garden, given about 15 minutes per day, will produce more than a big garden neglected. The minute amount of attention required of a small garden keeps it in the fun category instead of deteriorating into the four letter word, "work."

For a long time, I grew egg plants mostly because a garden ought to have egg plants. We ate it fried, of course, and tried ratatouille when it was the rage. Still, it gave more pleasure to the eye than to the palate. Conviction that a fruit so pretty and plentiful must somehow be delicious, led me years ago to try a dish called "Egg Plant Josephine" at the White Pillars restaurant in Biloxi, MS. **Shazam**!

Since then, I have enjoyed creating a variety of egg plant dishes. Some of them have been edible. A few have been dangerously delicious. Along the way, I learned a little more about the plump, purple pendant.

When it comes to egg plant, small is better. The fruit is firmer, the immature seeds are barely formed and it is less likely to be bitter near the rind. If you are buying instead of picking, make certain that the fruit is firm and that the stem is green and firmly attached. Before using larger egg plant, the slices are normally sprinkled with salt and allowed to sit for 20-30 minutes to draw out excess water; then they are rinsed and wiped dry.

Your fondest fantasies for egg plant and tomatoes can find fruition on the grill. With egg plant, having been known in Italy as *mala insana*, the "crazy apple," and tomatoes, called *pommes d'amour,* "love apples," by the French, you can love these crazy apples with

Grilled Eggplant and Tomato with Shrimp & Pesto Stuffing

For two:

2	young and tender eggplants about 2 1/2 inches in diameter and 6 inches long
2	medium-size, ripe tomatoes
1/2 lb.	Small/medium, shrimp peeled and chopped
1/2 C.	bread crumbs
1/2 C.	Mozzarella cheese, grated or sliced thinly

EGG PLANT

Cut off the ends of the eggplant and slice lengthwise into 1/4 inch slices. No need to peel I. Sprinkle with salt and allow to stand for 20 minutes; then rinse and pat dry.

Mala Insana Sauce

1 - 6 oz can	tomato puree or paste
1 T.	pressed garlic
2 T.	chopped onion
1 T.	fresh oregano
2 t.	fresh thyme
1 T.	olive oil
	salt and pepper to taste

Simmer for 10 minutes.

Prepare the grill for roasting - temperature about 350º - coals on one end or to one side

Brush the eggplant slices with extra virgin olive oil and place on the grill directly over the coals. Brown both sides and remove to the other side of the grill on foil or a flat pan. Using the largest slices as a base, build two stacks, layering as follows:

One slice of eggplant topped with

1 T.	shrimp
1 T.	sauce
1 T.	bread crumbs
1 T.	cheese

Finish the top layer of each stack with another layer of cheese and dab of sauce. Place on the grill, do not turn, but let the stacks cook until the cheese melts. Then remove to a warm plate.

TOMATOES

Core the tomatoes, taking out enough for the tomato to hold a couple of tablespoons of stuffing. Sprinkle in a little salt, turn down and let drain. Trim the other end enough that the tomato will sit stable.

Pesto Stuffing for the Tomatoes

1 T.	extra virgin olive oil
1/3 C.	fresh basil leaves,
1	small garlic clove
2 T.	roasted peanuts
3 T.	grated Parmesan
1/2 t.	fresh-ground black pepper.

Blend in blender until smooth

Stuff tomato with pesto sauce. Place tomatoes on the grill, away from the coals, in a shallow pan or on two layers of heavy-duty aluminum foil.

Close the grill for about 20 minutes while producing a medium smoke. Crazy, lovely and delicious.

Eggplant, sliced about 3/4th inch thick, basted with olive oil and broiled on the grill will make you hurt yourself. They are much cheaper than Portibelo mushrooms, but deliciously reminiscent. Don't overcook and experiment with favorite seasonings

Pit Roasting

In the natural world, there are rhythms and cycles which we have, after centuries of observation and thought, discovered the forces generating the changes. In the animal world, we are sometimes less certain why and how some behavior is activated. Wild ducks and geese, and some other fowl, migrate with the seasons: so do whales. Bears and ground hogs hibernate. However, in each of these cases, we can find logical reasons, patterns and signals which trigger each animal's activity.

There are some peculiar urges that arise in humans which drive them into activities which defy all efforts to discern the reason, the compulsion or the cause. One of the most remarkable is the urge to cook meat, covered with dirt, in a hole in the ground.

Perhaps it is the residue of seminal messages, fixed unknowingly, from watching "On the Road to . . ." movies, with Crosby and Hope, where a luau provided the ideal background for hula-hipped wahines and gave Dorothy Lamour a chance to wear another tight-fitting, two-piece sarong.

Whatever the reason, there are those in whom the urge to pit roast rises with all the uncontrollable force of a volcanic vent bursting out of the sea to make a new island. Pit roasting is, in my opinion, seriously misunderstood, or we have more under-exercised masochists running loose than I thought. First of all, it is not roasting. It is braising. Braising is cooking meat, enclosed, in its own or added juices— also known as pot roasting.

There are many good reasons **not** to cook meat in a hole in the ground. First, and foremost, you have to dig a hole. This resembles work so closely that it should give pause to those who have discovered that "work" is a four-letter word. Second, the labor does not end with the excavation. You have to burn down a pile of wood, then take out half the hot, glowing embers, introduce the carcass, properly encased (and that is, in itself, an onerous chore) replace the coals, cover with earth and wait.

Waiting for how long? That is the next problem. The process is unpredictable. It is an algorithm where the mass of the meat and the mass of the heat influence the time in an inexact and variable relationship. Unless you have an accurate thermometer with a remote probe, you risk premature excavation of a not-yet-quite-done carcass or discovering, too late, that it is cooked way passed its prime.

In the vigor and naivete of my youth, I pit roasted on a relatively small scale, but even in unripened wisdom of my childhood, I recognized this as unvarnished work. I knew how to pack a fresh fish in good river mud, stick it into the hot coals and take it out, when the mud was baked hard, for a delicious repast— even a duck or a dove served up succulently without a pot to wash or spit to split. I roasted potatoes in a shallow bed of sand beneath the embers of a camp fire and green corn, in its shuck in the ashes. But never, even flushed in the debilitating flux of my fieriest fever, did I hallucinate to the point of desiring to dig a hole in the ground big enough to enclose a livestock carcass, swaddle it in foil and burlap, shovel sand and hot coals around it and then, after hours and hours, dig it out again!

In an era when those evolving from generations of living sheltered lives, without the enjoying the exhilaration of exploring the ragged edges of danger in their childhood, now seek to round out their psyches in the pursuit of titillating thrills of "extreme" adventures, so are those, whose concept of "work" is a day at the office, wandering in search of Pit Roasting. That hermetically sealed meat is not at all influenced by its heat source is immaterial, and that, cooked in an oven, it would be identically, and infinitely easier, done is ignored. There is magic in the phrase: "Pit Roasting!" Some even more extremely misguided call it "Deep Pit Barbecuing!" It is related to barbecue only about as closely as is a camel to a horse.

So be it. If you are compelled, here's how. Start with a pit about 1 1/2 feet deep and 1 foot longer and wider than the meat. Stack 30-35 cubic feet of dry hardwood and burn down to coals. Remove 1/2 the coals and cover the remainder with about 3 inches of sand or gravel. Then cover with wet burlap. Place the pig/meat wrapped in aluminum foil or wet cotton sheeting on a piece of wire fencing of suitable size and lower into the pit. Cover with wet burlap, banana leaves, wet newspapers, etc., and then the dirt and return the removed embers. Go take a shower. After showering, you may even want to consider getting counseling.

189

Depending upon the amount and shape of meat, mass of the coal bed, temperature, clemency of weather and the compassion of the Saint of Errant Behavior, it will be done in from 8 to 24 hours. Unless you have inserted the remote probe of a thermometer in the meat, you will have no idea of the temperature until you uncover it, reclaim it from the earth (hopefully without serious burns to any of the parties involved), transport it to a suitable resting place and open it up.

This pot roast should be delicious and tender. Eating it should make you wiser.

You may choose to add garlic, onion, potatoes, carrots and other vegetablesv to the package before wrapping it up. That will produce a pretty complete pot roast or stew.

Chapter Six

Hot and Cold Smoking, Curing and Drying

Because it *sounds* so good, many newcomers to grilling were misled into calling what they were doing, or attempting to do, on a grill "smoking." As you know by now temperature defines the techniques of broiling, roasting and barbecuing. It also does the same with smoking.

Cold smoking, in the 70 to 90° F. range, is used to complete the process of preserving meat, fish and fowl— after it has been salted, brined or subjected to some other type of preservative. Continuing the preservation process by smoking accomplishes several things. First, the mild heat, administered over an extended period, further reduces the moisture content of the food, and, therefore, denies bacteria the moisture that they need to live and multiply. The low temperature and gentle smoke also deposit bactericides, such as phenol and cresol, on the surface of the food, thereby providing additional protection. Fortunately, it also adds delicious flavor. Cold smoking is best done when the outdoor temperature is cooler. With outdoor temperature in the 90's, hot smoking is the only practical approach to smoking on the grill.

Cured and cold-smoked food, can usually be eaten as is, but in the strictest sense of the word, cold-smoked food is not "cooked." Food preserved by curing and smoking can, in reasonably dry and temperate conditions, remain safe for consumption, and eminently edible, for long periods of time. Examples are the country hams produced in the Middle South and salmon preserved in Northern Europe and the Pacific Northwest. Bacon, hams and several sausages are cured and cold smoked.

Hot-smoked food is *cooked* in the temperature range of 90 to 190°—usually after some sort of cure which involves salt. The flavors and textures generated by the cure and the smoke combine to create exquisitely unique food. Hot-smoked food has a very short useful life unless refrigerated. Fish, poultry and many sausages are hot smoked, then refrigerated, or subsequently cooked again at higher temperatures.

Drying is another form of preservation, which can be accomplished with or without smoking, by drying food to the point that it lacks enough moisture to support bacterial life. Sun-drying meat, fish and vegetables is a venerable preservation technique which has been used by man for centuries in various climates and locations. Pacific Northwest Native Americans dried salmon, rock-hard, in great quantities for winter food. Jerky was sun-dried, heat-dried or smoke-dried. Salt drying cod, and later salmon, sped the exploration and exploitation of the North American continent. Salt cod is still a staple food in many areas.

Preparations and Precautions

While all of these techniques have been successfully used for centuries, even by primitive peoples, this does not mean that success is easily or automatically achieved. The curing process is essentially a race with death. The curing process must outpace bacteria to the center of the food. Every step of the process must be clearly understood, planned and executed as near perfection as possible.

Temperature measurement and control are vital. Below 34° F., very little curing can take place. But above 40° F., bacteria become much more active. At 40°, bacteria double every 6 hours; at 60°, every 2 hours and at 70°, every hour. The maximum temperature for dry curing is 38° F. but below 36° will extend the requisite curing time.

Fortunately, almost all meat that has not been extensively processed or handled by humans is relatively free of harmful bacteria. Bacteria is most likely transferred to the meat surface by faulty or careless handling. Therefore, the origin and condition of the food is extremely important for safety and quality.

When I was a chap, my mother canned and, later, froze much of our food. She was absolutely adamant that any food to be preserved must be of the best quality— fresh, without blemish and without fault. Woe be unto the one who was lax! It is dangerous and wasted effort to try to preserve questionable food. Eat it at once, or discard it, but do not try to preserve it.

This is not meant to be a complete and exhaustive manual on food preservation. This chapter is to provide factual basis for an introduction into hot smoking, cold smoking and drying. The cures for hams, bacon, fish, poultry and simple sausages are all old, time-tested techniques. If you wish to go beyond these basics, there are whole books devoted to sausages and/or hams and bacon.

At all times, make cleanliness, temperature control, accuracy and constant surveillance your constant companions. The work area should be maintained like an operating room. The temperature should be a cold as you can work in. When grinding meat for sausage, return the meat to refrigeration after each step. Wash all utensils frequently with hot water and strong soap; then dry them well before reusing. Keep your hands, knives, cutting boards clean. Don't forget to exchange the used towel for a clean one.

Smoking and Drying

After the preparation of the food and the salt/brine cure, the more relaxed part begins. Drying is very simple. I have dried beef jerky with the summer sun heating my black charcoal grill to an internal temperature of 150°. In dry climates, meat can dry at much lower temperatures. Hot smoking can be accomplished with most charcoal/wood grills or with makeshift temporary structures.

Cold smoking, however, requires lower temperatures for days or weeks. While the structure need be only large enough to enclose the food, the fire box or smoke generator must be so removed that the smoke is cooled to no more than 90°, or the food cooks rather than cures and does not preserve.

I currently use a recycled 32 cubic foot upright freezer which I rescued from the scrap metal yard. All the refrigeration elements had been removed, leaving only the stainless steel shelves. I cut a hole in the bottom to receive a 3" pipe which runs 15 feet to a small brick fire box. I cut another 3" hole in the top of the back for exhaust and covered it with screen to keep out the bugs. A small hole drilled in the top front to receive a bimetal thermometer probe completed the construction.

For optional heat, a 1000-1200 watt electric hot plate can be placed in the center of the floor of the smoker/smokehouse and a cheap stainless steel pan containing sawdust, resting on the heating element, will produce adequate smoke with little elevation of temperature.

Cold smokers can be made of any enclosure of most materials – even wood. The only essentials are that it enclose the meat and that the temperature of the smoke can be controlled. Metal clothing lockers, oak or steel barrels, recycled industrial boxes, old water heaters and the like have all been used by creative smokers. A small smoke house can be thrown up in an afternoon, or you can build as elaborately as you choose. Wooden or plastic dowels or stainless rods to support the food stand up better to the salty atmosphere where steel would quickly rust.

In the **Build Your Own** chapter, find several variations of smokers and smoke houses. The meat really doesn't care what the original use of the enclosure was nor what the neighbors think about how your smoke house looks. Functionality is the goal, and the easier and simpler that you can accomplish that, the better.

Temporary structures can be thrown together for a smoking session, then disassembled and stored until needed again. A simple frame covered with plastic will survive the mild temperatures, contain the smoke around the meat and keep out the insects. It won't, however, offer much protection from two-and four-legged varmints, marauding in the night.

The fuel for the smoke should be appropriate for the taste that you intend to impart. Light woods like alder, willow, birch are more suitable for fish, although oak and hickory, judiciously applied, turn out delicious products. Even juniper branches are used, to a limited degree, by some to cold smoke salmon in Scotland and Westphalian hams in Germany. Many a ham and side of bacon have been smoked with corn cobs.

With good food, good technique and the precise, persistent application of knowledge, curing, smoking and preserving can be rewarding activities that will provide tastes and textures that are hard to find.

You can tell that this ex-freezer has gotten a work out.

Notice that the plastic shelves on the front door have sagged a bit from a little over heating.

All metal construction would be much better.

Before getting into curing hams and bacon, you should understand the chemicals used in the "cure." Sodium nitrate and nitrite and potassium nitrate and nitrite are commonly used in commercial and private cure mixtures. The nitrate form is converted to nitrite during the curing process.

Some cures contain "Prague Powder" which is the name for a mixture of salt and nitrates which are dissolved together in water, then re-dried in order to form a more perfect union. Prague powder #1 is a mixture of 1 oz. of sodium nitrite to 1 lb. of salt. An equivalent using potassium nitrate would be 1.2 oz. per pound of salt. Prague Powder # 2 is 1 oz. sodium nitrite and .66 oz. sodium nitrate per pound of salt. The nitrates are essential in preventing botulism, but they can be toxic if used excessively.

Curing the Holiday Ham

Curing hams is considerably less trouble than one would think, and the rewards are great and various. Curing and smoking are two separate operations, however. A ham which had not been properly cured could not be preserved by smoking alone. Smoking, in this case, is cold smoking, performed at 70-90° F.

You need a thermometer long enough to reach the center and accurate scales. You will also need container/containers which are non-reactive to hold the hams (wood, plastic, stainless steel) which have either porous platforms in the bottom or drain holes and, of course, a smoke house.

Separate out the hams (and shoulders) leaving the skin intact. Hams keep better with the skin on. The next, and a very important step, is to chill the meat until it reaches 33-35° F. in the center— but don't let it freeze. An almost empty fridge at the lowest temperature setting, a freezer or a local meat shop will do the job in 1-2 days. If the outside temperature hovers about freezing, the chilling can be done outside. If it rises, put the hams in a wooden or plastic container on chunks of ice laced with coarse salt and cover with additional chunks of ice interlaced with coarse salt. Add water to cover, and keep a check on the temperature.

There are two basic methods of curing, dry curing and brine curing. Dry curing is the simpler and, in my estimation, produces a better tasting end product.

Mix a curing rub of 8 lbs non-iodized salt, 2 lbs of sugar and 2 oz of saltpeter (potassium nitrate) per 100 lbs of meat— the classic 8-2-2 recipe. Mix thoroughly, separate out 1/2, and reserve. The salt removes moisture from the meat and reduces some bacterial action. The sugar is a preservative, but also acts, in this case, to ameliorate the toughening effects of the salt. Brown sugar, molasses or honey may be added or substituted. Other seasonings and spices may be added. The saltpeter fixes the red color and retards some bacteria, notably botulism and enzymes. Morton Salt, among others, makes a ready-mix for curing. If you use one, make certain that it is for dry curing, and follow the directions carefully.

Clean, dry and trim all extraneous parts and residue from the hams. Weigh each ham accurately. Each ham should receive rub equal to 5% of its weight. Carefully weigh out the appropriate amount of the curing mixture. In a container large enough to hold the ham easily, rub the mix forcefully into all surfaces, especially the hock and the cut face of the butt. Use all the allotted mixture. Place the ham gently in its box/container atop the drain board. Continue with the other hams and shoulders. If you are putting more than one in a container, put the larger on the bottom. Cover with cloth and store in the 35-45° F. range. Do not let it freeze.

In three days, use the remaining mixture, in the same proportions, and meat from each container should be reversed, top to bottom. If you do not intend to keep the meat for more than 3 months, this second application can be reduced by 50%, but if there is any question, use it all.

Meat should cure for 2 days per pound for large (10+ lbs) pieces, but smaller pieces, such as bacon, require only 1 1/2 days per pound. Curing time is influenced by temperature in that it cures faster at higher temperatures and stops curing at all at 34°F.

After the cure is complete, remove the hams, scrub thoroughly clean, dry, and rub with fresh black pepper. Make an opening at the shank, insert a strong cotton cord, and hang overnight to drain. Hang in your smoke house, and after the hams are dry, apply a gentle cold smoke, (70-90°F.) 5-7 hours per day for 3-4 weeks. Longer is okay. Hams may be hot smoked at 100-120°F, but they will not preserve as long and will not have the same flavor. Use green hickory, maple, oak, ash, apple or pecan wood or sawdust. The smoke should not be dense, nor the amount great, and the fire should not flame. An 8x8 inch coal bed will be ample. Try to produce a deep amber, rather than a black, color.

During the slow smoking, moisture is driven from the meat, preserving it as well as producing a mellow flavor. It is permissible and desirable, after a week or so, to cut and use portions of the meat while the rest is left hanging. Meat cured in this manner may be left in a cool, dry smokehouse for at least a year.

Beware, this may become a Christmas tradition.

Makin' Bacon

Are you sure you want to do this? Making bacon is not a weekend job. In fact, it is dangerously close to work. But if you insist, here it is. I must advise that it is as easy to do 100 lbs. as it is to do 5 lbs.

There are two parts to the process. First, you have to cure the bacon. (I guess that, technically, that is the second part, since you must first bring home the bacon—even though it is not, strictly speaking, "bacon" at the time.) Second, you must smoke it.

First things, first. You need a wooden or food-grade plastic box, keg or barrel into which the amount of bacon which you intend to cure will neatly, but not loosely, fit. (That sentence is not nearly as complicated as the curing process.)

For each 100 lbs of pork bellies, mix well:

> **5 lbs of non-iodized salt** — sold as pickling salt or kosher salt. Use fine-ground, not coarse ice cream-type, salt. All, I mean **all**, salt is sea salt. So don't buy, at extravagant prices, anything labeled "sea salt."

> **3 lbs of sugar** I recommend dark brown sugar.

> **3 oz. saltpeter** (potassium nitrate) This is an essential preservative which also fixes the bright red color. Regardless of what ignorance you have read about it, it is safe and effective when used properly. It wasn't in the GI food either.

Put a layer of the mixture in the bottom of the container. (Are you still sure you want to do this?)

Pack in a pork belly and pound it flat. "Rub it in, rub it in!" Repeat with bellies and salt until you get a belly-full or the meat runs out. Cover the top with a good layer of salt. Pack everything firmly. Get all the air out. You do not want to eat pig with the vapors.

Close the lid and have a drink. If you have easy access to a dependable psychologist, you may want to casually discuss your fixation.

It will take about 1 1/2 days per pound to cure. BUT in about 7-10 days, depending upon the temperature, you will need to reverse the stack (top to bottom) and add any leftover mix. Drink some more. Check with the doc again.

After everything is cured, except you, take out the pre-bacon, wipe it down, stick a hole in one corner, put a 3-4' strong cotton cord through and tie it off.

Now, hang the pre-bacon in the smoker/smokehouse for about 2 weeks in a 40-50° F. dry atmosphere and let it drip. Wash the bacon with hot water and wipe clean and dry; then cold smoke at 70-90° degrees for 10-15 days. You may smoke longer if desired. Don't let the pieces touch or drip onto each other. White oak 80%, green hickory 20% are the preferred woods, but you may use maple, fruit woods or others.

Don't worry about the mold. That is natural. Wipe it off. Actually, the safety hazards are minute. Unless you have a "no knows" nose, bad pork will reveal itself to you in irresistible fashion.

Now, how about let's corn some beef— the only sensible use for beef brisket.

Let me know if you or the bacon gets cured first.

Country Sausage

Even in these days of prophets preaching polyunsaturated platitudes, there are still occasions that cry out for something other than polymerized sausage. In the days of yore, when Hector and I were still pups, almost everybody in rural America made their own sausage. Although some folks were, by then, using store boughten seasoning mixtures, many still seasoned their sausage from scratch.

The sharp smells of savory sausage samples sizzling on the stove perfumed the crisp, clear air of hog-killing weather. When the meat had been once ground and seasoned in the same proportions as last year, a sample was quickly fried to check the taste. There is no instance recorded where fine-tuning corrections to the seasoning were not made.

Even now, I do not know how to season a batch of meat that guarantees nailing the nuances on the first try. The freshness and potency of the individual seasonings provide too many variables. It may take several attempts to tweak the taste to its tempting best. That is one of the challenges of sausage making, but it is also one of the opportunities— a missed opportunity in most commercial attempts. It is quite obvious that nobody is fine tuning the seasonings in the vast majority of what is now sold as sausage.

Sausage making may seem a little awesome to some, but it is really about as simple as making biscuits. And well worth the effort for those who care enough to serve the very best. Once you ever try, you'll wonder why you waited so long.

The necessary tools cost less than a video movie and are guaranteed not to bore you after you have put it through its paces more than twice. Used meat grinders go for $10-15 at flea markets. Meat grinding attachments for mixers are only a little more, and the steel blade in a food processor chops meat well. That's all you need for patty sausage. A sausage stuffing funnel makes you a full-fledged sausage factory.

For beginners, we'll do a simple country patty sausage. Next you may want to stuff some and smoke them in your grill. Later you will want to do Italian (full of fennel), Spanish chorizos and maybe even boudin. The variety of tastes and textures will amaze you.

Country Breakfast Sausage

Sausage should be about 20-30% fat— less is tough and dry; more cooks away to a memory. Pork butts and shoulders have the ideal ratio.

5 lbs.	pork butt or shoulder
5 T.	non-iodized salt
3 t.	ground (not rubbed) sage
3 t.	cayenne pepper
2 t.	ground thyme

Trim fat and gristle from the meat and cut into grinding size chunks or strips. Mix the seasonings and sprinkle half onto the meat, then <u>chill until it reaches to 33-34° F.</u>

Grind the meat using your coarsest wheel. If using a food processor, leave the meat in 1/4 inch cubes. Mix in the remaining seasoning and grind the meat again with the 1/8 inch (hamburger) wheel.

Throw the skillet on the stove and fry up a couple of small patties. It would be nice if you had a pan of hot biscuits coming out of the oven about that time. Check the taste and judiciously correct. Fry up enough to satisfy your immediate cravings. Cover the rest and put it in back into the 'fridge for a couple of hours to chill. Shape into patties, store in ziplock bags and freeze.

If this doesn't make for some memorable breakfasts, you may want to check in for a palate overhaul.

Stuffing and Smoking Sausages

After making sausage country sausage, you, no doubt, will find or develop a recipe that is "as good as Mama used to make." You are probably wishing that you had some stuffed and smoked the way Grandpa used to do. Well, that's no hill for a stepper.

Stuffing sausage is easier than making molasses candy. All it takes is a little casing and a simple stuffer. Natural and vegetable-based sausage casings, while not in every supermarket, are relatively common. Smaller packages of about 50 feet and larger packages, packed in brine and frozen, can be found in meat markets and slaughter houses. Mail order sources are in the **Resource** section.

Casings are available in approximately 1/2 inch, 1 inch and some larger sizes. Choose the appropriate size for the sausage of your dreams. If you need 200 feet of 1 1/2 inch size for a summer sausage project, you may want to give your supplier a little notice to assure it is available when you need it.

Measure out the amount that you think that you will need for the project, soak it in fresh water and rinse it in several changes of water to remove the excess salt. Keep it in the 'fridge until needed. Return the unused portion to the freezer in its brine. Casings frozen in brine will keep indefinitely.

Now all you need is a stuffer. Stuffing attachments for food grinders are very inexpensive. These are plastic or metal cone-shaped devices that fit on the end of the grinder. A length of casing is pushed upon the tubular spout and a knot tied in the bitter end. (An old sailor's term that has nothing to do with taste.) As the food is ground, it fills the casing and pulls it off the spout.

A serviceable food grinder with a stuffing attachment is well worth the investment. It will pay for itself swiftly by allowing you not only to produce sausage but the finest ground meat available for hamburgers, meatballs and meat loaves. Later, when you start making boudin, andouille, chorizos and bratwurst, you'll be happy that you did not tarry.

Make it easy on yourself by carefully trimming all tendons, fibers and gristle from the meat. Such stuff is likely to foul up the cutting action, which not only slows the process terribly, but overgrinds the meat— reducing it to a liver pudding consistency. Not what we want in sausage.

Texture of the finished product is important. Grind the meat first with the coarsest plate available. That is the one with the biggest holes or slots. If the meat doesn't flow through easily, your blades may be dull. Most grinders have a four edged blade, looking somewhat like a Maltese cross, which rotates against the face of a steel plate having holes in it. The feed-screw forces the meat into the rotating blades and through the holes of the stationary plates. Good cutting action depends on the edges of the blades and the plate being sharp and like, sweethearts, true to each other.

Dull blades are a snap to sharpen. Lay 1/4 sheet of 400-600 grit wet/dry sand paper in the bottom of your sink. If the bottom isn't flat, place a board under the paper. Drip a small stream of water onto the paper. Find or make a square peg that just fits the hole in the back of the blade and rotate the blade on the paper in the direction of the sharp edge. After a few rotations, the edge will be sharp and shiny. Then place the plate on the paper and polish it thoroughly, using a circular motion. Just like new.

Mix in your seasonings and fry up a little to assure that the taste precisely pleases your palate. Attach the stuffing spout and load it up with casing. Add about a fourth of a cup of ice-water per two pounds of ground meat. This will serve as a lubricant. Prepare to stuff.

Control the fullness of the casing by holding the casing on the spout with one hand while feeding meat into the grinder with the other. Don't try to pack it too tightly or the casing will burst. If it does, simply cut out the split, tie both ends and return the meat to the grinder.

Every foot or so, pull off a little extra casing and give the sausage a little twist. This makes the links easier to handle. If you are doing bratts or wienies, of course, do this every five or six inches. With a little practice, everything will run smoothly.

Now is the time to go start a small fire in the grill and let is get going while you disassemble and clean up the grinder. Make certain that all the cracks and crannies get a good scrubbing. Finish off by bathing all the parts in boiling water and placing them on a rack to dry. When they are thoroughly dry, wrap the blades and plates in cloth or paper to protect their edges.

On with the Smoking

We will be cold smoking with temperatures less than 90° and heavy smoke. Oak and hickory are the basic woods. Fruit woods, sassafras and sweetgum may be added. Restrict the air supply to maintain low temperatures for long periods. If you start early one morning, you can decide by sundown whether you want to smoke through the night or eat the first batch.

As quickly as the sausage is stuffed, chill it down in ice water while you get the fire pit going. Remove the sausage from the water and dry it off; then hang it in the smoker/smokehouse. Sausages should be hung so that they do not touch each other.

Start with low heat and no smoke until the exterior of the sausage is completely dry; then gradually start the smoke and bring up the temperature to slightly below 90°. Maintain it there. Sausages started off too high will sweat, mottling the color and becoming hard.

For 3/4-1" diameter casings, about 15-18 hours should do the trick. You can decide by cutting off a piece, cooking and tasting. You can smoke as long as you like to get the amount of smoke taste that you want.

Remember that this meat is not cooked; it is not cured. It should be refrigerated as soon as it cools down. It must be cooked before being eaten. It can be stored for 2-3 days in a refrigerator, but must be frozen for longer storage.

Check out your sausage-smoking skills. The weather is right.

Grilling Sausage

3 lbs.	pork butt, with at least 25% fat
2 lbs.	beef chuck, with at least 25% fat
1 T.	garlic powder
1 T.	onion powder
1 t.	ground coriander
1 t.	ground bay leaf
1 t.	cayenne
5 t.	salt
5 t.	black pepper
1 C.	icewater

Cut pork and beef into 1" chunks. Mix seasonings and divide in half. Mix one half with meat; then refrigerate overnight. Grind meat, spread out and sprinkle with the remainder. Regrind and stuff in 3/4-1" casing. Refrigerate until ready to grill.

You may mix 2 cups of your favorite finishing sauce before the regrind and omit the water.

These make excellent grazing fare on the grill.

Venison Sausage

Venison and other big game meat need pork or beef fat added, about 30% by weight, in order to make acceptable sausage. Substitute venison equally for any meat, in any sausage recipe, but add 25% beef or pork fat.

Smoked Turkey

Long before that funny thing happened to Columbus on his way to India, and long before that motley crew of malcontents gathered around the Plymouth Rock, the turkey was held in high esteem among Americans. In addition to appreciating his tasty presence, his intelligence and wile, we respected him for saving fire.

"Long, long ago a great storm came and wind blew and rain poured for many days. The campfires were drowned out all across the land. It was the beginning of winter and our people were cold.

"We called on our friends for help to find any fire remaining. The birds held a council and offered their help. The eagles and the ospreys circled high with sharp eyes intent. The kites and hawks spread out across the land and gave shrill cries and hovered in likely places.

"One by one they returned— without success. And the earth grew colder and the sky became darker. And the people were afraid.

"Then a small brown sparrow found one faint, small coal flickering dimly in a half-burned stump. The people rushed to find fuel to keep the coal from dying, but all the wood was wet.

"Then the turkey stepped forward and began to fan the coal with his wing. The coal glowed and grew larger and larger. Finally it burst into flame. All the feathers were singed from the turkey's head and red blisters raised up. Because he saved fire for the world, his descendants have borne red blisters instead of feathers on their heads, in memory of his deed. To honor his bravery and service, we use a turkey wing to fan the camp fire." (From a Native American legend)

This delightful legend adds even more flavor to a spectacular taste of smoked turkey. Smoked turkey can be dressed up or down. It forms the center of an all-time- great sandwich and is the beginning of many delicious variations. Unfortunately, like most things, a good smoked turkey is hard to find. If you don't have a talented, generous friend, you just about have to do it yourself.

Turkey smoking is not for the intense "Type A" personality. It is the sort of activity that combines well with a triple-header football Saturday. It provides the perfect prophylactic to unwanted invitations, "I'd like to, but I'm smoking turkeys." And it would go well with a re-reading of *War and Peace*.

How to Smoke a Turkey — Right

Get a right turkey. I prefer fresh. Not "sort of" or "semi," but real fresh. And not a large one— 12-14 pounds is big enough. The heavyweight 20+ pounders remain too long in the dangerous 40° - 140° and can create too many problems. If the turkey is frozen, carefully follow the producer's instructions for thawing.

It is safer to assume that all poultry has some little salmonella bacteria lurking about. Poultry, properly prepared and cooked, is safer than a baby's teething ring. But large birds and low temperatures create opportunities whose knock you do not wish to hear.

Prepare the grill for hot smoking— temperature 170-190°, for prolonged periods: sweet smoke of fruit woods (apple, pear) white oak, hickory, hardwood charcoal.

Trim excess fat and skin flaps and wash thoroughly under running water. Wipe dry and place directly on the grill: no salt, no seasonings.

Close down the grill. Adjust your air flow to maintain about 170°. Establish a light, but continuous stream of pale, white smoke. Go taste your favorite beverage or check out your game plan.

Check back in about an hour to assure that your adjustments were what you thought they were. Adjust if required. Then find something to do for the next 15-18 hours. How often you need to check the grill depends upon how long your grill will maintain the proper temperature range without your attention. How long you carry on depends on how long it takes the center of the thickest part of the bird to reach 160°.

The bird should have the same color if he had spent the summer on the beach, not the blackened, creosote color of the inside of a neophyte's grill. The meat should have a pale pink band inside. When sliced, juices should run clear. The meat should be moist and tender.

Allow the bird to cool before slicing in your usual professional manner. Try not to eat it all before everybody gets a taste. Refrigerate after it cools.

You may never again be satisfied with what has previously passed as "Smoked Turkey."

Although the bird, seasoned only with smoke, will have the purest flavor of smoked turkey, you may want to experiment with added seasonings. I recommend that you begin with very mild flavors and keep it simple. Keep the bird's cavity opened. Do not pack it with stuffing and start a salmonella factory.

Is Brining the Cure?

There are those who engage in brining turkeys before smoking. In my opinion, this overly complicates the simple smoking process, and may lull some into thinking that they are curing the turkey for cold smoking. I believe that the more swiftly the turkey is heated through the 40° - 140°, the better.

Furthermore, the texture of the unbrined bird is more moist and tender and I have found that properly smoked turkey is delicious without any salt.

Smoking Fish

Smoked fish, whether they be salmon, mullet, bass or catfish and whether they be hot or cold smoked, are a true delicacy in every language. Hot smoked fish are actually cooked and should be eaten or refrigerated promptly— a caution which is probably totally unnecessary because they seem to evaporate as quickly as they come off the grill.

Cold-smoked fish are even more highly valued and only partially because of the investment of the additional time. The texture of cold-smoked fish is entirely different from that of hot smoked fish. Although they can be safely, and pleasurably eaten, as is, cold-smoked fish are not cooked. The cure, and the cold smoking, change the texture so that there is none of the flakiness of cooked fish; rather, the texture is quite similar to that of a thin slice of a fine medium-rare beef roast. The flesh can be sliced so thin that it is almost transparent, yet still retain its integrity. The tactile sensation is purely sensual and the flavors can be no less exciting.

Whether the fish are to be hot smoked or cold smoked, freshness is essential. The shorter the period between capture and cooking, the better. I do not recommend trying to cold smoke or hot smoke fish bought from the average grocery, and would want assurance of freshness from any fish monger.

Quick-frozen fillets can be thawed and smoked with excellent results. I have not had great success starting the cure with fillets which are not fully thawed. Fish should be thawed under running water or covered in water, and refrigerated until thawed.

Since smoked salmon is the most common and most widely available commercial product, it is also the one that most are familiar with. So we will start with salmon— cold smoking first; then hot smoking.

Cold Smoked Salmon

Cold smoking salmon is an ancient tradition practiced in Northern Europe since recorded time and in the Pacific Northwest by Native Americans for centuries. Initially, it was solely a means of preservation. How that has changed!

Scotland and the Scandinavian countries are where the science has been raised to a fine art. When we think of cold smoked salmon in the U.S., we generally have Scottish processed salmon in the memories of our minds and palates.

The actual process is quite simple, but like many of our highly prized commodities requires substantial investment of invaluable time. It also requires attention to detail and a good smoker.

As with curing pork, there is a brine cure and dry cure. I prefer the dry cure for cold smoking.

Cold Smoked Salmon

The process takes so long that it is hardly worth the effort for less than 10 lbs. After you have a couple of successful runs under your belt, you will, like me, not want to go through the exercise for less than 25 lbs.

For 10 lbs. fresh, gutted salmon, rinse and split lengthwise, along the back bone. Make slash cuts 1/4-1/2" deep, diagonally, in the skin sides. Weigh out pickling salt (non-iodized) equal to 15% of the fish's weight, in this case 1 1/2 lbs., and divide it into two equal piles. Rub the salt well into the upper 2/3s of each side, but none on the lower 1/3 tail section.

Run a stout cord or dowel through the shoulders of each side and hang, tail down, in a well-ventilated, cool, dry place for 2-3 hours— where it will drip. Rinse well under running water to remove all salt. At this point, seasonings may be added in a powder form or in a flavored alcohol mixture. Some seasonings used are garlic, onion, ground mustard, bay leaf, coriander, cardamon, cloves, mace, allspice, fennel, dill, etc.

Hang again in the well-ventilated, cool, dry place until a shiny surface, called a *pellicle*, is formed. A fan will speed the process.

After the pellicle is formed, hang the fish, tail down, and exposed to a rather dense smoke of oak, hickory, apple, (some Europeans even use a little juniper) at temperatures not exceeding 90°. The smoking should continue for at least 36 hours and may, (as in Finland where it may kept for several months) be smoked up to 3 weeks.

Smoking need not be continuous during the whole period, but a 70-90° temperature should be maintained. Fish prepared this way should have a firm yet flexible flesh that can be cut on the bias in sections thin enough to read through. It will keep in the 'fridge for months, but it never lasts that long. I seal mine in plastic bags from which I have evacuated all the air. But that is a waste of time. It all gets eaten very quickly.

Salmon fillets can also be cured and cold smoked. Just reduce the time in the salt and the cure.

Hot Smoking Salmon

Hot-smoked salmon is almost as delicious, but will not have the same texture as cold-smoked. It has the distinct advantage, however, of being ready to eat much sooner. As another bonus, it is practical to hot smoke in smaller quantities.

Fillet out 8-10 lbs. of fresh salmon into 1/2-3/4" thick fillets. Prepare a brine solution of 2 C. pickling or kosher salt to 1 gal. of water at 60° F. Soak fillets for 30 minutes, remove, and rinse thoroughly.

In a second brine with 2 C. salt and 1 C. brown sugar to 1 gal. water at a maximum of 60° F., immerse fillets for 1 hour. Remove, rinse and hang in a cool, dry place until a shiny film forms. Using an electric fan speeds the process. Seasonings in the brine— garlic, onion, lemon/lime and pickling spices are optional.

Heat the grill to 170-180° and add green wood— alder, apple, pear, white oak— to the coals. Place fillets on the grill and maintain temperature and a gentle smoke for about 8 hours.

Hot Smoking Salmon-Lite

Fillet the salmon into pieces of approximately uniform thickness. Place in a non-reactive container with cover, and coat thoroughly with a mixture of 1/2 lemon juice and 1/2 light olive oil. Cover and refrigerate for 1/2 - 2 hours or you may cook it as soon as the grill is ready.

To prepare the grill, load your smoker-gadget with green oak, hickory, apple, alder, or what ever turns you on. Dry wood or chunks should be soaked for 1-6 hours. Or, you could light up the gas grill, close the lid and turn to maximum heat. Remove the salmon from the 'fridge to allow it to warm up. You will need a spatula, with an opposing arm, for turning, a basting brush and a platter upon which to place the grilled fillets. When the grill begins to smoke rather generously, open it up; let the smoke clear enough for you to see what you are doing, place the filets carefully on the grill, and lower the heat.

If you had a very hot charcoal grill, you would leave the top open. With the gas grill, you will probably need to close the lid. Check the fish in about 3 minutes. The bottom surface should be beginning to firm up. Check one corner— gently— to determine if is it stuck. If it is, close the lid for a bit. If there is any browning, the fish readily releases the grill; baste the top side, and gently turn it over. Smoke should be rather heavy and constant. Relax for about 3 minutes. Repeat the inspection as before. Baste and gently turn when ready. After about 3 minutes, baste and turn for the last time.

Remove carefully to a warm plate. Serve at once. Salt and fresh ground pepper are optional. A chilled wine capable of contending with superb aromas and flavors would be welcome. Hot-smoked salmon may be eaten at once, refrigerated or frozen.

On subsequent occasions, you may want to lightly sprinkle the salmon before grilling with combinations of some of the following seasonings: garlic powder, onion powder, freshly chopped dill leaves, fresh thyme leaves, rosemary, ground bay leaves, ground coriander, freshly grated ginger, zest of orange, etc. I recommend that you add seasonings slowly, so that you do not overpower the natural flavor of salmon.

Salmon, of course, is not the only fish that takes smoking well. Many salt-water and fresh-water species turn into scrumptious, elegant, new creatures when judiciously smoked. The common and readily available mullet is one such. Fresh mullet is unappreciated and much under-utilized even by many who live near the oceans. Fresh mullet is a real delicacy fried, and it pickles and cans well, but it excels when properly smoked.

Hot Smoked Mullet

Fresh mullet may show some red body fluids, so they are first leached, soaked in salt water, to remove this. For 8-10 lbs. fresh mullet fillets, rinse thoroughly and treat as follows:

Leach brine: 2 C pickling salt per gal. of water at 60°.

For fillets:	Wt.	Leach	Brine
	6-8 oz.	20 min.	20 min.
	10-12	20 min.	40 min.
	14-16	30 min.	60 min.

Remove from the leach brine, rinse thoroughly and put into the curing brine.

Curing brine:

2 C.	pickling salt
1 C.	brown sugar
1/2 C.	lemon juice
1 T.	garlic powder
1 t.	onion powder
1 oz.	pickling spices
1 T.	Tabasco

Simmer for 10 minutes. Cool; then add to 1/2 gal. cool water and 4 lbs. ice to bring temperature down to 60°.

Remove from curing brine, rinse well and hang to dry— out of the sun. Using a fan speeds up the formation of the pellicle, as detailed previously. Move to the smoker and start with temp. of 120° for 4 hours with low smoke, then raise temp to 170° for next 4 hours with dense smoke.

You may discover why, along the Mississippi Gulf Coast, smoked mullet is called "Biloxi bacon."

Hot Smoked Catfish

The spring floods always bring an abundance of one of my favorite fish. Pond raised catfish are, of course, available year round at your friendly grocery. The fillets are individually quick-frozen (IQF), and their quality is retained. While I am sort of ambivalent about fried catfish, smoked catfish are one of my favorites.

Start with about 10 lbs. of fillets. If they are frozen, thaw them in the refrigerator, covered with water.

First bath:	2 C.	pickling salt
	1 gal.	unchlorinated water

In a non-reactive container, cool bath to 60°; then, rinse and drop in the fillets. Immerse the fish and refrigerate for 30 minutes.

During that time, prepare a second mixture of

	1 C.	salt
	1 gal.	unchlorinated water
	1/2 C.	brown sugar
	1 T.	minced onion
	1 T.	crushed garlic
	1/2 C.	lemon juice
	1 t.	liquid crab boil
	1 t.	Tabasco

Remove fish from first brine, rinse thoroughly under running water, and place in second brine. Leave for 15 minutes for thin fillets to 2 hours for whole fish. Remove and rinse again and hang (use bamboo skewers) in a cool, dark place with good air circulation for about 3 hours.

Using a fan will speed up the process. This drying allows a thin glossy sheen to cover the surface, which helps seal in the juices and prevents the oozing of protein to the surface. The surface should be completely dry to the touch.

Place the fish on the grill or hang them from the skewers. Start with a low temperature, just above 100º, for the first couple of hours. Thereafter, build up a heavy, dense smoke and allow the temperature to rise to 160º. In addition to oak, use apple wood, bay (or bay leaves), green juniper (or a few juniper berries) or citrus.

They should be completely cooked in about four more hours or when their internal temperature reaches 140º. Now, that's Smokin', Joe.

Cold Smoking Catfish

Sorry, but not yet ready for prime-time. A couple of years ago, I got the urge to cold smoke catfish fillets, and, thereby, to transform the rather common house cat into an elegant, exquisite exotic. After pondering for sometime, I prepared and picked up 15 lbs. of individually quick frozen catfish fillets.

It was my intent to render unto them the same tender, yet pliable, texture that distinguishes the finest cold-smoked salmon. There are, of course, to my knowledge, no instructions or recipes to do this. The producers and purveyors of this plebeian *poisson* had no clues, nor did the land grant colleges' agricultural departments. Likewise, the great federal bureaucracy was unenlightened on the subject.

Loving a challenge, as well as the chase of a taste, I threw together a process and whipped out about 5 lbs. during one cold streak. There are forces which smile upon the naive and the bold. Remarkably, the first batch came out 99% perfect, failing only in having a tad too much salt. The taste and texture was totally unlike fish. It could cut on the diagonal, so thinly that you could almost read through it! And the taste matched, or exceeded, the best $60.00 a pound Scotch-smoked salmon that I have ever tasted.

Being the scientific kind of guy that I am, I whipped out a **P**rocess **C**ontrol **C**hart, (a little appropriate fanfare here) with all sorts data points to collect, evaluate and refine. Quickly, and eagerly, I began processing the next batch, faithfully recording as I went, desperately trying to duplicate the first delicacy. **Flop!**

No big deal. I am a persistent guy. Making minor corrections, I charged into the third round. **Flop! Flop!** Then, in the middle of December, the weather became too warm. That winter was the warmest on record, so I never got a cold streak when I had the time to devote to the chase.

Since then, I have been too busy on the book, but the taste and texture are tattooed multi-colored in my memory. It is a chase that I will resume. You'll be the first to know the results.

Smoked Pickled Shrimp

"Times, they are a changing." The words of the old Bob Dylan song are almost always applicable. But who would have ever thought that we would see the day when seafaring men would have so much in common, with little ol'' ladies. It seems now that shrimpers, like little Ol' ladies, can't afford to be caught without their *teddies*.

Turtle Excluder Devices (TEDs) are no laughing matter to Gulf Coast shrimpers. Caught between the threat of $8000 fines, for excluding turtle excluders and loss of revenue from shrimp, excluding themselves from the net, shrimpers may, also, become an endangered species.

While the outcome of the battle on the high seas is, currently, unfathomable, the course, dead-ahead, will find consumers colliding with higher prices for shrimp. "It's an ill wind, that blows nobody good."

We who live close to the coast are spoiled with fresh seafood. The opportunity to purchase fresh shrimp almost year 'round is really a luxury few folks can share as much as we. The crisis on the seas is certain to make fresh shrimp even more of a luxury. Those who feel that life isn't complete without shrimp will find new ways to stock up and preserve shrimp when their cost is in the trough of the price wave.

Like fish, shrimp are better when frozen fresh and fully immersed in water. Handled quickly and carefully, shrimp can be frozen for at least six months and still retain their texture, taste and appearance. Since they rarely stay stored that long around these parts, I do not bother to remove the heads. For longer storage, the heads and fat should be removed.

When you do remove the heads and shells, throw them into a large pot with a couple of onions, a couple of garlic cloves, a celery stalk or two, a tablespoon or so of mustard seed, cover with water and simmer until the stock is reduced to a rich essence. Strain and freeze to flavor sauces, stews and gravies.

A savory shrimp butter or shrimp dip can be concocted by baking the shells and heads, in the oven— NOT IN MY GRILL — until fully dry, then pulverizing them in a blender or food processor. Add melted butter or cream and blend well. Pour into a coverable container and refrigerate for several hours to let the butter absorb the flavors. Then melt the butter again and strain through fine mesh or cloth. This produces a heady shrimp-flavored butter that can be served straight, combined with sour cream, cream cheese or convoluted with your favorite herbs and spices.

Until now, necessity had never mothered many inventive alternate methods of preserving shrimp. Orientals dry teeny-tiny shrimp, and they are tasty. I wondered if smoking would preserve them as well and render them even more delicious. Unfortunately, it is not a technique that I have yet perfected. However, how about smoked pickled shrimp.

Smoked Pickled Shrimp

Peel, devein and rinse 10 pounds of medium - large shrimp. Reserve shells and heads for broth or butter as above.

Brine:

1/2 C.	pickling salt
1 gal.	water
4 C.	distilled (white) vinegar
1 T.	cayenne pepper
1 T.	mustard seed
6	med. bay leaves

1 T.	black peppercorns
1 t.	cloves
2 t.	dill seed
1/2 t.	cinnamon

Simmer for 30 minutes, add shrimp and bring to a boil, at which point, remove from heat and pack shrimp into hot, sterilized pint jars and add to each jar

1 small bay leaf
a sprig of fresh dill
3 cloves
1 small clove garlic
3-4 peppercorns
1/2 teaspoon each of the following:
cayenne, thyme, mustard seed.

Fill jars to rim with a solution of 4 cups water, 2 cups white vinegar and 2 t. sugar. Seal tightly and refrigerate.

Shrimp are properly pickled in 3-4 days. I don't know how long they will keep; they seem to evaporate before the question can be answered.

For a unique flavor that you will never be able to buy, take out two pints of shrimp, drain and dry. Prepare the grill for hot smoking, temperature about 170°. When the coals are ready, add seasoning wood for a heavy smoke. Use citrus, fruit, oak and hickory. Place the shrimp on the grill and warm them up — they are already ready to eat.

Place shrimp on the grill, and smoke for about one hour— if you keep the temperature low. You will want to test occasionally to assure that the shrimp are not becoming overly dry. Take them up when you absolutely cannot eat another and still leave enough for each guest to have at least one. Count carefully, or you may find yourself in a pickle.

Jerky

Drying is the world's oldest and most common method of food preservation. Canning technology is less than 200 years old, and freezing became practical only during this century when electricity became available to people. Drying technology is simple and readily available to most of the world's culture.

Dried meat has been used at least since ancient Egypt. Humans dried meat from animals that were too big to eat all at once. "Biltong" is dried meat or game used in many African countries. North American Indians were masters at jerky making and mixed it, pounded into a powder, with dried fruit or fat to make "pemmican," a portable and highly nutritious food. Some think the word "jerky" came from the Spanish word "charque"; others think it came from the preparation, where the meat was jerked in strips from the muscles.

The scientific principal of preserving food by drying is that by removing moisture, enzymes are denied access to the food. Whether these enzymes are bacterial, fungal, or naturally occurring autolytic enzymes, preventing this action preserves the food from biological action.

Food can be dried, naturally, in the sun or in the shade or with additional dry heat. In the drying process, it is important, this day and age, to move the food through the danger-zone, between 40° and 140°, as quickly as practical. This gives the enzymes and bacteria less time to reproduce. Successfully and safely drying meat at home requires learning and applying some basic rules.

Apply all the rules for safely handling meat. Wash your hands, keep all surfaces clean and dry. Assure yourself that the meat was handled properly before you received it.

My personal favorite is to buy sirloin tip roasts, on sale— cheap, trim all exterior fat, and throw it in the freezer long enough for it to firm up. Then I slice it into 1/4" or less slices and trim out any fat and gristle. Fat will react with oxygen and become rancid with time, whereas lean meat will not. Gristle will just be very hard to chew and provides no taste. Cut larger pieces into snack-size bits for quicker drying, easier storage and practical eating.

My favorite recipe is the one I first learned, "Put enough salt on the meat to draw out the moisture and enough black pepper to keep off the flies." Then it goes into the drier. Over the years, I have used a black grill with no heat in the summertime. A gas oven set to 160°, a low temperature coal bed, with or without smoke, an electric food dehydrator. All have performed satisfactorily.

After the meat is thoroughly dry, and while it is still warm, store in heavy-duty plastic bags, expelling all the air, or in glass jars or other containers which will keep out moisture. Once I found a small sack which was at least five years old, that I had hidden from my children— who could knock off what was previously a 10 lb. roast in an evening. It was still delicious.

Some words of caution. There are gadgets on the market which extrude ground meat for drying, as in jerky. Some studies have shown that bacteria survive the drying process in ground meat. All the bacteria is covered in the **Meat** chapter, as well as the hazards of ground meat. All ground meat which I use, I grind. **I would not recommend any pre-ground meat for drying**, and even if I ground it, I would make certain that the dried meat reached 160°.

Read the ingredients label on so-called "jerky seasonings." Many contain monosodium glutamate and other adulterants, including potassium nitrate. You can mix your own much more cheaply and have a better product. While potassium nitrate is essential in curing hams and bacon, it is unnecessary for jerky.

As in other curing processes, the salt helps the low temperature to remove the moisture from the meat, and drying is the essence of preservation. Seasonings which already have salt, such as teriyaki, soy and Worcestershire sauces, require little or no additional salt. Garlic, onion, chili powder, ground bay leaf and minute amounts of cloves and allspice will perk up the flavor if you ever tire of straight jerky.

Any of the large game— venison, elk, moose, antelope— make excellent jerky. Bear meat should be dried to at least 160° because bears are susceptible to trichinosis. And, really, if you have access to the old "utility" grade beef, it makes the best jerky and chili because it has little or no interspersed fat.

Chapter Seven

Spices Seasonings and Sauces

Seasonings and sauces are an integral part of all cooking, but they are especially important in barbecuing and grilling. They not only make food taste good; they give it a particular identity. They may also tenderize the meat and/or keep it from drying out while cooking. No other form of cooking offers so many different methods of flavoring meats. There are dry seasonings, currently called **rubs**, for flavor alone — unless they contain a powdered artificial tenderizer; **marinades** for tenderizing, as well as for flavoring; **basting** sauces for tenderizing, flavoring and protecting; and the **finishing** sauce purely for flavor. **Glazes,** faddish, fancified finishing sauces, may be added for flavor as well as decoration.

It is the finishing sauce with a tomato base and a little sweetener that is traditionally considered "barbecue sauce." Unfortunately, "barbecue sauce" is the name given to that misbegotten marvel of malfunctioning taste buds mistakenly shown in advertisements being heavily applied to uncooked or overcooked meat. Obviously its producers, publicists and purveyors have deficiencies other than in their taste buds. Finishing sauces with sugar should **NEVER** be applied until the meat is already 90% cooked. The temperature must be carefully controlled or the tomato/sugar will quickly burn. Often, the finishing sauces are effectively applied after the meat is removed from the grill.

Seasonings should always be appropriate for the meat, the method of cooking and the result that you have created in your barbecue vision. It's the "vision thing" again. Seasonings should blend together — marry, if you will, becoming unified so that no part is separately identifiable from the whole.

Since seasonings and sauces are so important to the production of savory, succulent, delicious food on the grill, let's look at the individual herbs and spices, rubs, marinades, basting sauces and finishing sauces.

SPICES AND SEASONINGS

To put this subject into proper perspective, we should recall that Columbus, when he set out on his westward course, was looking neither for a new continent nor for gold. He was looking for a shorter route to the spice producers. At that time, pepper corns were sold individually in Europe, and a pepper corn was literally worth its weight in gold.

Spices and herbs are now much more readily available and, although not quite worth their weight in gold, they are still expensive. They are absolutely indispensable for fine cooking. However, all spices are not created equal. Some are inferior in quality and may have lingered on the shelves for years. **Buy the best and freshest that you can find and use them quickly or discard**.

For short-term storage, use a cool dark place. Store the more volatile in the freezer or refrigerator.

Here is a list of the more common seasonings used in grilling. Disregard neat little charts that prescribe which herbs can be used on what. Herbs and spices are being used and combined in new and exciting ways. Try the recipes; learn how each herb and spice tastes; how they combine; start mixing your own.

ALLSPICE. The ground up berry of a West Indian tree. The flavor is like a mixture of cloves, cinnamon and nutmeg. A little goes a long way. Use allspice in marinades and finishing sauces. A tiny bit ground onto the surface has a surprising effect. This is considered, by some, to be a "barbecue" spice.

BASIL. An annual herb of complex aromas, especially when fresh, almost essential in any tomato recipe or dish. It is essential in Mediterranean dishes. Use the leaves.

BAY LEAF. The leaf of the laurel tree (laurus nobilis) used in rubs, bastes,marinades and finishing sauces. Bay leaf is sometimes ground and applied dry. Some spice companies sell a leaf that they call "California Laurel." It tastes different and contains a neurotoxin.

BEER, COLD. Absolutely indispensable. It is rumored that several states are considering enacting laws to make it illegal to attempt to fire up the grill without cold beer. Frankly, I believe this to be rank governmental interference and totally unnecessary. I have never met a skilled barbecuer who did not enthusiastically utilize this essential ingredient.

BEER, HOT. Use as a marinade. Immerse portions remaining in ice to convert to "BEER, COLD."

BUTTER. First choice for supplying the oil requirements. I prefer unsalted because it is fresher and I can control the amount of salt going onto the meat. Do not use margarine. Margarine is nothing but cooking oil whipped to a froth with stabilizers to keep it firm. If you don't use butter, use oil.

CARROTS. For their unique flavor, add grated carrots to the basting sauce or marinade or include them in your cooked marinades.

CELERY. The stalk and leaves are cooked in basting sauces. Celery seed is acceptable, but will impart a bitter after taste if overcooked.

CHILI POWDER. A mixture of ground chile peppers, onion, garlic, cumin and oregano. It comes in different degrees of heat. The real problem with using chili powder in a recipe is that each manufacturer has its own mixture. Therefore, recipes which say use "x" amount of chili powder are misleading. It is better to add those ingredients that normally make up the chili powder mixture. That way you control the final product.

CLOVES. An intense, "high" flavor used in finishing sauces. Also can be used as a toothache remedy if you don't have any good whiskey.

CUMIN. A pungent spice essential for cooking chili and other Tex-Mex dishes. Cumin is used in marinades and basting sauces and it can also be rubbed on as a dry seasoning. Although recently popularized by Tex-Mex dishes, this is a very important spice in most of the world, especially Asia.

GARLIC. Don't leave for the grill without it. Learn the varieties of garlic available and enjoy. Roasted garlic is fantastic for flavoring. Fresh garlic is preferable but garlic powder is acceptable. The salt in garlic salt absorbs moisture and won't sprinkle.

GINGER. The root of the ginger plant combines well with garlic. It is considered an Oriental flavor. Ginger is used primarily for special effects in barbecuing, but finds wide use in other grilling. Fresh is much superior to dried.

HORSERADISH. Fresh ground horseradish root is good with beef, lamb, mutton and shrimp. Powdered horseradish provides a sharp, hot flavor shortly after being reconstituted.

LARD. Rendered pork fat has a flavor that has not been duplicated. It is an excellent baste or addition to a basting sauce.

MUSTARD. Dry mustard (ground up mustard seed) is used in rubs, marinades and finishing sauces. Mix with a little water to make a paste before adding to other liquid. Prepared mustard (dry mustard with vinegar, turmeric and sugar) is added to finishing sauces or painted on as a marinade or basting sauce.

ONIONS. Onions go in everything but ice cream. Use in rubs, marinades, basting sauces and finishing sauces. Get acquainted with the wide variety. Onion powder is acceptable.

OREGANO. A delicious herb and highly aromatic when fresh. Oregano is necessary for chili and tomato-based dishes and does magic with poultry and lamb. Essential in some Mediterranean and Oriental dishes. Dry is acceptable.

PAPRIKA. This is a finely ground, mild red pepper. Unless you can find one of the hotter Hungarian varieties, paprika contributes more color than flavor. When overcooked, paprika generates a bitter flavor.

PARSLEY. A beautiful little green herb that softens strong flavors. Fresh is best. A great breath deodorant. Chock-full of Vitamin C. It mixes well with other herbs.

PEPPER, BLACK. Fresh ground is better. Like other spices, pepper begins to lose its flavor once it is ground. There are several kinds of pepper corns, some vastly superior to others. Learn a little about the different black peppers and find a supplier who can provide fresh, high quality peppercorns.

PEPPERS/CHILES. It's time you got acquainted with several chile varieties. Their heat is measured in Scovilles, with the sweet bell registering 0 and the currently faddish habanero and Scotch bonnet topping out at from 100,000 to 300,000 Scovilles. The tasty jalapeno pepper, earns a 2500-5000 Scovilles while cayenne racks up a 50,000. Very good, but use with care. The grill is a great place to blister chilies in order to peel them. Chiles deserve a whole book, if not an encyclopedia, to explain them.

ROSEMARY. An aromatic herb used on salads and meats. Especially favored in Mediterranean dishes, it is gaining a wider audience. Makes a beautiful plant. Fresh twigs impart a delicious aroma when burned.

SAGE. A highly aromatic leaf used to flavor pork and poultry. Ground, it may be applied directly to the meat. Otherwise include it in the basting sauce. A must for Southern breakfast sausages.

SALT. Yes, salt. Salt is a conveyor of flavors as well as an intensifier. Salt transports, by osmosis, other flavors inside the meat. Regular salt is fine for broiling, roasting and barbecuing. Where it is used in a cure for preservation, use pickling salt, which has no iodine or flow enhancers. Sea salt is another faddish, high-priced, no-brainer. *All salt is sea salt.* The salt, mined from underground, is deposited from ancient seas, which, to the logical mind, would seem to have fewer pollutants than that made from current sea water.

SCALLIONS. Little green onions can be used in any of the sauces. Sometimes inserted in slits cut into the meat before cooking. They add color as well as a distinctive flavor to sauces. Do not confuse with shallots or chives.

SOY SAUCE. Indispensable in Chinese roast pork, soy sauce is also used in basting sauces for chicken. Most domestic soy sauce is way too salty. Visit an oriental grocery to try some of the great variety of soy sauces. You'll be amazed and delighted at the flavors — and prices.

STOCK. Bones and trimmings of whatever you intend to barbecue, or grill, can be boiled and the reduced (boiled down) stock added to your basting sauce. It makes a much richer basting sauce and reduces the need for additional oil. Wild game trimmings are not normally used, but stocks from other sources are very good on game.

SUET. Beef fat from around the kidneys. However, any rendered beef fat is excellent as a seasoning and as a tenderizer.

TARRAGON. A little tarragon goes a long way. Like rosemary, it makes a beautiful plant. Tarragon flavored vinegar is very popular.

THYME. This pungent little leaf is added to basting sauces for beef, pork and venison. It is sometimes put directly on the meat. It's an essential herb that has wide uses and seems to have the ability to augment other flavors. This is one of my most favorite herbs. It joins well with other herbs and, unlike some ladies I know, marries well.

VINEGAR. Flavorful and tenderizing, distilled, apple cider or wine vinegars are interchangeable. The acid content of distilled vinegars will be consistent. Vinegar should be discreet, not blatant. Balsamic vinegars expand the flavor spectrum and explode the price range.

WHISKEY. A controversial ingredient. Whiskey is effective as a tenderizer and a flavoring ingredient in marinades and basting sauces. Questions arise as to the proper utilization of resources. If it's good whiskey, why waste it in an undrinkable mixture. If it's not good enough to drink, don't put it on your food.

WINE. Use in marinades and basting sauces. Sometimes used as a substitute for cold beer.

WORCESTERSHIRE (WOOSTER) SAUCE. If this did not exist, somebody would have to invent it. It is used in marinades, basting and finishing sauces. Lea and Perrins brand is stronger than all the others. If you switch brands, make adjustments. Twenty years ago, I bought this by the case in gallon jugs — couldn't cook without it. Now I use it in much more modest amounts.

Recipes

At best, recipes are a starting place; at their worst, a delusion. A recipe is a snapshot, a recording of an assembly of measured ingredients, which, theoretically, together have the ability to produce and reproduce certain tastes and/or textures.

In fact, the effectiveness of the recipe depends upon many variable factors. The original quality of the herbs/spices — their conformity to and intensity of the expected characteristics is, at least, **doubtful**, until proven. Their condition and age is **suspect** — even true and potent spices lose their volatile flavors languishing in warm, humid warehouses or in lengthy exposure to bright lights on grocery shelves. Abandoned for years, aging above the stove in part-time kitchens, even the best deteriorate quickly.

If you are to succeed in cooking, indoors or out, you must learn to taste critically: to distinguish individual seasonings, their intensity, and their truth in conformity. You need not have the one-in-a-million tongue, which is loaded with receptors, but you must learn how to make the most of what you have.

Start with basic strong flavors, like garlic and onion. Taste the difference among fresh, raw and sauteed, blended with olive oil and refrigerated, compared to reasonably fresh powder and granulated. You can use a platform as simple as bread or a relatively bland dish — soup or eggs.

Then introduce, one a time, more volatile but regularly used ingredients, such as basil, bay leaf, oregano and thyme. Compare their intensity to allspice, cloves, cumin, mace and rosemary.

Acquaintance with the pure flavor/essence of the individual spices and herbs is the beginning. The next step is to discover how they blend, contrast or oppose each other. Some intensify during cooking; some lose parts, or all, of their flavors during long cooking periods or at intense heat; therefore, some should be added early, some late to the cooking process.

One effect to be watched is that flavors may become muddied. Remember what happened when you were water-coloring as a child and kept mixing different colors together to come up with a great new color. You wound up with a muddled grey/black, dull color. The same can happen with flavors.

Surely, there is a book somewhere that tells how-to and which and all the goodies that simplify learning to use seasonings. Sometimes, I wish I had found it, but then I would have missed all the pleasurable hours of discovering disasters and deliciousness.

If this is a little daunting, or you'd just rather not, we have recipes.

MARINADES

Metaphors and other inedible mixtures

Among many misinformed, myriad malodorous mixtures masquerade as meaningful marinades. Misuse of marinades, a common waste of time and resources, comes from a misunderstanding of the real purpose of marinating. Marinating is to either to tenderize or change the basic flavor of the *marinadee*.

In other words, if you don't like what you have to eat, marinate it to change or disguise its flavor. Marinades are meant to disguise the flavor of a piece of meat until its mama wouldn't know it.

So, if you like the taste of what you have to eat, no need to marinate. Add seasonings before you put it on the grill and/or into the basting sauce to be absorbed while cooking. Seasoning with herbs and spices and/or basting with highly flavored sauces can enhance the basic flavor. A marinade can dominate the original flavors.

Occasionally, you may marinate to add more of a distinctive flavor to a food which will be cooked but a few minutes. Be careful not to overpower the original flavor — unless that is your intent.

There are really two kinds of flavor-altering marinades. The first tames a strong flavor. This is for use on old venison and other gamey meats and fish with a slightly strong odor. These marinades are built to absorb. They will contain salt, vinegar, milk, buttermilk or combinations thereof. Milk is especially effective. Powdered milk works just as well as whole milk. These marinades are usually discarded while those containing acid may be boiled, then used as a baste.

The other reason for marinating is to tenderize. Frankly, most marinades are much more effective as flavorers than as tenderizers. Acids in vinegar, lemon and lime juices, wine, beer, milk, etc., have a somewhat limited tenderizing effect. Real success in rendering tough meat tender depends upon proper methods and temperatures in the cooking.

Fresh pineapple juice and fresh papaya juice contain an enzyme, papain, that is a very effective tenderizer. However, it is most effectively administered while the animal is still alive. That makes for a large marinade vessel. (Actually, it is injected.)

Papain, also available as a powder, is effective in a marinade and renders the meat less mushy than the other powdered tenderizer, monosodium glutamate. But either will turn meat into mush if applied too heavily or too long.

A friend of mine, who for his own protection shall remain nameless, recounted a tale at our judging table at a world famous barbecue cooking contest in Kansas City, MO. Nameless, along with others, was invited by a friend to partake of barbecued chicken breasts to show off his newly discovered marinade. With the guests gathered expectantly, the chef removed the chicken from the grill onto a cutting board and, expertly wielding his knife, made the first cut on a chicken breast. His blade was keen — as sharp as the assembled appetites — but, the unkindest cut was rendered upon the host. His ego was slashed when he discovered the meat was so mushy that it smashed instead of sliced.

The marinade of pineapple juices had been so good the first time the host had used it that he thought a few more hours would make the chicken even better. However, recovering quickly, he showed his good taste by declining to serve his guests chicken mush and called in an order for home-delivery.

Since most marinades are on the acid side of neutral pH, they should not be prepared or stored in any metal, other than stainless steel. Use porcelain, glass or plastic. Cover the meat with the marinade, to block exposure to air. Enclosing meat and marinade in a plastic bag will accomplish this with less marinade. The amount of marinade should correspond to the amount of meat. Don't expect two cups of marinade to perform the same magic on a ten-pound venison roast that you'd get from ten cups.

Use your judgment about how long to marinate the meat. The time can vary from a few minutes for a mild fish fillet to days for a large venison roast. Time and the strength of the marinade are somewhat interdependent. The opportunities for variations are endless.

Personally, I rarely find a need for using a marinade.

Marinade Recipes

All of the useful marinade recipes that I know of contain variations on the following ingredients.

Acids	Aromatic herbs and spices	Salty mixtures
lemon	allspice, anise, basil, bay leaf,	anchovy
lime	cardamon, celery, cilantro,	fish sauce
vinegar	cinnamon cloves, coriander,	oyster sauce
milk	cumin, dill, fennel seed, garlic,	soy sauce
buttermilk	ginger, juniper berries, mace,	teriyaki
yogurt	mint, mustard, dry or wet,	Worcestershire
sour cream	nutmeg, oregano, peppers -	
beer	chilies and *piper nigrum,*	Enzymics
wine	rosemary, sage, savory,	Papaya
whiskey	tarragon, thyme	Pineapple

It is easy to see that the acids are derived from citrus, vinegar, dairy and alcohol. Natural vinegar, of course, has gone through conversion, past the alcohol stage — as will any alcoholic mixture exposed to natural bacteria and allowed to continue fermentation. I am positive that there are other natural acids, such as cranberry or crab apple juice which would also work, but I leave those to you to discover and develop.

From these, you can produce your own recipes, adding or omitting oil as appropriate and water as needed. You will see them in use in the following recipes. You will find them, also, in every commercially available marinade — along with extenders, preservatives, tenderizers and other undesirables.

I have omitted tenderizers. Pineapple juice is a natural. Powdered papain is readily available. I just haven't found anything that needed them. If you will learn to not over cook your meat, you also may find them superfluous.

I urge you to consider the following recipes as beginning points and discover your own.

Flavor Tamers

Up and Down Fish Marinade

The fish needs a little perking up and the flavor, perhaps, taming down.

1/2 C.	lemon juice
1/2 C.	water
1/2 C.	chopped fresh parsley

Add water, as needed (within reason) to cover the fish. Refrigerate in a plastic bag, with all the air expelled, for 20 - 60 minutes.

This, added to melted butter or olive oil, can become the baste, with very good effect.

TLC Marinade

The fish needs a little tender, loving care to recover from abuse or neglect.

1 C.	milk/ yogurt/ buttermilk
1 C.	water
1 T.	lemon juice
1 T.	chopped fresh parsley
1/4 t.	ground cloves

Cover, excluding all air, and refrigerate up to overnight.

This one should be discarded after use.

Powdered milk, skim milk or sour cream may be substituted and vinegar or lime juice may be substituted for lemon juice. A dry white wine is an excellent substitute for the milk, but, personally, I'd use the wine otherwise.

Major League

Big Game

Personally, I don't marinate game — if I have cleaned it. But there may arise occasions upon which you think that you need to bring out the big guns for game or beef. This will do the job.

1 pt.	water
1 C.	Worcestershire sauce
1 C.	vinegar
1/2 C.	oil
2	bay leaves, crushed
6	juniper berries, crushed
1 T.	granulated garlic
1 T.	granulated onion
1/4 t.	ground cloves
1/4 t.	cinnamon

Bring all except oil to a simmer, remove and add oil. Let cool before covering the meat in a plastic bag and refrigerating for 4-24 hours. Can be brought to a boil and used as a baste.

Lubrication

Everything operates smoother with a little lubrication — even the cook. Some meats, fish and fowl lack enough internal oils to cook properly and easily on the grill. Soaking those in oil also gives an opportunity for adding flavors.

Passing the Buck

WD-40 is used for hundreds of things that were never conceived by its discoverers. I suspect the same is true of **Kraft Heavy-Duty Italian Dressing.** This has the ingredients of a good marinade and a good basting sauce — especially when time is short. This works well with fish, chicken, pork and lamb — that I know of, and perhaps others. Depend on your own wisdom for the time period.

Finessing the Flavor

Sometimes flavor can be finessed into food by a little subterfuge. Olive oil, especially virgin, seems to facilitate the infusion of flavors into meat. This may be a figment of my imagination, but I am a believer

The Italian Connection

1/2 C.	virgin or extra-virgin olive oil (depends upon how much olive oil flavor you want.)
2	cloves garlic, pressed
2	shallots, mashed
3 T.	prepared mustard
1/4 C.	water

Bring all ingredients to a simmer, cool and cover meat — a plastic bag works well — for 1- 4 hours, unrefrigerated.

Herbal Infusions

With the recent interest in herbal infusions, for medicinal reasons, this will seem less foreign than a few years ago.

3 C.	stock beef, chicken, fish — whichever is appropriate
1 lb.	carrots, julienned
1 lb.	onions, chopped
1 lb.	celery and tops, chopped
4	cloves, garlic, mashed
1 C.	fresh parsley, chopped
1/4 C.	fresh thyme
4	bay leaves
1 T.	pepper corns
6	whole allspice
1/4 C.	virgin olive oil
1/4 C.	wine — whatever is appropriate
	salt to taste

Saute carrots, onion and celery until clear then add garlic and continue until garlic is clear. Add to stock pot and bring to a simmer. Continue until stock is reduced by 1/2; then add parsley, thyme, bay leaves, pepper and allspice. Simmer for 15 minutes; then add the wine.

At this point, you may want to consider saving the meat for another day and just consuming this as a soup. However, if you choose, you can cool this down, and then use it as a flavoring marinade.

This would make an excellent court bouillon, pronounced *coobiyon* in Louisiana, for simmering fish fillets. It could also become the magnificent matrix of a mother of all stews. However, marinating your meat, fish or fowl in this for up to 2 days will imbue the viand with delicate flavors that are guaranteed to enhance, but not to overcome.

Don't dare discard! This can be reheated for basting, but could best be used as the foundation for a delicious sauce to accompany the meat. If you do, reheat, then strain to remove all the vegetables, allspice, bay leaves, etc.; then simmer to reduce.

Metamorphosis

There may be times when you just wish to change what you have into something different. We can do that. Sauerbraten is a good example. The mock crab recipe in the broiling chapter is another.

This calls for radical action — extreme, even. The goal is to so infuse flavor into the subject as to obscure, if not obliterate, its original identity. A pickled egg would never pass as a candidate for an omelet any more than a jugged hare would pass for fried rabbit.

The only way to do that is to use very potent flavorings which take over, in a revolutionary way, the original flavors and textures. This drastic action should, in my estimation, only be taken when one is pretty sure of the desired results and has a reasonable belief that this will achieve them.

Abracadabra Marinade

2 C.	vinegar
1 C.	water
1/2 C.	pickling spice
1/4 C.	oil
1 T.	black pepper, ground
1 T.	salt
1 t.	cayenne pepper

Bring the mixture to a boil — in a well ventilated area — then let cool. Place the meat, fish, fowl in a non-reactive container and cover with the mixture. After about two days, the marinade will have done its work.

This, by the way, is excellent for pickling eggs, pig feet, 'possum lips and other various and sundry items.

Pickling spice is a generic name for a collection of spices, typically as follows:

1/2 t.	cinnamon
1/2 t.	ground cloves, or 1 t. whole cloves
4	bay leaves
4 T.	coriander
2 T.	mustard seed
1 T.	pepper corns
1 T.	dill seed
1 T.	celery seed
1 t.	cayenne pepper
1 t.	allspice

Nowhere are these relationships or even identities written in stone, but this collection, and variations thereof, is used for sauerbraten, pickled eggs, pickled peaches, boiled shrimp, crabs and crawfish and boiled corned beef.

RUBS

A rub is a mixture of dry seasonings which is sprinkled or rubbed onto the meat. It may be put on a few seconds or a few hours before the meat goes on the grill. Because most rubs contain a significant amount of salt, I prefer to put the rub on shortly before the meat goes on the grill. Otherwise, the salt will begin drawing moisture out of the meat.

Some commercially available rubs contain monosodium glutamate (MSG) or powdered papain extract as tenderizers and flavor enhancers. I personally do not use the products and do not recommend them for several reasons. MSG is, first of all, a sodium. Those with hypertension and weight problems don't need another source of sodium. A percentage of the population, around 13% according to a recent study, has some reaction to MSG. Papain is a potent tenderizer and can easily convert meat to mush. The texture, resistance to the teeth, is part of the enjoyment of eating meat. There are many other ways to render meat tender.

Rubbing is an opportunity to coat the meat surface with an intense flavor. However, seasonings may change with exposure to heat and from their reaction with the meat. Therefore, the flavor of the finished product may not be what you expected from the raw mixture. You will need to learn by experimenting.

Rubs add no moisture or oil to meat or veggies; therefore they offer no protection to keep the exterior from hardening or burning. This shortcoming was apparently first expressed by a Dane of some note who, according to Billy Bob Shakespeare said, "Aye, there's the rub . . .."

Try some of the recipes for rubs and some of the commercial products, but begin to experiment with making your own.

I put all the ingredients into a gallon jug, closing the lid, then shake, rattle and roll until well mixed. Use the rub as you would salt. When the meat is salty enough, the rub should have the flavor intended by its maker.

237

The Basics

Since most folk were introduced to rubs by local custom or from commercially available products purporting to represent a certain style or geographical area, the first group of rubs will be generic representations of the known, or at least supposed types of rubs. Of those mythical or mystical genre, those who promote such consider that Kansas City, Texas and Louisiana have distinguishable characteristics.

While I personally consider this mostly mythology, here they are.

Generic Theoretical Rubs

Texas Style

1 lb.	salt
2 oz.	paprika
1 oz.	black pepper
1 oz.	red pepper

Some add sugar, cumin and chili powder.

Kansas City Style

1/2 lb.	salt
1/2 lb.	sugar
2 oz.	paprika
1 oz.	chili powder
1 oz.	garlic powder
1 oz.	onion powder
1/2 oz.	celery seed

Among other ingredients often found in K.C. style rubs are ground cumin, mace, coriander and allspice.

Cajun Style

1 lb.	salt
2 oz	onion powder
2 oz.	garlic powder
2 oz	paprika
1 oz.	cayenne pepper
1 oz.	celery seed
1 oz.	lemon-pepper
1 oz.	allspice

Remember that these rubs are *representative* of the different areas. There is no more a "right" recipe for a rub than there is for vegetable soup in the whole of Iowa.

Some Custom Rubs

Smoky's Legendary All-Purpose Rub

1 lb.	salt
4 oz.	garlic powder
4 oz.	onion powder
4 oz.	Hungarian paprika
2 oz.	ground thyme
2 oz.	ground bay
1 oz.	ground celery seed

This has been used on meat for barbecuing, roasting and broiling. People have reported using it on steaks, potatoes, popcorn, boiled/roasted corn. I use it as the basis for a basting sauce by adding 4 T. of the rub to 1/2 C. each of vinegar, water and oil and 1/4 C. Worcestershire sauce.

Smoky's Pork and Poultry Rub

1 lb.	salt
4 oz.	onion powder
4 oz.	garlic powder
2 oz.	rubbed sage
2 oz.	ground thyme
2 oz.	ground bay
1 oz.	ground mustard

This has proven to be a big favorite on pork roasts and chickens. I mix it in bulk, then fill small jars with shaker tops to dispense as needed.

Greek Rub for Lamb

4 oz.	salt
4 oz.	garlic powder
1 oz.	ground oregano
1 oz.	rosemary
1/2 oz.	black pepper

Big Game Rub

4 oz.	salt
2 oz.	garlic powder
2 oz.	onion powder
1 oz.	ground bay
1 T.	ground juniper berries
1 t.	celery seed
1 oz.	ground thyme
1/2 oz.	fresh ground black pepper
1/4 t.	cayenne pepper
1/8 t.	ground cloves

BASTING SAUCES

All other things being equal, basting sauce is probably the single most important ingredient in successful barbecuing. Marinades or rubs are used sometimes; basting sauces are used every time the experienced barbecuer barbecues. Even when rubbed or marinated beforehand, meat is still basted during cooking. The flavors in basting sauce are cooked into the meat, and if the meat is over coals, the sauces drip and come back up as flavored steam. This is a "secret" that separates barbecue from all other forms of cooking. It imparts a special flavor and texture that makes barbecue distinctively delicious. There are those who believe, with good reason, that a good basting sauce judiciously applied will make a pine knot tender and delicious.

Basting is also an excellent way to add flavor and keep the exterior moist when broiling or roasting on a grill. The sauce is applied with a mop, brush, spoon or spout at appropriate intervals while the meat is cooking. Basting frequency depends upon the type of meat and the cooking temperature. Of course, opening the grill to apply the basting sauce and the sauce itself will reduce the temperature. You can compensate for a hotter-than-desired grill temperature by basting more frequently, or vice versa. More frequent basting will also increase the amount of flavor absorbed by the meat. Generally, you baste more often during the early cooking time when the fire is hotter and flavors more easily penetrate the uncooked meat. To minimize the heat loss, keep the basting sauce warm.

The proper basting sauce will not only enhance the flavor of a particular piece of meat, but it will provide a liquid and oil to create a seal that will preserve natural juices and prevent formation of a hard crust. Properly done barbecue is evenly cooked from the outside to the center.

Regarding basting, the sauce for the goose is not necessarily the appropriate sauce for the gander. Basting sauce is tailored to suit the fattiness and flavor of meat that is being cooked. Basting sauce for pork will contain less oil than that used on venison. Pork has more natural fat, so it provides some of its own oil. Beef cuts vary in the amount of natural fat marbled into the meat. The basting sauce must be adjusted accordingly. Basting sauce prepared for a particular piece of meat should reflect sound judgment about the flavor that is best for that particular piece.

A robust, highly seasoned sauce appropriate for a venison roast would overpower the more delicate flavor of chicken, quail or domestic rabbit. Further, the basting sauce should agree with the finishing sauce. Both sauces should combine to present the finished product your taste buds have conceived. This opportunity to create so many different flavors is one of the aspects that has caused barbecue to continue to grow as one of America's favorite types of food.

Recipes

Most basting sauces, or bastes, contain water, oil and an acid with salt and seasonings. Most non-disposable marinades, those not using dairy products, make good basting sauces. Some of these will benefit from addition of oil.

We start with the delicate and move, progressively, to the heavyweights.

Baby-cakes Baste

For use on delicate fish, chicken breasts, domestic rabbit, veal, 'veggies.

1/4 lb.	unsalted butter, melted
2 T.	lemon juice
1/2 t.	salt
1/2 t.	white pepper

The butter protects, the lemon juice brightens the flavor and the salt and pepper enhance. Mild olive, corn or peanut oil may be substituted. I would not use sesame or canola in this.

Variations may include:

Fish: fresh dill, ground coriander, mint, and minute quantities of ground cloves, allspice, nutmeg, and cayenne pepper.

Fowl: all of the above, plus sage, thyme, bay, rosemary.

Rabbit and veal: all of the above plus black pepper

Veggies: all of the above

Saucy Seafood Sauce

Stronger fish, such as tuna, shrimp, lobster, soft-shell crabs.

1/2 C.	mild oil
1/2 C.	lemon juice
1/2 C.	water
1 t.	garlic powder
1 t.	onion powder
1/2 t.	ground coriander
1/2 t.	ground mustard
1/4 t.	ground allspice
1/8 t.	ground cloves
1/8 t.	cinnamon
1/8 t.	ground bay
1/8 t.	cayenne

Bring to a simmer and allow to cool.

Mid-Range Magic

For pork, veal, poultry when broiling or roasting. This is for broiling and roasting, not necessarily barbecuing.

1 C.	mild oil
1 C.	apple juice
1/2 C.	apple cider vinegar
1 T.	garlic powder
1 T.	onion powder
1 T.	salt
1 t.	thyme
1 t.	ground bay
1 t.	ground mustard
2 T.	Worcestershire sauce

Cut the salt in half to use soy or teriyaki sauce instead of the Worcestershire sauce, and instead of apple juice, use chicken or veal stock.

243

Ultimate Barbecue Basting Sauce

This will work wonders on pork, beef, goat or poultry.

1 qt.	beef or chicken stock
1 pt.	apple cider vinegar
1 pt.	Worcestershire sauce
1 C.	oil, butter is preferred
4 T.	salt
2 T.	garlic powder, or 3 cloves, mashed
2 T.	onion powder, or 3 med., chopped
2	carrots, julienned
2	stalks celery and leaves, chopped
2 t.	thyme
4	bay leaves
1 bunch	green onions, chopped
1	medium bell pepper, chopped
1	lemon, squeezed

Saute vegetables until tender, add other ingredients and simmer 20 minutes. Mop the meat well and let dry before putting on the grill. Keep the sauce warm and baste at 10 minute intervals for the first hour. Then, at 20-30 minute intervals until done.

Quick and Easy

1 bottle Kraft Zesty Italian Dressing

Oriental Express

2 C.	water
1 C.	soy sauce
1/4 lb.	unsalted butter
1 t.	grated ginger
2 T.	lemon juice

Baste and dry, before and frequently after placing meat on the grill.

Basic Eastern North Carolina Basting Sauce

This sauce is as old as barbecue and, like barbecue, has not changed for over 300 years. It may not perfectly fit your palate, but this is truly "The Mother of Barbecue Sauces." In the place of its birth, this is still the only barbecue sauce. In the beginning, no water was used. Vinegar, these days, is brought to a consistent 5% acidity. In the old days, vinegar was homemade and of variable strength so that the recipes called for pure vinegar. Current palates may find pure current vinegar a tad on the tart side.

1 qt.	water
1 qt.	vinegar
3 T.	salt
2 T.	cayenne pepper
1 T.	black pepper

This, by the way, is also the Eastern North Carolina finishing sauce, which is poured or sprinkled on the pulled or chopped barbecued pork.

Finishing Sauces

Finishing sauces put the final flair on appearance and taste to barbecue or add glazes which flavor and enhance the appearance of grilled dishes. The traditional barbecue sauce is a sweet/tart tomato-based combination of a variety of additional flavorings that create a full-bodied, spicy flavor to compliment the meat. A glaze, usually having a sweet base, may be added for appearance or to produce a complimentary or contrasting flavor.

Finishing sauce is basted onto the meat, or when it is almost finished cooking, the meat is dredged into the sauce. Because of the sugar and tomato, it is highly susceptible to scorching. Scorching (blackening) would give the meat a bitter taste; therefore, take care to insure that the temperature does not get to that point. A thick sauce would also tend to insulate the meat from the heat and retard cooking. It is preferable to baste with the finishing sauce for the last ten to thirty minutes over reduced heat (dying coals), but the meat may be removed from the grill, sliced and soaked with warm sauce before serving.

The finishing sauce may be omitted to achieve a certain taste or effect on particular meats. Fish rarely requires a finishing sauce. Chicken, domestic duck, Cornish game hens, quail, frog legs and other light and tender meats are often served with no finishing sauce.

Regional variations in finishing sauces may surprise you. If you have not been exposed to them before, try several. Then you can develop your own. Variations on the traditional finishing sauces are limited only by the baster's imagination. There are those to excite the savage or titillate the discriminating palate.

To some, finishing sauces are almost addictive. To many, they represent **the** taste of barbecue. I believe that the finishing sauce should be only one of the many elements of flavor and appearance and that it should neither dominate nor clash with previous seasonings.

I did not easily, or without some sacrifice, come to this persuasion.

On Getting Properly Sauced

One day I came upon three ladies in the process of getting seriously sauced — in the grocery store. Each clutched a bottle in her hand and they were engaged in animated conversation. It was pitifully obvious that they had sadly slipped into a state of confusion. Alas, we have too often seen that scene.

In my youth, I too wasted hours in such frivolous pursuits. Yes, friends, I also lugubriously lounged at the long, loaded shelves, lusting for the last, luxurious elixir. Seduced by the passionate promises of ecstasy, I became intoxicated by the invidious influence of sensuous shapes, comely colors and prurient prose.

Being still a recovering person myself, my sympathies were immediately aroused. Let us not be swift to judgement. Who among us has not also suffered. "There go I. . ." — but for the grace of God and *Barbecue Sauces Anonymous.*

A few years ago, before I took the pledge, I tasted 178 different barbecue sauces in one day. It served me right that I was sick for days. The occasion was the International Barbecue Sauce Contest in Kansas City. Despite that indiscretion, I was invited to judge the contest again. But now I prudently limit my tasting to 25 or 30.

This past year over 300 barbecue sauces were entered in the contest. While each judge is normally expected to taste and pass judgement on about 10 sauces, I was still compelled to check out some of the more popular versions that weren't on my list. The identity of entries concealed, the samples are served in numbered cups, and several judges taste each entry. Only when the totals are delivered by an accounting firm are the winners known.

Unfortunately for the majority of us, nobody passes out free samples of all the varieties of barbecue sauces lining the shelves of grocery stores. So the task of choosing the right sauce for your palate is a challenging chore — absorbing lots of time, energy, money and stomach-soothing remedies.

The three ladies finally solved their dilemma by selecting one bottle each and agreeing upon the choice of a fourth.

Their conversation convinced me that their barbecue would be delicious, regardless of the finishing sauce. This is perhaps the redeeming feature of commercially bottled barbecue (finishing) sauce. No matter how bad, it can't hide the taste of good barbecue. On the other hand, no finishing sauce will cover up incompetent cooking.

While many backyard barbecuers use a sauce straight off the shelf, some use the store-bought variety as a beginning point and add herbs and spices to tailor it to their taste. If you have never rolled your own or spiced up a basic blend, try these versions then follow your taste buds.

Eastern North Carolina Finishing Sauce

See Eastern North Carolina Basting Sauce

Basic South Carolina Finishing Sauce

Essentially, South Carolinians took the Eastern North Carolina finishing sauce and substituted prepared mustard, the main constituent of which is vinegar, for the vinegar and water and then whacked the cayenne pepper in half.

Basic Lexington-Style Barbecue Sauce

Lexington, meaning Lexington, NC, was the site of the first great barbecue revolution. Located westward up in the Piedmont (foot hill) Region, it was the place where some heretic, who shall remain nameless, first dared to barbecue the shoulder rather than the whole hog. Perhaps he was a native of the lowlands, forced to flee, light-footing it into the hills, for his heresy; we do not know. What we do know is that in Lexington, barbecuing less than a whole hog became acceptable in polite society.

Then, as sacrilege begat sacrilege, the sauce was changed! The insidious *love apple*, the plump, seductive scarlet fruit, suspected of inflaming passions, defiled the sanctity of the sacred sauce. Tomatoes and the extravagant sugar were added to the finishing sauce! Shades of Martin Luther!!

This heretical heritage is what move westward with barbecue over the Appalachians. Still maligned as illegitimate by East Coast whole-hog purists, it was accepted as gospel by the naive natives of the interior.

Lexington Style Barbecue Sauce

As revolutionary as this sauce was, it is still a little tart for modern tastes, suckled on sugar-tits and saturated in catsupy sauces.

1 qt.	apple cider vinegar
1 C.	catsup
1 C.	brown sugar
1 T.	Worcestershire sauce
1 t.	onion powder
1 t.	salt
1 t.	black pepper
1/2 t.	cayenne pepper

Simmer until well joined and allow to cool.

Most other traditional barbecue sauces show their heritage.

Basic Mid-South Finishing Sauce

1 C.	catsup	1 C.	water
1/2 C.	vinegar	1/2 C.	butter
4 T.	Worcestershire	2	lemons, juice of
4 T.	brown sugar	2 T.	prepared mustard.
1 T.	black pepper	1 T.	salt
1 T.	Tabasco		
	dash of cloves		

Simmer for 10-20 minutes.

249

Many folk start with a commercial barbecue sauce product and use it as a base to put their on flair to it. This can yield an acceptable sauce as long as the commercial sauce is not loaded with the odious liquid smoke.

Basic Doctoring Sauce

Start with any basic commercial barbecue sauce of 28-32 oz. and add:

1 C.	catsup
1 C.	water
1/2 C.	brown sugar
1	large onion, chopped
2 T.	garlic powder
1/4 t.	cloves

Simmer 30 minutes or more.

Remember that finishing sauce goes on late when the fire is low. Its purpose is to put on the final flair on fantastic flavors. Do the first part right, the last part light and you can't go wrong.

Texas Black Jack

This is included because it is the only barbecue sauce, of which I am aware, that uses coffee in a barbecue sauce. Perhaps its original purpose was to try to cover up the sour-smelling mesquite wood smoke

2 C.	catsup
1 C.	strong, black coffee
1 C.	Worcestershire sauce
1/2 lb.	butter
2 T.	brown sugar
1 T.	salt
2 T.	black pepper

Combine and simmer for 30 minutes.

Mama's

What kind of guy could write a book like this and not put his mama's barbecue sauce in it? From my earliest memories, barbecue was regular fare around our house. Dad did the barbecue, or at least supervised it, but Mama made the sauce. She was a skilled and creative cook and well-known for those talents. This recipe was in her vast repository of family favorites.

1 qt.	catsup
6 oz.	mustard
3 T.	vinegar
1/3 C.	Worcestershire sauce
2 T.	brown sugar
1	lemon, juiced
1/2 lb.	butter
1/2 t.	salt
1/2 t.	black pepper

Blend well, simmer about I hour. Refrigerate if kept for more than one day.

These are beginning points. Mix your own to match your palate.

Chapter Eight

Accompaniments

"Man does not live by meat alone." The successful barbecue will offer some appropriate accompaniments. Traditional dishes associated with barbecue are baked beans, often erroneously called "barbecued beans,"cole slaw, and from ancient times, hash. Close cousins, Brunswick stew and burgoo, are also traditional in their respective areas.

The broader spectrum of grilling vastly increases the range of accompaniments. Anything that can be served in an indoor meal, can be as easily joined at the grill. As with planning any meal accompaniments to the main course should offer contrasts in taste, texture, color and nutrients, yet compliment, rather than clash with the main course.

Offered here are a few suggestions, accurate renditions of some traditional dishes and a few avenues for pursuit.

Salads

Caesar: "The Ides of March have come."

Soothsayer: "Aye, Caesar, but not past, and if you go into the senate today, having a salad named after you will be small consolation."

Or, I think that's the way the conversation went.

Although salads were popular with the Romans, as they had been for centuries with Greeks, Persians and Chinese, I doubt that Julius Caesar ever tasted a salad comparable to the one that bears his name.

There are many good reasons why salads have been popular for centuries in many civilizations. They provide some welcomed crunch contrasting to softer textures and the fresh colors give the appearance of wholesomeness and health. They can complement flavors or cleanse the palate before a change of tastes.

It is unfortunate that salads these days have often become a motley melange of empty crunch and a counterfeit collage of colors, pleasing neither the eye or the palate.

Of my three least favorite food substitutes, the common salad has two: iceberg lettuce and hothouse tomatoes. The third is "light" bread."

Lettuce began as a robust weed that grew well in cooler weather — which made it a welcomed gift of early spring. It was cultivated extensively by the Persians and Chinese. Columbus brought seeds with him on his excursions to the Americas. But we have improved upon it cosmetically until now like the Irish setter, it is only a pretty parody of what it used to be.

Hothouse tomatoes should, by law, be required to carry a different name. They bear the same resemblance to a real, juicy, tangy tomato as a plastic reproduction. With the passing of vaudeville, so bad that it required the hurling fruits and vegetables, the last useful function of hot house tomatoes faded away.

253

Despite all these improvements of modern agribusiness, the determined cook can still turn out a proper salad using lesser-known ingredients that have not been so "improved."

Fresh spinach, though less crunchy, is richer in color and in food value. Curly mustard has a tangy taste. Sorrel adds a tart flavor and vitamins. Rocket, a.k.a. *roquette, arugula, rugula,* is getting a big play in the trendy set of food fashion faddists. These are the same people who are currently on a radicchio rage.

Salads should be built to requirements of the meal. They should always be pleasing to the eye, healthy and tasty. But they should also complement the main dish. The big, boisterous salad that can hold its own beside a brawny steak would overmatch a fragile fish filet.

Get off the food fashion freeway and meander through some stranger scenes. Capers, olives, anchovies, artichoke hearts, carrot slivers, grated cheeses, pickled peppers - mild or hot, nuts, mushrooms, water chestnuts, radishes and other less-used ingredients add flavors, textures and shapes.

One of my favorite big-time salads, I inherited. It's called

Novy Lee's Salad

For 6-8 hearty eaters.

1	big bowl of iceberg, romaine and endive lettuces.
1-6 oz. jar	marinated hearts of artichokes - with marinade
1	tin anchovies, chopped
2	firm, real tomatoes, chopped
2 T.	Parmesan cheese
1 T.	capers
10	small Salonika peppers
12-15	stuffed, Spanish olives

Toss together with a dressing made of

1/2 C.	water
1/4 C.	apple cider or wine vinegar
1/4 C.	extra virgin olive oil

1	T.	tarragon
2	T.	chopped fresh parsley
2		scallions, shopped fine
		black pepper and salt to taste.

Serve immediately after tossing.

This one can hold its own in any kind of brawl.

Pig Salad

This is a great use for that leftover pulled pork or as a preamble to a meal.

4 C.	fresh mixed greens
1 C.	tomato, seeded and chopped
1 C.	barbecued pork, pulled or chopped

Wash and drain greens and mix all ingredients.

The dressing options are open. A "ranch-type," or Russian, works very well, but you might try a slightly altered version of your favorite barbecue finishing sauce.

Hand Salads

Outdoor cooking and eating should be relaxed and relaxing affairs. A hand salad fulfills the function and fits the informality.

Serve spears of asparagus spears, broccoli, carrots, celery, broccoli, cucumbers, radishes, scallions, spinach, pickled beans, and/or whatever strikes your fancy with individual dipping cups of appropriate salad dressings. This means that one doesn't have to lick the fingers in order to pick up the salad fork.

Cole Slaws

Cole slaw is a traditional accompaniment for barbecue. There are thousands of recipes— sort of like barbecue sauces. They just start out with good crisp cabbage and take off like a sunburst. We will include several variations that start out in different directions. Then include some alternative ingredients that offer logical developments on those basic themes.

The variations are made in the texture ingredients as well as the sauce ingredients. The texture of the cabbage is very important. Personally, I have never cared for real coarsely chopped cabbage in the slaw. However, I don't often take the time to render is extra-fine in the style that some call "angel hair."After you have tried a few variations in texture and taste you will probably want to "roll your own." Remember that your slaw should fit your barbecue. You don't want to serve a tart, robust slaw with a delicately flavored barbecued fish. And you wouldn't match up a "featherweight" slaw with a "heavyweight" venison roast. Cole slaw, like barbecue finishing sauce, is a balance between sweet and tart. Play with the ingredients until it fits your palate and your menu. Always give the ingredients time to marry.

Cabbage and Apple

2 C.	shredded cabbage
1 C.	tart apple, julienned
1/4 C.	mayonnaise
1/4 C.	lemon juice
1 t.	sugar
1/2 t.	salt
1/2 t.	black pepper

Combine and adjust for sweet/tart.

256

Basic Cole Slaw

3 C.	shredded cabbage
1/4 C.	mayonnaise
2 t.	sugar
3 T.	sour cream or 2 T. vinegar or lemon juice
	salt & pepper to taste

Combine and adjust sweet/tart taste

Potato Salad

It is hard to write down a good recipe for potato salad because those people who make the best not only don't go by a written recipe, they also never do it the same way twice. And if you want to see a really blank look on someone's face, just ask a good, creative cook to write down the recipe for an especially tasty dish in their repertoire. So again, I'll just throw in a basic recipe and some recommendations as a starting point.

Authorities on potato salad seem to agree on at least a couple of things. Choose good "boiling" (not "baking") potatoes. Boil the potatoes while in their skins until done. Peel and dice as soon as they are cool enough to handle. The size or shape you cut them into is a matter of personal choice. I have a neighbor who cuts his into little 3/8 inch cubes as precisely consistent as the dice on a Las Vegas craps table. That sure looks good. But I've eaten some mighty good potato salad with chunks as variable as a handful of river rocks.

A word of caution about potato salad. Once you mix it, serve it hot or refrigerate for storage. Many a "picnic panic" has been caused by overripe potato salad.

Basic Potato Salad

8-10 medium	boiling potatoes
1/2 C.	chopped sweet pickles
1/2 C.	finely chopped onion
1 T.	prepared mustard
1/4 t.	celery seed
3	hard-boiled eggs, diced
1/2 C.	mayonnaise
	salt and fresh ground black pepper.

Prepare potatoes as described above. Combine with everything except eggs, coating all the potatoes. Carefully mix in eggs without breaking them up. Serve hot or cold.

Baked Beans

Baked beans, for some reason or reasons, became a staple at outdoor cooking events. Why not? They are delicious, healthy, economical and don't require a lot of attention. Baked beans were served so often with barbecue that they are often mistakenly called "barbecued beans." But we know better, don't we?

In any case, here are a couple of versions for starters.

Old Fashion Baked Beans

1 lb.	navy or Michigan white beans
2 C.	brown sugar or molasses
4 C.	tomato juice
1/4 C.	minced celery
1 C.	chopped onion
1 t.	ground mustard
1/4 t.	cloves
1 T.	fresh grated horseradish
1/8 t.	cardamon
1 t.	black pepper
1 lb.	barbecued pork

Cook beans until tender; pour into bean pot or casserole. Mix other ingredients, except pork, and pour over beans. Chop the pork fine and mix into beans. Bake at 300° F. until tender.

Old Fashion Baked Beans Number 2

2 lbs.	navy or Michigan white beans
1	medium onion, diced
1/4 C.	brown sugar
1/2 C.	molasses
1/2 C.	catsup
1/4 C.	vinegar
1/4 C.	chopped bell pepper
1 T.	prepared mustard
1 t.	black pepper
1 t.	salt
1/2 lb.	sliced salt pork

Cook beans until tender; then mix beans and other ingredients into a casserole dish with liquid to cover. Lay on the salt pork and cook at 275° for 3 hours, adding liquid as needed.

Hashes, Stews and Such

Pork Hash

Pork hash has been an old Southern custom which usually coincided with hog killing time in the fall, or barbecuing time, anytime. Originally starting out as a means of using all of the hog, "except the squeal," early hash recipes used the internal organs. Later, hash recipes, as with other dishes, began the inevitable evolutionary cycle.

In the Carolinas, there developed distinctly different "upland" hashes and "flatland" hashes. Pursuit of their origins, as well as their ingredients, had been an unsatisfied hunt.

One year, at the Blue Ridge Arts Festival and Barbecue Contest, in Tryon, NC, I was fortunate to meet Raymond McLees, a fellow judge, who related the following South Carolina Upcountry hash recipe and its origin. The story is as tasty as the hash. Now a financial advisor, Raymond, as a youngster, worked occasionally for Mr. Landy West, who owned a sawmill in West Springs, SC. Mr. West would "throw" a barbecue and cook hash for his "hands," customers and friends. While he might let others tend the barbecue, he trusted nobody else to oversee the hash.

The hash became as famous as the West Spring mineral waters, a ladle of which, Landy always put into the hash.

Landy West's Upcountry Hash

3 lbs	lean beef cut into 2-3" chunks.
1 lb.	lean pork cut into 2-3" chunks
1 C	onion, chopped and ground
1/4 lb.	unsalted butter

Put the meat into a heavy cast iron pot, cover with water to cover and simmer until falling- apart tender. Add water as necessary. When tender, remove the meat to another large pan, and when cool enough to handle, pick out and

remove connective tissue, veins, slivers of bone — "skivin's, according to Mr. West, and pull the rest into small bits.

While the meat is cooling and being picked, quarter and grind the onion in a meat grinder or food processor. Place in pot and boil gently, without burning, while it becomes thick soup. Return the meat to the pot, add 1/4 lb unsalted butter, continue cooking and stirring, removing any "skivins," until the meat becomes one with the onions. It should become a light grey color.

Raymond said that Mr. West was extremely vigilant, and adamant, about the skivins, as his helpers were quick to learn. Because of the light color and mildness of flavor, his would-be copiers accused Landy of adding milk to the hash. Raymond says it just wasn't so, but that carefully removing the darker connective tissue lightened the color, as well as improving the taste and texture.

Low Country Pork Hash

There are probably as many hash recipes in the Carolinas as there are gumbo recipes in Louisiana. The search and collection of authentic originals, as well as popular restaurant recipes has just begun. The following is a recreation from ancient memories and ephemeral flavors. It was put together from pieces of a picture-less puzzle, found scattered in the trash bins of time.

I fondly recall stews and/or hashes from hog killing times and enjoyed their tastes by either name. Webster's *New International Unabridged Dictionary* defines "hash" as "to cut into small bits" and, sort of, infers that hash is made from meat that was already cooked, whereas, stews are made from previously uncooked meat and/or vegetables heated in a small amount of water.

In the vast majority of cases, I would fully agree. I recall that one of the minuscule number of dishes that my mother cooked that I did not absolutely relish was hash made with left-over roast. (I think the only other thing was cooked spinach.) Even now, the only hash of precooked meat that I eat is corned beef hash: the second use of beef brisket.

But I recall those pork dishes called "hash" which were made from fresh meat — as was Landy West's Upcountry Hash. So, to satisfy my curiosity as well as report, here are a couple of recipes for pork hash that only the adventurous are likely to ever taste.

Uncle Earl's Low Country Hash

Dot and Danny Livingston,from Harleyville, SC, introduced me to uncle Earl Hartzog's low country hash who said that it was his mother's recipe. This recipe makes 15 gallons of delicious hash.

3	hog heads
15 lbs.	boston butts
12 lbs.	ears
12 lbs.	tongues
12 lbs.	ground beef
11 lbs.	pork liver
20 lbs.	white potatoes
12 lbs	onions
3 gal.	catsup
3 qts.	mustard
12 oz.	tomato paste
8 oz.	white vinegar
4 lbs.	light brown sugar
4 oz.	salt
4-8 oz.	black pepper

Peel, quarter and boil potatoes until barely soft. Boil beef separately in enough water to cover until done then drain. Boil all other meat, except liver, until done, about 1 1/2 hours, then add potatoes, chopped onions, beef and continue cooking. When done, remove bones and run everything through the meat grinder. Put in a double boiler, add boiling liquids, catsup, vinegar, 1/2 each of brown sugar, 1/2 salt and pepper. Stir constantly until thickened. Add salt and pepper to taste.

There are lots of folk in this world who would not willingly share an old family recipe, especially one that wins prizes. We owe a special thanks to Dot and Danny for sharing.

Old Timer's Country Hash

At hog-killing time, prudent pioneers let nothing go to waste. While hams and bacon were put into the cure, the sausage meat was being ground and the fat was being rendered into lard and cracklin's, lesser known activities were carried on. The hog heads were put it a great kettle to be converted into souse meat and the feet which accompanied them would, after boiling, be pickled and preserved. The intestines would be thoroughly cleaned and covered with salted water, in preparation for the sausage stuffing.

The back bone and neck bones were put into a large pot, covered with water and brought to a gentle boil — this would become the mother's milk of hash.

Smoky's Ol' Time Pork Hash

Neck bones, hearts, lungs, kidneys and liver from 1 hog
2 lbs	onions, chopped fine or ground
2	carrots
1/2 lb	lard
2 T.	black pepper
2 T.	salt

Put bones in a large pot, cover with water, add onions, salt and pepper. While the bones are simmering, there is work to do.

Hearts

Slice the heart down one side, cutting away the arteries and veins at the top and the fibrous chamber membranes on the inside. Wash well, then cover with water and 1/2 C. vinegar for 30 minutes.

Kidneys

Wash the kidneys thoroughly and cover them in salt water for at least 1/2 hour. Then remove the thin, tough covering membrane, split the kidney, then remove the fatty core and the heavy tubes.

Lungs

Wash the lungs carefully, cutting away the windpipe, major veins and arteries. Cover the lungs with salt water and soak for at least 30 minutes. Rinse as necessary to remove all blood.

Liver

Pork livers are delicate and delicious, but they are also optional. If you don't like liver, don't add it. Remove the membrane covering the liver and remove the tubes. (Loosen one end, grasp and pull out.)

Constructing the Hash

After the bones have simmered at least 1 hour, cut the hearts into approximately 1" cubes and add to the pot. Next, at your leisure, do the same to the kidneys. Follow this with the lungs, cubed. No need to be in a rush.

When the meat begins to fall off the bones, remove the bones to a separate pan until cool enough to pick the meat and return it to the pot. Continue to stir and add water as necessary.

After about 4 hours of simmering, the meat should all be tender, and the liquid should be reaching the consistency of a thick soup. At that point, add the butter and stir it in well. About 10 minutes before ready to serve. add the liver. As soon as the liver loses its pink, shut down the fire and get out the bowls.

You'll wonder how you got all those good flavors — with so little effort.

Unless you really make the effort, you are not likely to find pork lungs and you may not even find pork back bones and neck bones. Obviously you can substitute pork butts or other parts for the meat — trim the fat first. Chine and brisket bones would add flavor, but not much meat. Hearts and kidneys are more readily available and liver is usually always available. All will have some preliminary processing done. Good luck.

North Carolina Pulled Pork Hash

This comes from the memory of J.C. Stevens, barbecue judge, writer and Associate Editor of the *National Barbecue News* and calls for barbecued pork.

1 lb.	picked barbecued pork
1 lb.	cold, boiled potatoes
2 oz.	bacon drippings or lard
1 med.	onion, finely chopped
8 oz.	cooked greens — cabbage, turnips, mustard or collard sprouts, chopped
	salt and pepper to taste

Finely chop potatoes and crush slightly. In a number 10 frying pan, melt half the fat and lightly fry the onion. Mix in the other ingredients and add more of the drippings. Press the bubble, from the center outward, to form a cake in the pan and fry until brown. Spray a plate with oil and use the plate to turn the cake out and slide it back into the pan upside down. Add the remainder of the drippings and continue to cook until medium brown. Slide out of the pan and let cool for 5 minutes. Slice into 8 or more pieces and serve with fried egg on top, sunny side up.

Brunswick Stew

Of course, it would be as ridiculous to try to give the "one true recipe" for Brunswick Stew as it would to be to propose a one-and-only recipe for gumbo or barbecue sauce. Yet a stew that stirs such strong sentiments should be shared, simmering in all its stout and savory semblances.

Who knows whence it came. What is known is that it is one of the few indigenous dishes whose ingredients are detailed with equal ardor from Mississippi to New York. Brunswick stew early became a staple and favored prelude to barbecue at outdoor gatherings.

Of the things that can generally be agreed upon meat, corn, tomatoes, onions and peppers are central to the stew. There is even controversy among those. In Mississippi and several other southern states, squirrel is an essential meat. Rabbit is an acceptable alternative or addition. On the east coast from Georgia to New York, chicken has been the primary meat, with pork a frequent companion in most areas. Beef has never been sanctioned in any region by conscientious keepers of the pot.

Green lima beans and okra have gradually become acceptable to all but hardcore purists. But potatoes, rice and noodles continue to be forbidden by serious stewards of the stew.

Brunswick stew is not to be confused with Burgoo that birthed beside the Ohio river and gained prominence in Kentucky and Illinois. Burgoo begins with beef and squirrels and contains a variety of vegetables banned in Brunswick stew.

Traditionally, Brunswick stew was cooked outdoors in cast iron kettles that sat simmering for hours over hot coals until the meat disintegrated and joined the juices. That is still the best way. Since a simmering pot makes a good outdoor gathering place, invite over about twenty friends to share.

BRUNSWICK STEW

6-8	plump squirrels (substitute domestic rabbit), quartered
6-8	frying chickens cut into frying pieces
1 lb.	smoked bacon, sliced
24	medium onions, thinly sliced
1 C.	plain flour
1 Gal.	tomatoes, chopped
1 qt.	cream-style corn
6	red peppers, chopped
6	green peppers, chopped
2 qt.	green lima beans
2 qt.	cut okra
1 C.	parsley, chopped
5	bay leaves
3 T.	thyme
2 T.	black pepper
2 T.	cayenne pepper
1/4 C.	Worcestershire sauce

Fry the bacon until crisp in a suitable-size cast iron pot. While the bacon is frying, salt an pepper squirrel and chicken and dredge in flour.

Remove the bacon, bring the temperature of the rendered fat to 375 degrees and fully brown the meat. Set meat aside and brown onions. Reduce the heat and add tomatoes, corn and peppers. Return meat to pot and add water to cover.

Simmer until the meat falls off the bones and correct seasoning to taste. This can take from two to ten hours, depending upon the wishes of the cook.

Add green limas and cut okra about an hour before serving, if desired. Marylanders would add a quart of sherry or Madeira to the stew just before serving.

Sit yourself down and taste some history.

How to Succeed in Stocks

Trading in stocks is something that most of us think has to be left to the professionals. Nothing could be further from the truth. Actually it is all very simple, and everybody with reasonable intelligence and decent taste ought to participate in the stocks market.

There are **COMMON STOCKS** and **PREFERRED STOCKS**. There are **OPTIONS, PUTS** and **CALLS.** There are your basic **BLUE CHIP** stocks and there are **HI-FLYERS**; then there are those that appeal to a particular interest.

We can all **PROFIT** from stocks, and most of the time the **DIVIDENDS** are tremendous.

Amongst it all, there is nothing that an accomplished outdoor cook cannot handle with style and panache. If you don't have panache, it is always trendy to use pecan or pistachio nuts.

Truth is, that some stocks are about as common as three-day-old underwear. I am about to tell you how to recognize the good from the bad. Obviously, you have to use your nose.

267

The **CARDINAL RULE** in stocks is: **Don't try to cook good stuff without them!**

It is always surprising to see folks throwing away parts of fish, veggies and animals that, given a little boiling water and accompaniments would transpose themselves into a delicious stock. (If not a dish)

Stocks, which are the basis of all good sauces, (and soups, gravies and stews) are also the SOLE authentic basis for any French claim to fame in cooking. Everything else, except arrogance, they learned from the Italians. In essence, stocks retained the essence of the food by preserving it in the stock.

Americans, by and large, (I like that phrase because it is so apt) consider ourselves amateurs. We are a little put off, even afraid, of investing in stocks that require any semblance of effort and expertise. Truth is, investing in proper stocks is the safest, tastiest investment we can make.

Let's look at the basic **PORTFOLIO** of real **BLUE CHIPS**.

In the normal course of events, stocks represent four main markets: beef, poultry, seafood and veggies. Incorporated under beef are lamb, veal and some game. Pork sort of floats between beef and poultry. On the other hand, poultry may float chicken or fish. Fish or seafood covers a wide variety of stocks from clam or oyster juice to fish heads and pounded shrimp shells.

Vegetable trimming are often given no respect. The delicious (and expensive) flavors in asparagus, broccoli and mushroom stems are, woefully, often wastefully discarded. Carrot tips and tops may not make the cut for the table, but are fine for the pot.

Americans are generally skittish, at least, about using the trimmings from edible foods to contribute flavors to what we cook. If it exceeds pot likker and bacon grease, we are inclined to look upon it as "furrin" and, therefore, suspect. Let me disabuse you of that notion.

Any soup, stew, sauce, and most other dishes, will benefit from the tasty enrichment of a good stock. While any good cook could write a book on stocks, and most likely someone already has, not many folk are taking stock of what has been written.

Shortage of three things contribute to this in America: time, taste and frugality. We run so hard that we have not time, have lost our taste and "frugality" is just a foreign word for "Save Me!" (Frugal me! Frugal me!)

Saving is the essential ingredient of stocks. Using what you save is the essence of good tasting.   Save the bones of whatever fish, foul or beast. If beast, brown them well — unless you are making a white stock. Cover with water and bring to a gentle simmer. Skim off the froth. In all cases, skim off the froth and discard. Season according to your planned use.

I make stock when I cook. When stock is left over, I freeze and label it. Sometimes I make stock just because I have some trimmings left over and I don't want to waste all that good taste.

Without a special use in mind, flavor the stock lightly so that it can be used for several dishes.

You will be amazed at the collection of neighbors (and strangers) that will accumulate in your back yard when you are just enjoying yourself and cooking up a batch of stock on your fish cooker.

Try this **IPO** (Initial Public Offering)

Stock to Stew Transition

The Sunday paper is an integral part of the ritual around our house. Publishers allow interesting things printed which, in their infinite wisdom, are unworthy of weekday space. Sources of hardcore information and entertainment are Sunday fare.

The classified ads section is the definitive indicator of economic conditions. If auto dealers are advertising heavily for salespeople, it means that sales are so bad that the current crew has gone on welfare. Ads for geologists means that the oil business is about to pick up. Right now there is a bounty on any moving body with nursing skills, but bankers need not apply.

Then there is the comic section. I am so old that I remember when this was called the "funny papers." Who knows why or when they began to appear in color. But there is always a laugh or two.

But the greatest source of amusement, for me, is the food section. Having spent a significant portion of my life informing folks how to grill chicken without burning it black, I find it hilarious when "blackened chicken" shows up featured in living color. And some of the combinations of fruits and nuts commingled with an otherwise promising lamb stew raise stimulating questions about the proper place of fruits and nuts in modern society.

I mean, if I am to remain on the cutting edge of outdoor cooking, should I be doing really creative things like an elegant Sunday brunch of "**Pickled piglips stuffed with pate of 'possum livers and prunes, served on wheat short crepes with hickory nut and balsam-clabber sauce?**" These are heavy thoughts which weigh as mightily upon my bosom as a spinach quiche*.

Alas, I am constrained by my inadequacies, condemned forever to stew in my plebeian juices, sans fruit, sans nuts.

On the other hand, a hefty stew is not a thing at which to sneeze. It satisfies the simple stomach, royally pleases plebeian palates and comforts the cackles of the country heart. Nor is its concocting complicated.

The simple secret to a savory stew is in the stock. It is the essence of the bone which warms us to the marrow. And bones, browned in the seasoning smoke of the grill give new dimensions to this gastronomic gift of gods to simple folk. The smoky stock will also serve as the starter for stout soups to fend the winter winds.

*After a contentitious relationship with Charles DeGaulle, during WWII, Winston Churchill is reputed to have uttered, "Of all the quiches I have had to bear, the heaviest was the Quiche of Lorraine."

Stout, Smoky Stock

Start with 2-3 pounds of meaty bones. Neck bones and tail bones are readily available. Other bones can be trimmed from cuts of meat at home or bought from the butcher shop. Venison bones add a distinct flavor to game stews. Break large bones with a hammer, cleaver or saw into short lengths.

Remove excess fat and any small bones or chips and place in a pan large enough to contain in one layer. Prepare the grill for roasting - 350 degrees for about 2 hours with a little more smoke than normal.

Use white oak, hickory and fruit woods. Put the pan of bones on the grill, close the lid and find something else to do for about an hour. Check and turn using tongs. Close the grill and check back in about 30 minutes. The meat on the bones should be thoroughly and deeply browned. Remove when thoroughly done.

Place bones and meat in a large pot and cover with water. Deglaze pan with hot water and add to pot. Turn heat to highest and cover pot. When the pot begins to jingle, remove it and reduce the heat to a low, rolling boil. Using a long handled spoon, begin to dip off the fat and foam. When most of the fat and foam are removed, add

2	med. onions
4	cloves of garlic
3	bay leaves
3	carrots, scraped and halved
3	stalks celery, with tops, halved
1	med bell pepper, seeded and quartered
1 T.	thyme
1 T.	black pepper corns

Simmer, adding water when necessary until meat, falls off the bones. Remove the bones, dig out the marrow, chop the meat. Reserve meat and marrow. Remove all veggies from the stock and return the meat and marrow. Return pot to flame and continue cooking until the liquid is reduced by one half.

Adjust seasonings with

1	med. onion, chopped fine
2	cloves garlic, crushed
1	bay leaf
1 t.	powdered thyme

salt and fresh ground black pepper to taste

Continue simmering and tasting. There will come a moment beyond which it cannot possibly taste any better. Stop!

At this point, the stock can be frozen for future use, if you are equipped with such will power. Or it can be used immediately as a base for the soup or stew that you had in mind.

Only a nut would add fruits — and vice versa.

CHOWDER

There are times when nothing brightens the grey of a winter's day as much as a good fish soup. Or chowder. Or stew.

Actually it's hard to tell them apart without a score card. Webster says that chowder can be either as long as it contains milk.

> *Whether bouillabaisse*
> *or pot-au-feu,*
> *pray, when does a soup*
> *become a stew?*

Anyhow, the name is immaterial. It's the taste that counts.

One of the special delights of seafood/fish soup or stew is that you build it to suit your taste from a wide variety of ingredients.

Don't be intimidated by the gall of Gaullists, insisting that bouillabaisse can only be made from 12 different species found only in the bay of Marseilles. Or the California chauvinists complaint that cioppino can only be made with Dungeness crab.

Both dishes owe their fame to the variety of flavors, textures and visual stimulation which can be produced, in essence, if not reproduced exactly.

The most widely known version of seafood soup is of course clam chowder. A favorite of early settlers in New England, it has survived unchanged: salt pork, diced potatoes, onions, clams and milk with a little salt and pepper.

Once they discovered that tomatoes weren't poison, somebody in New York added them to the chowder. As far as New Englanders are concerned, tomatoes may as well be poison if added to chowder because they consider the result the same. Chowder with tomatoes is called "Manhattan" and without "New England" style. To my knowledge, this is the only fish/seafood soup/stew where anybody gets tight-jawed about a particular ingredient.

273

One ingredient that is essential in all soups and stews is stock. Clam juice and oyster liquor are tasty additions that should always be used when available. Fish stock can be made by gently boiling the bones and trimmings of any lean (not oily) fish with onion, carrot, bay leaf, thyme, parsley, salt. Shrimp and crawfish shells and heads make a tasty addition. Skim foam carefully and discard. After about 1 hour, remove from heat and strain. This can be frozen and kept for a couple of months.

If the dish will be cooked for longer periods — more than 30 minutes — fish or seafood can be added to the pot for flavoring rather than having to cook a stock separately. That is, we sacrifice some fish by allowing it to be cooked to pieces, in order to flavor the liquid in which the fish we intend to eat will be cooked.

Next time your day needs brightening, try this stew. It serves 12.

Seafood Stew

Firm fleshed fish:

> 1 lb. each of at least 4:
>
> > Spanish mackerel, wahoo, pompano, red snapper, grouper, drum, eel, flounder, sea bass

Tender fish:

1 lb. each of at least two: mullet, perch, whiting, speckled trout, croaker

1 pt.	raw oysters, with liquor
1 dozen	clams and juice
12	jumbo shrimp, unpeeled
12	gigantic crawfish, live
6	blue crabs, top shelled and cleaned
1 C	chopped onion
1/2 C	chopped scallions
4	cloves garlic, peeled and crushed
5-6	tomatoes, peeled, seeded and chopped
2 T.	chopped, fresh parsley
1 t.	fennel seed

In a large pot (12+ qt), heat 1/2 cup olive oil. Saute onion until transparent, add garlic, scallions, tomatoes and fennel.

Stir for 1 minute, then add clam juice, oyster liquor and enough water to cover. Bring to a boil and add crawfish. Arrange crawfish and add firm fleshed fish. Add water to cover and bring to boil. Simmer for about 8 minutes.

Add parsley and remaining fish, oysters, clams and shrimp. Bring to a boil and allow to simmer about 8 minutes.

Remove fish quickly, but carefully, to a large serving dish. Add salt and pepper to soup and adjust seasoning. Remove to tureen when ready.

Serve each guest a selection of seafood in a large bowl with a generous amount of soup. A hearty French or Italian bread and a robust wine will make the meal memorable.

Bread

Bread is the stuff of life. More than just a plate or palate cleaner, good fresh bread, has sustenance, taste and texture that so distinguishes it from the commercial pap that the other should be called another name — which I frequently do.

My wife and I cook all our bread. Dianne is adept at the bread machine, turning out her delicious tubular loaves. She bakes 3 days a week and shares her wares with friends and those whom she thinks need a little perking up.

I use a mixer with a dough hook to knead my favorite rustic Italian breads, with a "sourdough" starter that is old enough to vote. We buy bread flour economically in 25 lb. bags and yeast in 2 lb. bags at a warehouse and buy whole wheat and rye flours in smaller quantities. Some whole wheat and rye go into feeding my starter; some whole wheat goes into loaves for enrichment. The rye loaves are essential for soothing my periodic craving for a real Reuben sandwich.

Bread making, like barbecuing, requires long time periods to complete, but does not require attention for all that time. Once you develop the schedule and technique that fits your life, it is as simple as cooking grits.

Dianne rarely lets the bread machine do the baking. Instead, she removes the dough, after the second rise, to shape it for cooking in the oven in a regular loaf pan or shaped into rolls. Most often, however, she makes it into tubular loaves with diagonal slices that allow them to fatten into plump, crusty morsels.

The time that she is personally involved is minimal — less than 5 minutes for two loaves. She dumps the ingredients into the bread machine and sets the alarm. When the alarm sounds, she plops it onto the bread board, divides it, and shapes it for two loaves which she sprays with a water mist, covers with a light-weight cotton cloth and sets in a quiet place for the third rise.

When risen, she pops the loaves into a 350° oven, and after about 25 minutes, out comes delicious hot bread. If you can resist immediate consumption, bread can be refrigerated or frozen and brought out and heated as necessary. Enough loaves can be cooked in one day to serve fresh bread for the week.

Dianne's Long Loaves

Makes two loaves about 3 inches in diameter and about 20 inches long.

23 oz*	**bread flour (hard wheat)**
1 1/4 C water (unchlorinated)**	
3 t.	**dry yeast**
2 t.	**salt**
1 T.	**sugar**
2 T.	**olive oil**

Dump all ingredients into the bread machine, set it on "dough" cycle and let it go through 2 risings. Remove and shape into rolls or loaves. Long loaves need to be slashed diagonally 4-5 times about 1/4" deep to allow the bread to rise to the fullest. Spray with water and cover with a light cloth until fully risen.

Bake in a pre-heated oven at 350° 25 minutes, or until the crust is the color that you like.

* Successful baking requires measuring by weight because the moisture in flour can vary considerably — especially in the humid South.

** A tablespoon of whole milk or a teaspoon of powdered milk will deactivate the chlorine which would, otherwise, kill or retard the yeast bacteria; otherwise, use bottled water.

This may be a mistake. You will never again be satisfied with store-bought bread.

Hefty Home-made Bread

Over the years, my "personal" bread gradually evolved into what I eventually discovered was characteristic of what is called "rustic Italian" bread, which is, if not the mother, the grandmother of what is now, generically, termed "French" bread. Once I learned how to produce a decent "French" bread, decent being an acceptable substitute for the fabled Reising bread of New Orleans, I began typically to tinker with recipes. I found that although the "French" bread was tasty, delicious and versatile in its usage, I hungered for different textures and tastes for different occasions and reasons. I had maintained and used "sour dough" starter for years, but meandered away from the traditional West coast style bread, which uses white wheat flour, into a mixture of unbleached and whole wheat flours, with the added tang of a little rye.

This develops a hefty loaf with a strong texture that is great for sandwiches, as well as its primary function, just tasting good by itself. This bread keeps longer without refrigeration and has that sort of primitive, rustic look, and, after all, I am a rustic kind of guy.

It has enough character to stand up to the robust flavors of barbecue sauces, horse radish, mustard and similar creations. One of its major pleasures for me, though is the texture. It has a good, chewy texture that lets you know that you are eating something of substance. It gives a feeling of dependable sustenance — a bread that you can trust.

This bread is, at least, a two-day affair, but you can make enough to freeze or refrigerate and enjoy the fruits of your labor over a long period. Except for the relationship of the temperatures and the water to the total amount of flour, the recipe is as elastic as the dough.

Once alive and healthy, the starter can be kept alive for years by regular feeding, refrigerating for short periods or freezing indefinitely. From the freezer, it can be restored to action by thawing, adding a little warm water, then additional flour. From the frozen state, it can be ready for action in about 4 hours.

This starter is simple, resembling the *lievito naturale*, natural yeast of Italian bakers, by whom it is called *biga*. Itsa biga starter!

It's a Biga Starter

1 C	warm water
1 t..	dry yeast
3 C	bread flour
1/2 C	rye flour
1/2 C	whole wheat flour

Warm a large bowl, pour in the water and mix in the yeast and let this sit for 7-8 minutes. Meanwhile, mix all the flours together. Then gradually begin working the flour in, about 1/2 C. at a time. Scrape down the sides well and keep adding flour until you have a very thick, dry dough. Knead it just enough to mix well, 6-7 minutes. This can be done with a dough hook on a heavy duty mixer.

Then cover with a damp cloth and stash in a warm quiet place for 24 hours. The dough will have risen and fallen. It will look like a sticky, soupy mess, but this is *good stuff*. We will use half of it and freeze the rest.

When you go to use the stored half, remove from the freezer and allow to come to room temperature. Then add 1 C. bread flour and 1/4 C. each of rye and whole wheat flours. Stir, cover and allow the little yeasties to feed. Repeat after 2 hours. Then the batch is ready to halve again.

You can get by with freezing smaller amounts of the starter, but it takes longer to build it back to the volume needed for the following recipe. Always remember to separate out that portion that you intend to save *before* any salt is added. Salt retards the growth of yeast and slows the rising process.

Hefty, Hearty Bread

1/2	biga from previous recipe
2 C	bread flour
2 t.	salt
1/3 C	ice water
1 t.	dry yeast

Put the biga starter into a mixing bowl, sprinkle in yeast and mix well. Then add the salt and 1 C. flour, and while mixing add in the water. Knead/mix until thoroughly incorporated; then begin to add the remaining flour, 1/4 C. at a time. Knead until smooth — about 5 minutes.

Remove to a floured board or bowl, cover with a damp cloth and let rise for 2-3 hours until doubled in size. Punch down, pound it a bit, reshape and replace. When doubled in size, divide and shape into two round loaves or 2 long (20") loaves. Slash the top 1/4" deep with a sharp knife – cross-hatch on the round loaves or diagonally on the long loaves.

Spray with a water mist, cover and place in a warm, moist, still place until doubled in size. Bake in a 350° oven until crusty.

Tip: One of the little-known secrets of bread baking is moisture. We keep two water bottles with spray nozzles, one set to mist, the other to stream. While the bread is rising, we keep it moist by misting the covering cloth. When the bread goes into the oven, a pan on the floor of the oven gets 6-8 streams of water until steam starts boiling out. Keeping steam in the oven for the first 4-5 minute, allows the bread to rise more and also produces a thinner, crispier crust.

A lighter loaf and quicker rising can be had by doubling the yeast. A more authentic, tastier, chewier loaf can be produced by eliminating the yeast and allowing the natural yeast to work. A soupier biga, which has a different name *poulish,* makes a faster rising dough and a lighter bread.

If you plan to bake 2-3 times per week, just leave the starter in a cool place and feed, once a day, with water and flour. This starter will begin to develop a character of its own, giving off a delicious aroma. If left out too long, without reducing and replenishing, it will begin to become more sour, and, at some point, would be come a little too tart. Use or refrigerate, before this happens. If it does, use up 3/4 ths of the starter for sourdough pancake batter and replenish the remainder.

Bruschetta

If you go through life like everyday is a treasure hunt, you won't be disappointed. Serendipity will strew your path with gems.

As an example, Bob Lyon and I were making the long drive from the National Barbecue Association convention in Orlando, FL., back to the homestead, in the woods near McComb, MS. The radio was tuned to National Public Radio, as usual, and the narrator was in Tuscany, describing Italian bread slices, toasted on a grate in the fireplace, then rubbed with fresh cut garlic and drizzled with olive oil, so freshly extracted that it was *turbinado* — still turbid from the pressing.

It sounded delicious to me! Bob said, "Been there, done that." Bob and his wife, Sandra, were visiting a former student (Bob and Sandra are retired English teachers) in Italy. She had obtained some fresh olive oil from Tuscany, and she and Sandra toasted slices of unsalted Tuscany-style bread in the fireplace, rubbed them with garlic, drizzled them with olive oil and sprinkled little salt. I salivated for at least the next 100 miles.

When we got to the woods near McComb, my wife, Dianne, as usual, had loaves of fresh-baked French-type bread. Naturally, it was not too long until we cranked up a small grill, brought in fresh garlic and selected an extra virgin olive oil. Since here bread had salt, we used no more. For the first time, I fully understood the meaning of the word *synergism* — the whole is greater than the sum of the parts.

These simple basic components, combine to become a remarkably enjoyable trove of taste and texture. As good as it was with the run-of-the-mill olive oil that we used, I would be wary of using Tuscany *turbinado* for fear of becoming a *bruschetta* junky. (For the correct spelling of the word, by the way, Bob deferred to Sandra.)

I highly recommend this as an hors d'oeuvre, a snack, a tidbit with wine, or just because you think about it.

Chapter Nine
All About Grills

What you need to know to decide which is best for you

Barbecuing and grilling, like many pleasurable activities, have their own list of equipment —some mandatory, some optional, some worthless, never even coming close to the promises of their purveyors.

Second in abomination only to the mass of misinformation bastardizing the word barbecue is the melange of malapropos merchandise mendaciously misrepresented as "barbecues" or barbecue grills. One has to wonder if it only ignorance that produces such malfunctioning marvels.

I will lead you through the maze of misinformation to provide you all the factual information needed to make informed decisions for selecting, buying, building and using grills. We will look at the functions a grill must perform when cooking with different techniques and discuss the distinctions of different types, pointing out their strengths and weakness in design, construction and operating capabilities.

Grilling started out in the pits. Some of it has never gotten out. Originally barbecue was — still, in some places, is — cooked over a shallow hole in the ground in which hardwood had been burned down to glowing embers. Even well into the 20th century, Southerners were cooking on the same equipment as the Greeks at Troy and the Taino in Florida — wooden posts, supporting wooden sticks as racks.

Later, more permanent masonry pits were built and put to good use. Metal pits did not come into widespread use until millions of welders, trained in the WWII effort and under the G.I. Bill, began to tinker with their torches. Used 55 gallon steel drums were sliced, shaped and fashioned into thousands of designs to produce instant grills. More good meat has probably been cooked in converted 55 gallon drums than in all other manufactured grills combined.

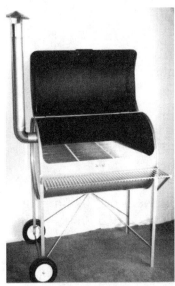

Several manufacturers still produce grills with the same shape. Some use the thin-walled drum; others, like the makers of the Hathorn, illustrated, use special, thicker- walled material.

Despite the great convenience of charcoal-fired metal grills, there are those of us who believe that none produces barbecue with the succulence and flavor of that leisurely cooked directly over an open bed of coals.

Gas and electric grills have gained popularity in the past decade. They are clean, neat and convenient. Properly designed and constructed they can, in the hands of a competent griller, produce excellent flavors and textures.

Which Grill Is Right for You?

Probably the most frequent question directed to me is, "What is the best grill for me?" That is a question that only you can answer. Choosing the right grill requires that you first determine your needs. The most important questions to be answered before choosing a grill are

1. **What do you intend to do with it: broil, roast, barbecue, smoke?**
2. **How often do you expect to cook on the grill?**
3. **What is the greatest number of folk that you intend to feed from the grill?**
4. **How much are you willing to spend on a grill?**

Different Techniques Require Different Capabilities

Different grilling techniques require different capacities in a grill. The right grill for you is the one which will allow you to cook what you want, when you want, with the least amount of hassle and expense.

Broiling, done with radiant heat (see Heat) requires only a fire grate and a meat grill. A simple hibachi or other small portable grill such as the "Sportsman" made by Lodge Cast Iron can do an excellent job. Mine was made by Atlanta Stove Works many years ago before Lodge acquired it, and I probably broil on it more often than any two of my several other grills. A grill lid or cover is normally neither required nor recommended for broiling. Broiling requires very high temperatures for a short time. It is a brief, intense affair like a single passionate chance encounter. Restocking the coals would be wasted effort— it is done.

For broiling with wood or charcoal, simply build a fire and burn the fuel to embers. Most gas grills, however, need to be closed before putting the meat on in order to build up the temperature of the grill structure to radiation temperatures. The heating coils of electric grills will provide the radiant heat— if they have the capacity. The necessity and characteristics of radiant heat are discussed in the Heat chapter.

Roasting that duck, rib roast, turkey or pork loin will require a covered grill that has enough space above the meat grill to accommodate the largest thing you ever intend to cook. Because roasting may take 2-4 hours, the charcoal/wood grills must also allow replenishing the coals easily and conveniently. The ability to control the temperature and the placement of heat sources is also important. A gas grill should have burners on each side which can be individually controlled and, like the electric grill, should have a reliable, variable thermostat.

Roasting can be done without a cover by turning the meat frequently or impaling it on a rotisserie spit. Rotisseries, covered later in detail, add complexity and noise that I prefer to live without.

Barbecuing requires using either wood or charcoal to maintain consistent heat at proper temperatures for up to 24 hours. This demands bigger firebox capacity, more mass in the grill, the ability to replenish the coal bed easily and an effective means to fine-tune the air supply — which controls the temperature. Barbecuing can be accomplished, with unequaled results some say, in the open over a bed of live coals. Most barbecue, however, is cooked in enclosed pits.

This is one of the finest designs and products ever produced for the back yard barbecuer/griller. It is the "Cue" Cart, which was produced by Atlanta Stove Works. I acquired mine in the early '60's and cooked tons of food on it. The fire grate could be adjusted very close to the meat for broiling or distanced for roasting or barbecuing. Both the fire grate and the meat grates were cast iron. If I had known that the company would abandon it when the fuel shortage got them so deeply into the wood heater market, I'd have kept it and had parts rebuilt.

Hot Smoking requires temperatures in the 90 - 190 degree range for a few hours to a few days. A well-designed grill capable of barbecuing can most likely perform hot smoking and drying — as when making jerky.

Cold Smoking is a whole different chapter. Cold smoking requires the ability to maintain smoke and temperatures between 70° and 90° for up to 6 weeks. This can hardly be done on the back yard grill. A smoke house or smaller unit designed especially for smoking is essential. This Pitts & Spitts design can do it all.

Frequency of Use

If you intend to grill three to four times a week year round, you will want a substantially made grill that performs consistently flawlessly with the least effort and is most economical to operate. If you grill a limited menu and only on special occasions, simplicity of operation should be high on your list of attributes.

Capacity

If your grilling is limited to serving parties of two, then the smallest gas or electric grill or a sturdy hibachi will cover your needs. If you like to throw large barbecues to show off your prowess, then you need a couple of medium or one large grill. Actually, if you are already throwing barbecue bashes, you probably have more than one grill.

If you grill often, it is preferable to have more than one grill of different sizes. It is wasteful in time and fuel to heat up a large grill just to broil two steaks.

Grill Economics 101

Grilling cost is a combination of the initial cost, operating and maintenance costs and the useful life span of the grill. The shoddily made sheet-metal, bottom-end grills—I call them disposables—will last about a year before they disintegrate from the heat, the ashes and the elements. Carefully cleaned and kept indoors, they may be coaxed into two years.

An aluminum or stainless grill can function for decades if the internal parts are replaced as needed. Cast iron costs substantially more than sheet metal, but will outlast it many years.

The decision— *your* decision— needs to be based on the first three factors. If you need more grill than you feel that your budget will allow, check the plans for making your own. Even a semi-handy guy can make a useable grill which can out-perform some of the commercial models.

Grill Construction Materials and Design Considerations

Steel, stainless steel, cast iron, cast aluminum, sheet iron and sheet aluminum, ceramic and masonry products are used in grill construction, and each has its strengths and weaknesses.

Cast iron is, in my estimation, the best material for meat grates and not bad for fire grates. When properly seasoned — like a cast iron skillet — food will not stick to it unless you wash it with soapy water. (Elsewhere in the book, I explain how to eliminate the sticking problem altogether— along with the extra cleaning that burned food requires.) The major problem with cast iron is that making single-use molds for casting it into shapes is labor intensive and, therefore, expensive. Its virtues are that it has lots of mass, heats evenly and, cared for, will last many years. Cast iron is not normally used for the body of the grill because of weight and expense, but, when it is, it makes a great stationary grill.

Steel is an excellent material for larger grills. Its mass retains heat well so that when the grill is heated it maintains even temperature more readily. It is heavier than sheet metal, will last much longer and, in general, performs better. Steel is used for the grill body as well as meat and fire grates. Normally, thicker is better.

Stainless steel is strong, durable and beautiful, but, like some other beauties, expensive. Its strength/weight ratio is much higher than steel, so stainless parts will be much lighter than a comparable steel part; however, even stainless will rust and stain to a minor degree. It does not conduct heat as well as aluminum or iron; therefore, not as much heat is lost through conduction and radiation into the atmosphere. Because of its cost, most large grills have little stainless steel on them. Stainless steel is much more practical and popular with manufacturers of smaller charcoal and gas grills. Some manufacturers of high end grills, such as Pitts & Spitts, use stainless for doors and lids and some, like HastyBake, use stainless entirely.

Cast aluminum is a popular material for gas-grill bodies for good reasons. It does not corrode, and the final product is relatively inexpensive because large parts can be cast in an automated process with reusable molds, and smaller parts can be extruded to shape. This reduces the manufacturing costs. In my opinion, cast aluminum is the all-around best material for small to medium size grills using gas or charcoal.

A few manufacturers produce ceramic egg-shaped grills, and they value them highly—to an unwarranted degree, in my opinion. The ceramic shell, which is thick, 1 1/2"+, and heavy is a very good insulator. Once heated, it preserves the heat very well so that it operates very economically. Ceramic grills are most effective for roasting. They are an expensive and somewhat fragile platform for broiling burgers.

The ceramics do not easily satisfy the functions required for long-term barbecuing and are generally too small for the average regular barbecuer.

Brick and masonry pits are regaining some of their past popularity. Although some folk want a brick structure to put their gas grill in, many want to be able to barbecue and roast. Even though I try to discourage folk, the requests for plans keep coming in. For old-fashioned barbecue, brick pits deliver outstanding flavor and texture — but at a price. First, the construction is expensive.

Even a modest-size pit consisting of low walls on three sides and a meat grate costs more than the average full-size metal grill. With no top, more fuel is needed— wood, naturally, because charcoal would be even more expensive. Wood requires a separate pit to burn it down to embers before adding to the coal bed. A masonry pit is distinctly non-portable and after a few years seems always to have been built in the wrong place. Filled with good soil, they do make good raised herb and flower beds—and most of them do end up that way.

All masonry pits are custom made. Those who want to be able to broil, roast and barbecue will find that acquiring the doors, vents, grates and covers is an expensive and almost impossible task. In order to properly perform the various cooking techniques, fire grates or meat grills should be vertically adjustable.

Since many folk seem to want them, I have included some designs in the **Building Your Grill** chapter.

Design Criteria

As we have shown, different cooking techniques require different functions from the grill, but, regardless of the technique, there are some considerations applicable to all techniques. Design should fulfill the functional requirements for the cooking techniques and, the capacity needs and support the planned frequency of cooking.

Capacity

Strength, heat and volumetric capacities are important considerations. The meat grill should be large enough and strong enough to handle the largest cookout that you can conceive of doing for next year or two. The fire grates and fireboxes on wood and charcoal fueled grills should have the volume and strength to provide adequate temperatures over the expected cooking periods. Gas fired grills should be capable of sustaining at least an output of 30,000 British Thermal Units (BTUs) — 50,000 BTUs is preferable. Electric grills should be able to sustain 350º F. with an 8 lb. roast when the ambient temperature is in the low '40s— don't expect much more. You can test this by seeing how long it takes to boil a gallon of water, which weighs 8.34 lbs. If it can boil a gallon of water, it can cook an 8-pound pork shoulder to 185 degrees.

Mass

Consistency is essential for relaxed grilling. Under identical conditions, the grill should deliver identical performance. This is largely a function of design and construction, but mass is an important factor. In general, the thicker and heavier the construction materials, the more durable and effective the grill. The thicker material will not only be stronger, but will also resist the unhappy results of speeding up the oxidation (rust) with high temperatures. The greater mass will provide more consistent heat over longer periods.

The obvious limitations and disadvantages to more and more mass are higher costs and massive weight. If you plan to use a grill mostly for broiling, roasting an occasional chicken, or barbecuing a couple of racks of ribs, the smallest grill that can accomplish those is the best one for your uses. It is wasteful of time, and resources to have to heat up an overly large grill just to cook small amounts.

While the greater mass is important in long-term cooking techniques, it is really immaterial in broiling. Broiling depends upon radiant heat; therefore, for broiling, the ability to adjust the fire grate or meat grill to bring them closer together is more important than mass. Mass should be controlled by function. Don't buy an18-wheeler, when a pick-up truck will better do the job.

Fuel Based Criteria

Functional Considerations

Different fuels present different design criteria because fuels determine what cooking techniques can be performed and influence the size and portability of grills. As already expressed, the popular fuels are wood/charcoal, gas (natural and bottled) and electricity.

Hardwood/Charcoal Burning Grills

Wood can fuel all forms of grilling, from low-temperature smoking to a 1000° bed for quick broiling, but successfully cooking with wood makes a definite set of demands upon the grill as well as the upon the griller.

Wood-burning grills must of necessity be larger and more massively built than those using other fuels. Unless the wood is burned to coals in another location, the fire box capacity should be at least four times as large as for charcoal, and it must stand the intense heat of the wood burning down to embers. Therefore, although several models are available in the modest price range, wood burners, unless home made, are generally the most expensive of the grill types. Most wood-burning grills can also be readily heated by charcoal.

Wood has other obvious disadvantages, the first being that it should be reduced to coals or embers before exposing meat to it. When burning, even dry wood gives off a mixture of noxious fumes and gasses, which can quickly taint the taste of the food. For long-term cooking, such as when barbecuing, a separate fire pit must be maintained to burn the wood to coals before adding to the grill. This can be just a pile of wood burning on the ground, a 20-30 gallon drum with a shovel-wide hole cut in one side of the bottom to take out the embers or a separate masonry or metal structure.

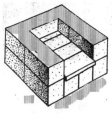

Another potential problem is availability. Not everyone has ready access to suitable woods, the storage facilities, or the time and facilities to burn it down to coals. However, several varieties of woods are now available from various retail channels, and friends can join together to buy hardwood in cord lots (4'x4'x8') and really reduce their fuel costs.

Charcoal-burning grills are, in my estimation, the most versatile of all grills. They come in all sizes from little hibachis with room for two skewers of shrimp, to giant rigs mounted on 8' x 20' trailers and big enough to cook whole hogs. With the exception of cold smoking, they can be used for the full range of grilling.

For techniques requiring long term cooking, wood and charcoal grills require ready access to the heat source and to the meat without one access interfering with the other. During the longer cooking periods, the coal bed must be replenished, and the meat may require basting and turning. Lack of easy access to the coals is a major failing of the kettle-type grill and most of the tin can, bullet-shaped, "smokers."

Since temperature is a function of the rate of burn, a means of controlling the air flow to the fuel is essential for wood and charcoal grills. When air intake is reduced, the fuel will burn more slowly, reducing the temperature or maintaining a lower one and lasting longer. Therefore, if you intend to roast, barbecue and smoke, the grill must be tightly constructed to prevent uncontrolled air influx and have some simple, effective means of metering the air flow. This means some sort of opening *below* the fire grate, the area of which can be varied as needed. Pass up any grill which does not have an air-tight firebox door and a variable air vent which can be tightly closed.

In order for air to enter the cooker, there must also be an air exit. A wood/charcoal fueled cooker that does not have an exhaust vent is worthless. *Believe it or not, there is one on the market!* Pass it up! Also, pass up any advice which suggests that while cooking you close, even partially, the exhaust vent. When cooking, this vent should be fully open, or the air flow is retarded. This results in reduced temperature, leading to condensation of phenols and cresols on meat and the cooker walls. This makes the meat unpalatable to anybody but a creosote junkie.

In a grill where the meat is directly above the heat source, thus within the flow of the heated air, placement of the exhaust exit is hardly important. However, in wood/charcoal fired grills with fireboxes offset from the cooking chamber, placement of the exit point of the exhaust is the subject of much conjecture. Because hotter air is less dense and, therefore, rises, the hotter air will rise to the top of the cooking chamber, and if the exhaust vent exit is at the top of the cooking chamber, the hotter air will exit without flowing past the meat. **The temperature at the level of the meat grill may be 50-100° cooler than at the exhaust.**

Some manufacturers have sought to counter this early escape by putting the exhaust entry below the meat grill at the end of the cooker opposite from the firebox. Some think the ideal placement is at the same level as the meat. In either case, the theory is that the air should not exhaust until it has cooled and moved to the lower exhaust point.

Unquestionably, the lower exhaust entry prevents the hottest air from exhausting immediately, and therefore, more efficiently uses fuel. However, the lower exits have their risks. If one has been cooking over burning/smoldering wood in a top-exhausting horizontal grill, most of the smoke has been going out the exhaust without fouling the meat. Using that same faulty method in a grill with a lower exhaust exit will allow more of the unpleasant constituents of smoke to be deposited on the meat.

Observe in the Anatomy of a Grill illustration that the exhaust exit, item 18, is lower than the meat cooking surface and that the flow of heat is down through the meat grill.

The Anatomy of a Grill

1. Exhaust cover	2. Exhaust damper	3. Grill lid	4. Handle
5. Thermometer	6. Grill lid handle	7.Work area	8. Drip pan
9.Grease drain	10. Tool rack	11. Firebox	12. Wheels
13. Firebox door	14. Fuel storage	15. Air vent	16. Handle
17. Upper and lower cooking surface		18. Exhaust entrance	

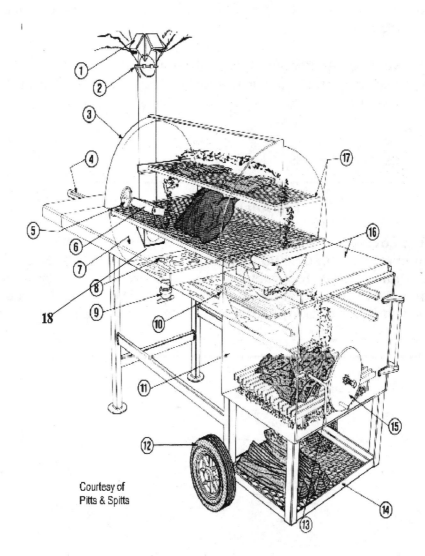

Courtesy of
Pitts & Spitts

Breaking in a New Grill

Many folk are concerned about breaking in (seasoning) a new grill. Start with a clean grill, taking the temperature up gradually to a maximum of 450 degrees — with all vents open. This burns off any volatile residue and solvents. After it has cooled somewhat, wipe the inside with a damp cloth. Then wipe or spray on a thin coat of cooking oil.

The metal will expand considerably during the heating. After it has cooled, check to see that everything opens and closes easily and tightly. If there is any warpage or the paint has flaked, take it back for replacement or refund.

Cleaning and Maintenance

The combination of hardwood ashes and water form a caustic potassium carbonate — similar to the commercially available product, lye. It has a seriously corrosive effect on sheet iron, and wet ashes left in the bottom of a sheet iron grill, will rust it away in one season. Always empty the ashes as soon as they are cool and keep the interior of the grill dry. Make certain that the coals are all cold! (An Internet correspondent removed his ashes, neatly contained in aluminum foil, and left them in the snow, overnight, before discarding them in a plastic garbage can in a garage. Fortunately he lost only part of the building.)

Hardwood ashes have several good, and surprising, uses. Distributed in the garden, they add potash to the soil and reduce the soil's acidity. American Indians taught the pioneers how to collect their hardwood ashes to leach the potash into lye-like solution for making hominy from dried corn. Pioneers also used the solution to mix with melted fat for making soap. In an even more creative use, wood ashes were piled upon a bed of straw in a wooden trough. Human urine poured or deposited over the ashes caused potassium nitrate crystals to form on the straw. Potassium nitrate (saltpeter), charcoal and sulphur are the constituents of black gun powder.

Rinsing or spritzing with a solution of 1 tablespoon of vinegar to a pint of water will neutralize the residual caustic effect. Cast iron and steel plate are less susceptible than sheet metal, but still need to be kept clean and dry. Sheet iron is obviously thinner and cheaper than the other common materials, but with proper care can last many years. Occasionally after cleaning, I oil the hinges, pins and such with lard. A mineral oil would work as well. A thin film of cooking or mineral oil, sprayed or wiped on the inner surfaces will help prevent rust.

Remove accumulated grease drippings periodically. Once after several weeks of heavy cooking without cleaning, I fired up my big Pitts & Spitts grill with wood and closed the lid so that the grill would heat up while the wood burned to embers. When I came back, I was surprised to see that the thermometer only read 250°. As I stepped closer, the radiant heat told a different story. The fat was in the fire, and the temperature had driven the thermometer around past the maximum 1000° mark and up to the 250° mark. I'll never know just how hot it was, but I know that it was way too hot! I shut down the air intake to smother it. **Don't ever open a flaming grill!** Shut off the air. This incident is one of the reasons that I caution against ever firing up a grill under a carport, porch or other wooden structure. A flame-up can be a disaster.

One thing I did not have to do after the fire was to spend much effort cleaning the meat grates. The easiest way to clean grates is not to get them soiled. If the grill is allowed to reach the proper temperature before meat is put on, meat will not remain stuck to the grill. When meat hits the properly heated grill, it seizes. Left alone, it will shortly release without leaving any residue on the grill. Glazes and finishing sauces applied to meat on a cooler grate will stick and char.

The total extent of meat-grate cleaning that any of my grills get is a light brushing with a wire brush after it is heated. The other care that I take is to scrape the grate with a spatula just after I have removed food to which a glaze or finishing sauce containing sugar was applied. Sugars char into a very hard carbon residue that when cooled clings like welded metal to the grates. Use sugars only after the temperatures are well below 200°. I occasionally season cast-iron meat grates by rubbing them while hot with a piece of fat impaled on a fork, which I have trimmed from meat in preparation for grilling.

Gas and Electric Grills

Gas grills, whether fired by natural gas or bottled propane gas are neat and convenient. Whether they are the relatively cheap $89.95 disposables or the gussied up $2000 grills burdened with bells and whistles, their functions are quite similar — all have gas burners much like gas kitchen-stove ovens. The more expensive will, or should, deliver more heat, have more space, be sturdier, have sideboards and accessories. But if the *el cheapo* can deliver at least 30,000 BTUs, it will broil a steak and cook a roast—which is about all any gas grill can do. Some smoke flavor may be added by various means but don't expect to produce real-barbecue.

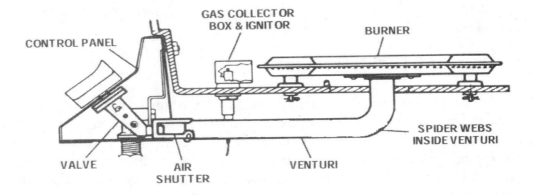

Gas-fired stoves have been safely used in homes for more than a century. During that time, there has been little change in the technology. The entire operating system consists of a gas valve, an orifice (read "small hole") attached to the valve, a venturi, which is merely a tube having a variable opening (shutter) to draw in air, and a burner—a hollow plate or other shape which has holes in it for the gas/air mixture to exit and burn.

There is nothing complicated about the process—except in the mind of the manufacturers. As a class, manufacturers know less about what a grill is supposed to do than a fifth-grade social studies class. Apparently their consuming interest is in manufacturing products which will satisfy the retailer and, thereby, generate sales and profits for their companies. You have only to read their brochures to discover that they are unburdened by the weight of obligations to the consumer to provide complete and accurate information. They can tell you how to assemble it, maybe, but not how to cook on it. Follow their recommendations for operation and maintenance, but ignore their cooking hints, recipes and extravagant claims.

A couple of gas-grill manufacturers have incorporated the new ceramic burner technology, which, although much more expensive, is more efficient in converting gas to usable radiant heat. Such grills are capable of producing temperatures almost as high as their prices, but I am not convinced that either is justified for the backyard broiler. If any heat source can produce temperatures in the 7-800° range, it is entirely adequate for broiling a steak. I know of no other cooking use which requires a higher temperature. I suspect that the boasts of grill manufacturers and restauranteurs of 1500-1800° for broiling steaks most likely comes from hot air. Iron begins to soften at 1530° Fahrenheit.

Safety Considerations

Auto-ignition systems for gas grills should have either a time limit or other shut-off device which would prevent the continued release of unlit gas. Otherwise, a deficient igniter which takes a minute or so to generate an ignition spark may allow enough gas to accumulate to cause an explosion. If there is an igniter, the grill should also have a clear, convenient passage for lighting by other means after the ignition system fails. Igniter systems on gas grills have about the same life span as a fruit fly.

Since propane gas is heavier than air, any leakage along the supply line will accumulate in the lowest area and will explode when it encounters an ignition source. Check all connections with a 50/50 solution of water and soap/detergent. Spray or brush on all connections. Open the valve on the gas bottle or on the natural gas supply line, but do not open the gas valve on the burner. Soap bubbles at any point will indicate a gas leak. If you cannot eliminate the leak by tightening, replace the part.

Cleaning and Maintenance

Gas fired grills are really very simple. Propane fired grills have a regulator on bottle end of the gas supply hose. Beyond that, propane and natural gas-fired grills are almost identical — the only difference being the size of the hole in the supply orifice.

A gas grill should be designed and constructed so that the venturi, burners, their covers and valves can be easily accessed for cleaning, maintenance or replacement.

Insects and spiders like to build nests and webs in the venturi tube. If the flame on your burner begins to burn yellow, this is probably the cause. Take out the venturi — carefully — and clean out the venturi with a small bottle-type brush. A clogged venturi may allow unburned gas to escape and create an explosion hazard.

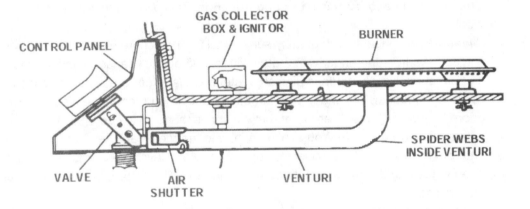

Sometimes the small holes in the burners become stopped up. If there is no flame at any hole, it is stopped up. Turn the grill off, allow the burner to cool, then remove it. Brush it well with a wire brush; then hold a water hose tightly to the entrance of the burner and flush it out. With a small wire awl or pin open any clogged holes. Inspect for any split seams or burned-out holes.

Periodically, remove the gas control knob on the grill and spray a lubricant such as WD40 into the stem. Replace the knob and turn the valve on and off a few times. If the valve binds severely, it should be replaced.

If the grill does not have a grease-trapping system, you will need to remove the burners periodically to clean out the grease before it causes what may be more than a minor conflagration. Ceramic briquettes and lava rocks which collect grease can be scrubbed or merely turned over for the flame to clean the greasy side.

Gas-grill replacement parts are available from the manufacturer and several other sources. A well-built, cast-aluminum gas grill can be kept in service for a lifetime. With an occasional touch up with high-temperature tolerant paint, it can continue to look good, too.

What to look for in selecting a gas grill

Aluminum (cast) body: review materials above.

Cooking area of meat grill: more is better.

Grill levels: Multiple levels add versatility. The ability to raise and lower are a plus.

Dual controls and burners on opposite ends. This allows much more control and, thus, flexibility.

Meat grates should be adequately substantial for their chore. Porcelain's propensity to flake from the underlying metal, with or without just cause, puts it on the bottom of my list. Cast iron, stainless or steel, in that order are my preferences. Cast iron grates will be wider than the others and when properly heated conduct more heat rapidly to deliver the attractive stripes that signify good grilling.

Glass viewing port: No. You can't see in, and the meat can't see out.

Mass: There should be sufficient ceramic briquettes, lava rock or metal between the flames and the meat rack to absorb enough BTUs to produce radiant heat for broiling.

Piezo igniter: Only if you get a 5 year warranty. Should have easy access to light manually when igniter fails.

Thermostat: Should have at least a 5 year warranty.

Thermometer: Should be bi-metal probe rather than a coil. It should be easily removable for checking its accuracy. It should have numbers rather than some nonsensical ranges and words.

Valves and burners: Look for United Laboratory (UL) seal and good bright brass. Burners should be easily removable. Stainless steel is a plus.

Hinges, tightness of lid fit: The lid should open and close easily, have adequate strength for the task, and make a tight fit.

Rotisseries: Worthless for most cooking and only complicate an enjoyable task. The bird or butt will cook just as well sitting still and quiet.

Side burners: Not worth the price for the function. Only for beginners who are not likely to have a separate cooker. Most are too small and only produce 9M BTUs. Cook it on the stove, or get a separate cooker which has the appropriate capacity for frying and boiling.

Grease Trap: A plus; otherwise you will have a cleaning chore.

Electric Grills

Electric grills, whether in the kitchen stove or on the patio, can provide clean, adequate, controllable heat for broiling or roasting. With adaptation, they can also produce smoke from wood chips and sawdust. Their relative low price and convenience do not, however, in my opinion, overcome the inherent shortcomings of most of the offerings—poor design and cheap construction.

A very few companies produce what they call electric smoking ovens to higher commercial standards. They are essentially well-constructed electric ovens which have a container for wood near the caloric (heat) rod. Their performance and price, beginning around $425.00, easily distinguish them from the hot-plates-in-a-bucket.

Heating electrically is not normally economical, especially if the heating element is 110 volt. A 220 volt circuit is more economical and more likely to have adequate heating capacity for broiling. *I don't know why they are not readily available.* In any case, the electrical supply circuit should be installed by a licensed electrician and contain a **Ground Fault Interrupt (GFI)** for protection against the hazard of electrical shock. If an extension cord is used to connect to current, it should have at least #12 wire—#10 is better. The unit should not be left out in the weather, and the insulation and isolation of the conductors should be inspected—**WHILE UNPLUGGED** before each use.

Chapter Ten

Heat and Light

The Myths of Direct and Indirect Heat

Those to whom the **Basting Mops** were passed by the ancient **Keepers of the Coals** also bear the burden of sharing of the truth in barbecuing. This is why I am compelled to state unequivocally that there is no "direct heat," there is no "indirect heat," there is only heat.

Over the years, I have bitten my tongue, until it is more scarred than a politician's conscience, when otherwise competent, and well-meaning, people passed along, as valid, these pernicious phrases of misinformation.

According to the irresistible laws of physics, heat moves from regions or objects of higher temperature to regions or objects of lower temperature until a state of equilibrium is reached. Heat moves in only three ways, by **conduction, convection** or **radiation.**

Conduction is the transfer of heat by *intimate contact*—who among us could oppose that—and moves from molecule to molecule. For example, the grate or grill upon which the meat rests, having a higher temperature than the meat, conducts heat to the meat. That is why, when the grill is right, that the beautiful brown stripes magically appear upon the surface of a steak. Then the exterior of the meat conducts heat to the interior, molecule by molecule. Conducting is extremely important in barbecuing because we must conduct the heat from the exterior to the center so slowly and gently that we do not dry out the exterior. Using low temperature over the long period is the essential distinction of barbecue from roasting or broiling. This longer period also allows for more flavoring and more fun. Let's hear it for conduction!!

Convection is the transfer of heat by movement of heated masses, i.e., air, water, oil. A political speech is good example of convection. In an oven, an enclosed grill or in the path of heated air, convection is at work. Convection allows us to remove the meat, from directly over the coals, and, therefore, tend the coals without disturbing the meat. Also, the amount of meat which can be cooked simultaneously is no longer restricted to the surface area of the coal bed, and fat dripping from the meat does not drop into the coals. The last is not necessarily and advantage in barbecuing, where fat and juices hit the coals and return to the meat as flavor bombs.

Radiation is the transmission of heat in waves of energy resulting from vibration of excited molecules—as when your tongue trembles at the taste of succulent, savory barbecue, it radiates ecstasy to your brain and other pleasure receptors. In a closed grill, meat receives radiated heat from the coals, if it is over them, and from the heated mass of metal in which it is enclosed, if hot enough.

This may be more than you really want to know about it, but *"the intensity of the radiated heat is directly proportional to the temperature of the source and inversely proportional to the square of the distance."* In practical terms, this means that meat on a grill over coals and below a metal cover may receive equal heat radiated from both. Those who have cooked on a grill with tiered racks have, no doubt, observed that those pieces of meat on the top rack (nearest the metal) may brown more quickly than those on the lowest tier directly over the coals. Likewise, if you cook bread on the top shelf of an oven, the top browns faster than the bottom, and conversely.

This is critical knowledge for those seeking to broil the perfect steak. Short term exposure to extremely high radiant heat produces the best results. Therefore, knowledge of the effects of distance is essential. **A glowing bed of embers, which produces 1000° of radiant heat at a distance of 1" will produce only 110° at 3" distance.** Instead of quickly searing and sealing, the steak just sits there and simmers—losing juices and tenderness. This is one reason why the heat grate or the meat grill needs to be vertically adjustable.

For the mathematically challenged, 3 x 3 = 9 and 1000 degrees divided by 9 equals 110 degrees.

As a practical matter, in an enclosed grill, unless meat is suspended from or resting upon a non-conducting surface, it is at all times receiving heat by all three transfer methods.

What does all this mean to the barbecuer? Meat does not care how it receives the heat. What is essential in barbecuing and roasting is that the exterior of the meat does not overcook, dry out, burn, blacken, or char, before the interior reaches an acceptable temperature. This requires that meat receive a constant flow of heat, in any form, at a temperature low enough to permit conduction within the meat, time to work.

In this respect, water is the great ally. Water absorbs and conducts heat much better than dry tissue. **Therefore, the more moisture that we can retain within the meat, the faster it will conduct heat to the center.** Also it will be more tender when it is finished. Most, who have done any cooking, have learned that a damp hot pad conducts heat to the hand so quickly as to be useless, whereas a dry hot pad insulates and allows one to safely handle a hot pot.

Everybody knows that at sea level water boils at 212° Fahrenheit. It, therefore, follows that, for barbecuing, if we keep the temperature of the exterior of the meat slightly below the boiling point of water, conduction is improved and tenderness is retained. This does not mean that no moisture will be lost, but it does reduce the amount of loss.

The one saving grace of the ubiquitous, tin can "water smoker" is that water in the pan acts as a heat sink, reducing the temperature of the air reaching the meat. Among its numerous defects is that it encourages neophytes to over-power the taste of good meat with excessive smoke and has confused many about what is meant by "smoking."

Putting water in a grill is an absurdity. Water pans were introduced by manufacturers of cheap charcoal cookers, which lacked any means of controlling the air flow—and, therefore, the temperature of the grill. In an open vessel, the water and steam can never rise above 212°. Therefore, whether the equipment or its operator are competent, the water acts as a thermostat. But what a waste! **It takes more BTUs to boil a gallon of water than it does cook the center of an 8 lb. roast to 185º!** Water in the grill is a waste of fuel and a waste of time. Besides, barbecue is "meat cooked in the dry heat of wood coals."

For a barbecuer, the effective grill is one which will allow its operator to present heat by all three forms in a controlled fashion over long periods of time and have ready access to the meat and to the coals—each without disturbing the other. The greater the mass of the cooker and the coal bed, the more consistent the transfer of heat, and the more time for enjoying all the ancillary activities, for which barbecue has become famous.

For roasting, the grill should, likewise, provide heat by all three forms. One which provides convection will do the job, but radiant heat from the cooker walls help to brown the exterior. For broiling, radiant heat is essential. The fire grate and/or meat grill should allow varying their proximity, as needed, to provide the appropriate temperature.

In the final analysis, there is no direct heat. There is no indirect heat. There is only heat. The judicious use of heat in any form and the creative use of the time during which it is applied is what barbecuing and grilling are all about.

Chapter Eleven

Cooking with Wood and Charcoal

Burning Wood & Blowing Smoke

The question of proper heat sources for grilling has fueled many heated discussions, and overheated enthusiasm has produced enough hot air to keep an armada of balloons inflated for an around-the-world voyage. The recent rage for exotic woods and excessive smoke has, naturally, generated more smoke than light. It's time we clear the air and look at some facts.

The temperatures required for grilling normally range from 70° at the bottom end of **cold smoking** to 900°+ for **broiling**. Wood and charcoal can fuel the entire spectrum. Gas is used for **broiling** and **roasting**. Electricity can produce the entire spectrum, with the exception of **barbecuing**, which by definition is cooked over wood or charcoal. .

Wood

Burning questions regarding the characteristics of particular woods have traditionally been confined to wood workers and their clientele and those folk who heat with wood. Except for Macbeth's fate resting upon whether or not Great Birnam wood came up Dunsinane hill, particular woods have never seemed like a life or death situation. But lately, with all the smoke blowing going on, the fad for cooking over exotic woods and the extravagant claims of smoke blowers has reached outrageous proportions.

Actually, it wasn't the discovery of fire that was so important, but the discovery of the uses of fire. Probably shortly after man discovered that fire could warm as well as burn, he also found that meat could be rendered tastier and remain edible longer if properly exposed to a fire. It was surely only shortly thereafter that we discovered that meat tasted better if it wasn't dropped directly into the flames and ashes and dirt. So we rocked along, warming up the caves, cooking up the meat on sticks and, generally, enjoying the good life and growing taller.

A strange thing began to happen. As we ate more meat because it tasted better and remained edible longer, the protein rich diet caused our brains to develop. We started discovering things and developing perceptions. Those whose palates had developed beyond the most primitive stages discovered a phenomenon. Meat that was cooked in the heat of wood coals tasted eminently better than that cooked in the flames and smoke.

As long as wood was the primary cooking fuel, this knowledge was proudly passed from generation to generation. But as we moved indoors with gas and electricity becoming the favored fuels, there occurred what is known in scientific circles as a discontinuity. There was a missing link in the chain of knowledge. For more than a generation, this precious information was lost to most of the population. It was kept alive by only a small cadre of Keepers of the Coals.

Suddenly, those in whom there arose an inexplicable, instinctive yearning for meat cooked over wood coals, and thereby imbued with the essence of purified flavors of the wood, lacked the lore to create it. Into this Dismal Swamp of ignorance rushed the demons of disinformation.

Unveiling their newest buzz work, they flung meat into the ghastly gasses of burning wood, blackened it in the phenolic resins of wood smoke and pronounced it **"SMOKIN!"** They flooded television and magazines with depictions of meat lapped by flickering flames, and created nonsensical, but appealing, phrases like "Flame Broiled!" Palates dulled by generations of feeding on fast-food burgers, TV dinners and prepackaged pap rushed to join the frenetic frenzy—believing, with the ardor of innocence, that **"BURNT IS BEAUTIFUL!"**

Like a virulent, swiftly moving plague, the misologyous message swept the land. Even those with more competence, than confidence, became seduced by the idea of **SMOKIN**! So for a dark period, cooking technique regressed hundreds of thousands of years. Good meat was burnt upon the altars of ignorance. Children, who formerly could eat from their father's grill, were forced to eat pizza. Those allergic to phenols, or not wishing to embrace benzene, were driven from the patios and back into the kitchens.

But even the dullest palates, and most naive minds, began to question. Slowly, the latent instincts, which have guided mankind from the savannahs of Africa to the mares of the moon, became aroused. Among the more discerning, the first reaction was, "What am I doing wrong? Good meat is not supposed to taste bitter. Dare I doubt the priests of PR!" But gradually, the truth became unavoidably obvious, **"Over-smoked meat does not taste good."**

Recovery, like the taste of over-smoked meat, is harsh. It requires that one accept responsibility for a temporary loss of critical thinking, a susceptibility to the herd instinct and an uncertain palate. The outlook for individual recovery, however, is excellent.

Fortunately, the lamps of enlightenment have been relit, and coals of sanity have been rekindled. More and more people are relearning a verity: meat cooked in the smoke stream of burning wood gets marred with cresols and phenols and other noxious volatiles—which make good wood preservatives and disinfectants but don't taste very good, even to an unskilled palate.

Besides unbounded enthusiasm spurred by abject ignorance, what permitted this travesty to good taste even to start was the development of the horizontal cooker with an offset firebox. When meat was cooked directly over the heat source, the results of flames and wood smoke were immediately apparent to even the dullest pates and palates. Even users of the tin can water smokers quickly deduce that it is very easy to turn what was a fine piece of meat into a mummified creosote fossil, unattractive even to flies and maggots with taste.

In the sidewinder cookers, the heated air, however baffled and directed, still flows in strata according to the temperature. **(See Anatomy of a Grill in the chapter All about Grills.)** This means that the hotter air flows up to the top of the cooking chamber, and out the stack, without necessarily coming into contact with the meat on the grate. Although some cookers are designed so that the heated air must exit below the meat, the flow is up and over, rather than under, around and through, so that the meat does not normally come into intimate contact with grossly excessive smoke. Rather, as the smoke cools, some of it is deposited on the sides of the cooker and builds up layers of creosote. This shiny black, acrid layer is an indication of an inexperienced cook. Sometimes, however, even this serendipitous air flow cannot prevent too much smoke being deposited on the meat. Eventually, even to those whose reasoning is as dense as the smoke they produce, there comes an awakening — "Less is more better."

Regardless of the species of wood, excessive smoke is offensive. It is truly amazing that those, whose palates do not rebel at creosote-contaminated meat are the same ones who claim that they can discern the flavor of grape leaves, determine the vintage of wine-barrel, French oak, and distinguish wood of Mackintosh apple from Northern Spy. Fact is that, **except for a few wood species, such as hickory and mesquite, less that 5% of the palates in the world can tell what kind of wood was used to cook.**

When you hear or read pretentious puffery describing the nuances of various bouquets of different woods, what you are experiencing is smoke blowing. Only a confirmed and experienced *kapnzophile* (lover of smoke) could identify, from the taste of the food, more than 3-4 species of the most common woods used for cooking.

Besides being distasteful, cresols and phenols are hazardous chemicals and suspected carcinogens. Creosote, a product of cresol, was used as a wood preservative and the active ingredient in sheep dip, until the EPA ban. Phenol is the active ingredient in a long-time-favorite bathroom disinfectant, Lysol.

Here is another's facts and opinion.

****

"Did a little research on the combustion of wood recently. Turns out it's an interesting subject that has undergone quite a bit of study in recent years.

Seems that wood is the world's most widely used industrial raw material and the third most commonly used fuel. The hardwoods used in the preparation of barbecue are composed primarily of cellulose (39%), hemicellulose (35%), and lignin (19.5%), extractives (3.1%) and ash (0.3%). The cellulose and lignin are primarily in the cell walls.

The extractives, primarily in the cells and walls, are such things as tannins, starches, resins, oils, dyes, alkaloids, and sugars. These vary widely among wood species and give each its distinctive characteristics. Up to 80% of the weight of green wood is retained water. Dry wood reaches an equilibrium at 20%.

Wood does not burn directly. Rather, when heat is applied it first undergoes a process of thermal degradation called pyrolysis in which the wood breaks down into a mixture of volatiles and solid carbonaceous char. The cellulose and hemicellulose mainly form volatiles while the lignin mainly forms the char. Exactly what products are formed by each depends upon the temperature, heating rate, particle size, and any catalysts that might be present.

The solid char remains in place. What goes up with the volatiles are a gas fraction (carbon monoxide and dioxide, some hydrocarbons, and elemental hydrogen), a condensed fraction (water, aldehydes, acids, ketones, and alcohols), and — here we go! — a tar fraction (sugar residues from the breakdown of cellulose, furan derivatives, phenolic compounds, and — pay attention here — airborne particles of tar and charred material which form the smoke.

If oxygen is present and the temperature is sufficiently high, burning of the volatiles occurs. When temperatures are too low or when there is insufficient oxygen for complete combustion of the volatiles, smoldering occurs. This is characterized by smoking, the emission of unoxidized pyrolysis products. (This is the awful tasting stuff, creosote, that will give barbecue a bitter taste.) If the temperature is high enough and sufficient oxygen is present, then flaming combustion occurs with less smoking and more complete oxidation of the pyrolysis products. Further pyrolysis of volatiles during flaming combustion may cause char particles (soot) to form.

The remaining lignin char burns in the presence of oxygen in glowing combustion. These are my beloved coals that yield the thin blue smoke that makes great barbecue! And that's why it is so important to pre-burn the wood to coals.

Commercial charcoal, on the other hand, is produced by heating wood at about 1000 deg F in the absence of air to produce a porous solid containing 85-98% carbon. Accordingly, this stuff is fundamentally different from live coals and should not be expected to produce similar results.

QED"
Dave Lineback
http://www.sunsetridge.com
Included by permission
North Carolinian, Dave Lineback is a scholar and defender of what he terms "traditional" barbecue.
****

According to a study published by the Environmental Protection Agency, wood smoke has more than 100 compounds. The list is included as Appendix "A." Most notably undesirable are the cresols, phenols, ketones, toluenes, aldehydes, all of which are considered hazardous materials by the EPA.

Let's clear away some smoke with:

Five reasons why wood coals are superior to flaming wood for cooking:

1. Green woods are 20-40% water. This must be boiled off before the wood can burn. This means that British Thermal Units (BTUs)—a measure of heat — are used to boil water (971 BTUs per lb. of water) rather than to cook.

2. Dry wood still has 8-20% moisture and contains many compounds which must be cooked out—absorbing BTUs—before the temperature can rise.

3. As long as there are moisture and volatiles to boil out, the temperature cannot rise above the boiling point of the substances. Therefore, in order to reach broiling temperatures—700°—all the moisture and volatiles must be driven out. At that point the wood becomes embers/coals.

4. Successful broiling—steaks, burgers, chops—requires very high radiant heat. Flames of burning wood do not generate radiant heat at temperatures as high as that of live embers. A handful of green twigs, nuts or leaves will add a short burst of smoke to provide intense flavor without overpowering.

5. In the hours' long cooking periods, as when roasting and barbecuing, the smoke flavor in the coals, alone, is more than ample. Visible smoke is too much smoke. Anytime that you see a full plume of smoke coming out of a barbecue cooker, you know that the cook in making a serious error. **A faint wisp of white smoke is the signal of a competent cook.**

Useful Common Wood Species

Almost any hardwood makes very good embers for cooking. Normally, the denser the wood, the more lignin, and, therefore, more BTUs per cubic volume. Resinous woods such as pine, fir, juniper, cedar and yew are not normally used, with few exception. Some Scots use small amounts of green cedar boughs as a part of their final stage of cold smoking salmon, and juniper branches are used in some Middle Eastern dishes for flavoring, much like they are used to flavor Syrian latikia tobacco during the drying process, and in some smoke cures for Westphalian ham.

Most commonly used woods, in alphabetical order:

 Apple/pear, ash, beech, birch, cherry, hickory/pecan, maple, oak.

Regional, specialty and miscellaneous woods:

Mesquite, alder, citrus, any edible fruit, nut or berry, persimmon, sassafras, gum, pimiento, grape leaves and vines, hackberry, elm, chestnut, bay, fig, guava.

Questionable: Parts are poisonous, cause physical reaction or produce bad taste.

China berry/mahogany, Osage orange, teak, tung, madrone, buckeye.

Definitely don't: Even the smoke can be poisonous!

Poison oak, poison sumac, oleander and other resinous woods.

Flavor quotient for common woods suitable for broiling, roasting and barbecuing.

Ignore any presumptuous "suitability" chart for woods—I have seen some dillies. Use common sense instead. Wood flavors, like other seasonings, should enhance the natural flavor, not overwhelm.

Hickory, and to a lesser degree, its cousin **pecan**, are powerful flavoring woods. A little goes a long way. The wood makes great coals for broiling. When barbecuing or roasting, I use about 20% hickory and 80% oak/apple/etc. Excellent for cold and hot smoking.

Mesquite has a potent flavor that some like and many dislike. I am of the latter group. The wood makes excellent hot coals for broiling and, used in this manner, does not overpower the meat flavor, becoming offensive. I do not recommend it for long-term cooking—roasting and barbecuing. Certainly not for cold or hot smoking, unless you grew up fixated on its flavor.

Oak is the wood most commonly used for outdoor cooking. It imparts excellent flavor without becoming too strong with normal cooking techniques. Oak is outstanding for all forms of grilling and smoking. I prefer white over red, but use them interchangeably. I just don't tell the meat which color I am using.

Fruit woods—apple, pear, quince, cherry, etc., and maple, beech, birch and ash are mild flavored, excellent choices for roasting and barbecuing and make excellent coals for broiling. They are especially suitable for mild meats, fish and veggies, but good for any grilling or smoking.

Alder, **mulberry**, **citrus**, **willow**, **birch** are mild flavored woods that are excellent for fish, poultry and seafood. They are softer woods and, therefore, their embers do not produce as much heat as those of harder woods. Birch, by the way, is of the same family as alder and may be used interchangeably.

Sassafras, bay and pimiento produce identifiable flavors which some might find intrusive. Use sparingly with other woods until you are familiar with the taste.

Faddish fire fodder includes grape vines, oak whiskey barrels and oak wine barrels. Their greatest value is in conversation.

Herbals can make an instant impact. A few green rosemary limbs thrown own the coals can add a distinctive and delicious flavor to food. Green tops of garlic and onion impart an amazing flavor. Bay leaves, citrus leaves and lemon grass assert themselves quickly when tossed onto the coals. Fresh herbs are best. Dry herbs, already bereft of most of their volatile flavors, burst into flame with little effect.

Using Woods for Flavor

If you live in a deforested area without easy access to wood, use an insipid charcoal and want to spruce up (just kidding - spruce is a no-no) the flavor for broiling, try the following. Bring the coal bed up to proper temperature—700°+—and add a mere handful of green wood chips or small limbs or wood chunks soaked for a couple of hours or sawdust soaked likewise. Wait until the smoke is intense and the temperature has returned to the proper level. Plop on the meat and close the lid—with good draft top and bottom. In a couple of minutes, turn the steak/burger and close the lid again. You should have plenty of smoke flavor. Be aware that the meat will cook much quicker with the lid closed. Don't over-cook.

For roasting and barbecuing under the same circumstances, the cheapest route is to go in with a few friends and buy a cord (4'x4'x8') of dry hardwood. Then you can burn down some wood for the coals while it is heating up the grill. You won't need to add any smoke flavor.

Lacking that opportunity, when the grill is ready to start cooking, toss in a double handful of wood, as above, throw on the meat and close the lid. Do that once again in about 30 minutes. That is probably all the smoke flavor that you need, but if you have become hooked on creosote, you can do it one more time. Beyond that, the meat has sealed and will absorb no more smoke flavor. Smoke will, however, continue to pile up on the outside with bitter results.

According to several scientific studies, wood smoke flavor is deposited and absorbed best in the early stages of cooking when the meat has the most moisture. Solid particles from heavy smoke are deposited on the surface as tarry deposits. Therefore, the competent cook will attempt to establish the level of smoke flavor early and make certain not to create conditions which allow tarry deposits.

It is my studied opinion that if the would-be griller spent at least as much time learning technique as he did chasing exotic fuel, he would be a 10 times better cook. And that ain't just blowing smoke.

Firing Up

Wood will lose about 80% of its bulk, depending upon how dry it is, when reduced to embers suitable for grilling. The moisture content, size and configuration of the pieces, density of the wood and such will determine how long it will take to burn the wood down to coals. How much to start with depends upon several factors. How big is the grill? How much and how long will you cook? A small bed for broiling is a simple matter. Building a bed for long-term cooking is a bit more complex. Best bet is to burn down ample woods to build a big bed of coals in the grill, that is "big" in relation to the grill, then reduce the air intake to lower the rate of burn. Thus, you can maintain an even temperature for a long time.

When the wood in the grill is burned to embers, start another fire, in an auxiliary pit, so that fresh embers will be available as needed for replenishment. **This separate pit is absolutely necessary for authentic barbecue results.**

Cooking with Charcoal

Commercially produced charcoal is that which remains when wood has been heated in an enclosure lacking sufficient oxygen for it to burst into flame. The wood sits there smoldering like a mother-in-law—giving off lots of hot air and vapors but no light. Having said that, let me also add that charcoal can be made by burning wood, in open air, to the point where the moisture and volatile gasses are driven off. Jack Daniel's distillery produces all of the charcoal used for filtering and mellowing their Tennessee whiskey in this manner.

Water, cresols, phenols and other noxious gasses are driven off, leaving the lignin structure of mostly carbon ready, willing and able, eager even, to combine with oxygen to produce heat. These virtues are why charcoal has a long history as a favorite cooking fuel. Folk found a long time ago that it not only burned cleaner, but was much easier to transport. In parts of India, Pakistan and other developing nations, charcoal is still the primary cooking fuel.

Charcoal can be no better than the wood from which it was made. The best charcoal for outdoor cooking is made exclusively from hardwoods. Regardless of what misguided or misleading manufacturers of gas grills and misinformed magazine mavens say, hardwood charcoal does impart excellent smoke flavor.

When random-shaped pieces of wood are charred, the product is called lump charcoal or raw charcoal. In this form, charcoal burns rapidly, producing clean, intense heat. But, like Dorothy Parker's candle, ". . .it will not last the night." It is great for broiling, where an intense heat is required for a short period. Lump charcoal burns rapidly because it has so much surface area to react with oxygen. Surface area the reason is that charcoal is such an effective filter. A pound of lump charcoal probably has about the same amount of surface area as Lake Superior.

A great advantage of lump charcoal over briquettes is that lump charcoal can be added to the hot coal bed without first burning it off. Most briquettes, filled with odious, odorous adulterants, must have the noxious fumes burned off or it will foul the food while producing deadly carbon monoxide.

Charcoal compressed into briquettes is more dense and has less surface area and, therefore, burns more slowly and consistently. Most charcoal these days is made of sawdust and other by-products of manufacturing operations using hickory and oak woods. Then it is milled, mixed and formed into the briquette.

The horse puck shape of the briquette is credited to Henry Ford. He had the hardwood scraps from early automobile frames reduced to charcoal and compressed into a shape that suited the grip of the coal tongs his blacksmiths used to pile it in their forges. Determined to protect his reputation of not being a wastrel, he added the dust from the coal bins into the mixture. The shape and the mixture that was appropriate for blacksmiths has, unfortunately, stayed with us until this day.

All commercially available cooking charcoal briquettes produced in the United States by major manufacturers is a malodorous, misbegotten mixture of wood coals and miscellaneous adulterants. The most odious of these is mineral coal.

Charcoal manufacturers also load down the briquette with clay and limestone. They vehemently deny that this dross is included, just to add the weight of a cheaper material. They insist that the only reason they add it is so that we dumb and dumber backyard cooks can tell when the charcoal has ignited! The white of the incombustible limestone/clay stands starkly as the covering charcoal burns away, announcing to simpletons that the briquettes are ready for cooking. **If you**

believe this, I have some property in South Mississippi that just seems to be prone to flooding, but really would make a great investment. That grey to tan gritty residue left in the bottom of your grill after the ashes are gone is the useless clay you paid for, and, from which, you got not a single BTU of heat.

Another secret ingredient, which would be unnecessary if they left out the coal and clay, is sodium nitrate or potassium nitrate. They add this, "to make it light better." Since we are so stupid that we can't build a fire, even with a highly flammable lighter fluid, we have to have an explosive ingredient to help us. The real reason this is included is to offset the fireproof rock and clay. Potassium nitrate and charcoal, by the way, need only a little sulphur to become the classic formula for black gun powder.

What this country really needs is an all-hardwood charcoal product, mixed and shaped, for the purpose of cooking food on a grill. With any luck, we can have it. I have applied for a patent on a method of producing charcoal in shapes and densities that eliminate the problems of stacking, starting and containing all the mess. Until it is available, we need to discuss how to choose and use what is available.

The Manufacturers

There are only two manufacturers whose product is readily available nationally. The biggest player is Kingsford, the outgrowth of the Henry Ford operation, and now a division of marketing giant, Clorox. Number two, Royal Oak, a product of a Utah-based lignite (soft coal) mining company. Next in size is probably Hickory Specialties, a Brentwood, TN, company which is also the leading producer of liquid smoke. Their brand names are Old Hickory, Natur-Glow and Wild Fire. They also produce the Jack Daniel's brand, and package their charcoal as house brands for several food store chains and manufacture for several smaller labels. The charcoal operations and brand names of Hickory Specialties have recently been acquired by Royal Oak. A Royal Oak representative told me that they would continue the brands.

Choosing Charcoal

Charcoal briquettes are priced as a commodity —somebody is always running a sale at prices substantially below normal. If you know which brands work for you, that is the time to stock up, if you have adequate storage. Charcoal soaks up moisture like salt, and once saturated takes more BTU's to dry it out than it will produce. Throw it in the garden. It will sweeten the soil and probably improve the carbon/nitrogen ratio.

Since freight becomes a significant part of cost, each section of the country has local brands from small manufacturers. These vary in widely in quality, but **some may be best in the country**. The best charcoal is that which supplies the maximum hardwood charcoal per unit cost. Hardwood coals are, after all, what we really want to cook our meat on. Hardwood charcoal also lights much easier than mineral coal—especially without the worthless rock.

My first criterion is to buy charcoal which says something like, "all hardwood," or at least, "hardwood," prominently on the bag. You can bet your sweet pork butt, if it were made of hardwood, that would be boldly stated on the bag. If there are any local products which do claim to be made on hardwood, by all means check them out. When I can find a new brand which seems to offer real charcoal, I buy and compare it to my current favorite. How do you compare charcoal briquettes?

The first thing to do is to pick up the bag and shake it. If there is a lot of dust swishing around in the bottom, pass it by; you will not get many BTUs from dust in the average charcoal grill. If it passes the shake test, take it home and look at the individual briquettes.

Are they mostly whole and of uniform grain? Broken briquettes may indicate that it has an overload of clay/limestone. Irregular grain may mean that the charcoal will not burn uniformly. This is not necessarily a fault. Less compressed charcoal with larger particles will probably burn faster than denser charcoal with uniform, small particles. This is very desirable when broiling, where you need intense heat for a short time. But these are not the ideal characteristics of charcoal for roasting, barbecuing or smoking.

Logically, the next test would be to compare the BTU output of 1 lb. of your current charcoal with 1 lb. of the new. You will probably not do this, but, if you do, the easiest way is to put a quart of water in each of two cans. Let them sit for 15 minutes for the temperature to stabilize, then check and record the temperature of the water. Fire the briquettes, in your normal manner, in the grill. Record the time you light up. After 10 minutes, record the time again, and place the cans on the grill. At 10 minute intervals, check the water temperature until it begins to decline. Compare results with your current brand. If your grill is large enough and you can provide equal air flow to both samples, you can run both tests simultaneously.

The last test is to look in the bottom of the ashes and observe how much inert residue is left. This will be clay/limestone which only benefits the miners and manufacturers.

Building the Fire

In a nation where thermostats automatically light our daily fires, the art of fire starting has almost become lost. It is actually very easy to get dry charcoal started — even that stuffed with incombustible clay. The simplest, cheapest, most effective for most is the starter chimney (described in the **Auxiliary Equipment** chapter). You simply crumple a little newspaper into the cylinder, pour in the charcoal, light the paper from the bottom, set it on the fire grate and walk away for a few minutes. The charcoal will light quickly, and when it is properly glowing — **and you can see the white of the clay** — pour it out on your fire grate.

Of course you can use the stinking charcoal starter. If you must, be sure to let it soak in for 2-3 minutes before lighting. Don't dare cook on it until all the stench is gone. A cheaper, less odorous product, but still unnecessary, is odorless mineral spirits, a paint thinner.

My personal favorite, which I readily admit is not an option for everyone, is to use a handful of dry twigs picked up from under hardwood trees. Break them into suitable lengths, pile them up, stack on the charcoal and light with one match. You can collect a six months' supply just picking up the dead limbs in a walk in the park, or from a few neighborly yards.

Sometimes I help the incipient fire along, with a little cube of pork or beef fat, which I have trimmed, rendered down and poured out on a flat pan to cool. I cut those into cubes, put them in a bag and store in a cool place until needed. A salutatory side effect is that when the fat starts burning, I immediately get the delicious aroma associated with grilling.

If you are in a hurry (and I hope not, since that is bad form), the fire can be helped along by several simple means. Turning a hair dryer on the base of the coals will get more oxygen in, and get things going in a hurry. Beware of hot sparks.

Another handy tool for hastening is a propane torch. Directed at the base of the pile, the propane flame will bring the stoniest briquettes to a glowing red, in a very short time. I wouldn't recommend this as a regular habit, but it is available when you need it. Frank Boyer, President of the California Barbecue Association, starts the firewood in his giant cooker with a 150M BTU propane fired weed burner.

There are several fire-starter cubes, sticks and wads on the market with various prices and characteristics. If you use them, make certain that all odor is gone before exposing your food to the coals.

Chapter Twelve

Cooking with Gas and Electricity

As a fuel, gas is clean, convenient, economical and efficient. Gas grills excel for roasting and baking. Those that can produce 700° + of radiant heat can also broil. Except for those using ceramic, radiant heat grids, most gas grills need a heat sink of some sort. Ceramic, rock, or iron mass can absorb heat over a relatively long period and give it up quickly — when you put the steak or burgers on. Even a grill capable of no more than 30,000 BTUs can broil effectively if it has adequate mass below the meat grate and is allowed time to heat properly.

For grilling, propane or butane (bottled) gas will usually produce more BTUs than natural (methane) gas in grills because propane is delivered at a higher pressure, and therefore more gas is available for burning at any given time. It also produces more BTUs per cubic foot of gas.

Bottled gas pressure is adjustable by a pressure regulator which normally provides gas at 6.3 ounces per square inch (11 inches of water column). Additionally, with a variable regulator, the delivery of propane to a grill may be increased or decreased. I do not recommend this for those who are not fully informed of the hows and whys. But increasing the BTU output when an occasion may call for it is an available option. Natural gas is normally delivered to households at 4 ounces per square inches (7 inches of water column) past the regulator—corrected for elevation.

****

Gas Facts

Three gasses are used in cooking: butane, propane and methane. Butane and propane are bottled in their liquid phase; methane is delivered by pipe in gaseous form. Because liquid is more dense than gas, butane and propane are compressed and bottled under pressure in their liquid state. Their low boiling points cause them to make a *phase* change from liquid to gas when the bottle valves are opened. For heating/cooking purposes, methane is delivered in its gaseous state by pipe because methane gas requires tremendous pressure and cooling to change it into liquid.

Propane's (C_3H_8) boiling point at atmospheric pressure is -44° F., while butane's (C_4H_{10}) boiling point is 31° F. The lower boiling point is one of the reasons why propane is more widely used as bottled gas than butane. Natural (methane, CH_4) gas boils at -260° F.

Propane produces 2488 BTUs per cubic foot of vapor (gas), while methane produces 1000 BTU per cubic foot. The ideal air-to-gas ratio for combustion is 24 to 1 for propane and 10 to 1 for methane. That means that propane burns most efficiently when it has 24 times as much air to combine with.

Without getting too deeply into physics, boiling points rise with pressure. Bottled gas fuels are under varying pressures, depending upon the quantity of gas in the tank and temperature. Therefore, while propane boils at -44° at atmospheric pressure, (14.7 pounds per square inch [psi] at sea level) the boiling point of the liquid under 100 pounds of pressure per square inch will be much higher.

Thus, when the propane bottle is left outdoors and the outside temperature gets down below the 30°s, the propane liquid does not vaporize (change to gas) as well and your grill may not be able to produce as much heat. To remedy this, store the bottle in a heated area overnight, wrap it in a blanket to take it outdoors, and the gas will vaporize much better. An option is to wrap the gas bottle in a small electric blanket. **Do not, however, expose the tank to high temperatures.**

Propane gas is 1.5 times heavier than air, while natural gas is only 60% as heavy as air. Butane is 2 times as heavy as air. This means that propane or butane gas will flow to the lowest point available and, when it accumulates, presents an explosion hazard. Natural gas will dissipate in air and can still be ignited, but it presents less of a hazard than propane or butane because it would be less concentrated.

Typical Properties of Propane

Formula	C3H8
BTU/gal	91,500
BTU/lb. of gas	21,560
Range of inflammability: gas-air ratio*	2.15% to 9.60%
Lbs. per gal. of liquid*	4.23
Boiling point of liquid*	-44 F.
Cu. ft. of gas/lb liquid*	8.59
Cu. ft. of gas/gal. liquid*	36.5
Specific gravity of gas (air = 1)	1.53

*at 60 F and , atmospheric pressure)

****

If you have an otherwise satisfactory grill that doesn't broil well, add mass. One of the cheapest and longest lasting is a slab of cast iron or steel which sets just above the flames. It will continue to absorb BTUs until its temperature rises to the point where it can effectively radiate. It also keeps drippings from going into the flames. If it is tilted slightly to one end, the fat runs off and collects. This should be cleaned out regularly to prevent an unwanted flare up of significant proportions. If your gas bottle sets at one end of the grill, make certain that the slab tilts to run the fat to the other end. Check to make certain that the slab does not stop up holes in the burners and prevent combustion.

Another option is to pick up a few fire brick; broken ones work just as well as whole ones. They never wear out, don't rust and do their job faithfully like an old family retainer.

There are several means of adding smoke flavor to the gas grill. Some companies make ceramic briquettes infused with wood smoke. These work for a finite period. Small pieces of green or wet wood can be dropped directly upon the metal slab. Sawdust or wood chips may be wrapped in aluminum foil with a few holes punctured and placed above the burners — below the meat grill.

Safety Considerations

It is dangerous to connect a burner built for natural gas to a propane source. Because the natural gas delivery pressure is lower, the supply orifice (hole) is larger for natural gas burners than for propane burners. Therefore, connecting a natural gas grill to a propane bottle can cause a couple of unpleasant things to happen.

If not enough oxygen is available for the additional fuel to fully burn, carbon soot and carbon monoxide—a poisonous gas—will be produced. (Remember that butane requires 24 parts of air for each part of gas.) If enough oxygen is available for the fuel to fully burn, the flame will be much higher than anticipated. In either case, the results can be dangerous.

Grill orifices can safely be converted from one gas to another, even though some manufacturers deny it. They want to sell you a new grill. Some natural gas suppliers will tell you that it costs too much because they, also, want to sell you a new grill. It is a simple, inexpensive task. If you need to convert, the first step is to talk with your local gas supplier. Replacement/conversion orifices can bought for most older grills. Modern gas stoves have an adjustable orifice which I have never seen on a gas grill.

Gas flames should always burn clear, bright blue with, at most, a small yellow tip. Yellow color in the flame indicates incomplete combustion and produces deadly carbon monoxide and other polluting, but less dangerous, compounds. Normally, the problem is caused by lack of sufficient oxygen getting to the point of combustion. Most often this can be corrected by a good cleaning. Refer to your owner's manual for cleaning—but not for cooking. I recommend that the gas bottle be located so that if there were a serious flame up or a regulator failure (a remote possibility) allowing uncontrolled gas flow, the bottle valve could be safely operated. On my bottle-fired cookers, I use a 3-5' hose to connect to the bottle.

Lighting the Gas Grill

I frankly prefer to use a disposable or refillable lighting wand rather than depend upon a built-in igniter. From reports that I have received, the built-in gadgets have a very short life span.

Learn how long it takes your grill to reach the temperature for the grilling technique that you intend to use. Broiling temperatures will take the longest and, quite often, it may take longer than a small charcoal-fired grill to get ready.

When preparing to roast, bring the temperature up to 350°—or whatever the recipe calls for before adding the food. It is actually better to exceed the temperature by at least 10% because you will lose heat when you open the lid.

After adding the food, wait to see if the temperature stabilizes at the desired level before leaving.

Electric Grills

According to the 1997 Barbecue Industry Association survey, about 3% of American families own an electric grill. It may be because the market is so small that it is extremely difficult to find an electric grill that would perform as well as a 1000 W. electric hot plate in the bottom a 20 gallon metal garbage can.

Many electric grill owners are denied, by circumstances beyond their control, ownership of a gas or charcoal grill. They have my sincere sympathy.

Check the grill by turning the thermostat to the highest setting and putting a quart container of water on the grill. Close it. Come back at 10 minute intervals, open the grill and insert your trusty thermometer into the water. Record the temperature. See how long it takes for the water to boil. This is about how long it would take the grill to reach 350° if it didn't have the water in it. If it won't boil water, give it to an enemy.

If it has no thermostat, you are probably wasting your time and energy. You might check with a local electrical supply house for an in-line thermostat. They will also have replacement heating elements and hot plates.

My condolences.

Commercial quality electric smokers produce ample heat for roasting and will churn out more smoke than you could possibly need if you put in too much wood. They are not for broiling or barbecuing.

If your electric heating element dies, you can normally pick up a replacement elemnet in your local electrical supply store or just set and electric "hot plate" in place of the deceased unit. You can also convert from a charcoal burner to electricity by the same method.

Chapter Thirteen

Auxiliary Equipment

Thermometers

Even 50 years of experience at the grill are not a satisfactory substitute for accurate thermometers. Fixed and portable thermometers are essential for consistently good grilling. My first and best advice is: Never trust a thermometer that hasn't been tested within the last week. Therefore, any thermometer installed in a grill should be easily removable so that it can be tested. Don't trust the thermometer that comes installed on the grill — even when it is new. As a rule of thumb, thermometers on the average grill, are accurate for about 38 nanoseconds. My test procedure for calibrating thermometers is simple but effective:

1. Put a pan of water on the stove and fire it up.

2. Fill a whiskey glass with ice cubes and pour in 1 1/2 ounces of fine Tennessee whiskey. Don't use a good single-malt Scotch because it shouldn't be iced. However, if you have a good single-malt Scotch, you might have one in preparation for the test.

3. Carefully clean the thermometer probe, then stir the whiskey and ice. The thermometer should read below 32º.

4. While sipping the whiskey, wait for the water to come to a vigorous boil. Then insert the probe into the water — not touching the pan. The thermometer should register 212º — less 1 degree for each 500 feet above sea level.

Caution: Do not reuse the whiskey mixture for a second test. Accuracy demands that you formulate a fresh solution for each test. (I think that is an ISO 9000 rule. If it's not it should be.)

It is permissible, however, to re-use the boiling water. If you are testing several, I recommend checking the boiling temperature reading on all, then testing the freezing reading at your leisure.

Good thermometers are cheap insurance against failure. Buy industrial quality thermometers with at least a 6" probe. Since I wear out about 10 per year, I buy them in quantity when the price is right. It is always good to have a back-up thermometer on hand. If you take a reading and it doesn't seem right, check it with a second thermometer. Keep them clean and protect from sudden shock.

Remove the thermometer attached to the grill, and test as above. You can check it with a small dial thermometer that sits on the grill or, if you know the difference between the temperature of the exhaust and the temperature at the meat grate level, you can insert your pocket thermometer into the air stream, take a reading and adjust for the known difference.

Use the thermometer **first** to determine the temperature at the center of whatever you intend to put on the grill. If the center is still around freezing, the food will take a lot longer to cook. You may even want to wait until it reaches around $60°$ before putting it on the grill. If you are sharpening up your skills, take and record, readings of grill temperatures, and the center of the meat at regular intervals. This practice, alone, will teach you more about grilling than you ever thought there was to know.

While frequently checking temperatures is good as a training aid, I do not recommend it as a regular practice. Normally, I probe the center of the thickest part at about the time I anticipate it being ready to remove from the grill. Excessive probing only makes better conduits for the juices to escape.

The new digital readout thermometers are accurate, but they are slower than the bi-metal thermometers at providing a final reading. Another new product has a probe on the end of long wire. The probe is inserted into the meat and the thermometer sets outside. This is very effective for reading the internal temperature, but does not provide the temperature at which the meat is cooking.

Charcoal Starter Chimneys

If you cook with charcoal, a starter chimney is an excellent investment. They are shaped like a large sheet-metal beer stein without a solid bottom. Stuff in a crumpled sheet of newspaper, fill the chimney with charcoal, light the paper on the bottom and set it on the fire grate. Quicker than you need them, the coals are ready. Costing $4 - $10, they will pay for themselves with savings in starter fluid and eliminate all the offensive odor.

There are several on the market. Buy the one which best fits the amount of charcoal that you normally use. Make certain that the handle is adequate for the task and is well attached. Before they were available, I used to take a #10 juice can and, using the triangular end of a can opener, cut air holes around the sides and the bottom. It worked the same way, but wasn't nearly as safe or convenient.

Tongs and Turners

There are enough tongs and turners on the market to fill a good-sized catalogue. The main considerations for choosing what you need are:

1. They are strong enough to do the job. Don't ask a burger-weight tool to turn a pork shoulder.
2. They don't pierce the meat. The fewer holes in the meat, the more moisture retained.
3. Find a spatula with an opposing arm to clamp together to make burger and steak turning easier and more controllable and they are essential for fish fillets, chicken breasts, etc.
4. Cast iron coal tongs or tongs built for commercial crab fishermen are strong and large enough to handle most cuts of meat. They can do double duty for stacking and maneuvering hot coals.
5. Use the fork only for carving — after the meat is done.

Bear Claws, are handy for turning large chunks of meat. Bear Claws come in pairs and are handy for handling hot meat and excellent for pulling pork.

Knives, Sharpeners & Cutting Boards

The sharp edge is one of man's oldest tools. Unfortunately, man and his edges appear to be getting duller and duller. Cheap knives kept loosely in a drawer full of miscellaneous stainless steel utensils are worse than worthless; they are dangerous. A dull knife requires excessive effort and sets up a scenario where a slight slip can cause serious injury.

While expensive, German made, knives are all in vogue, I find them too brittle. I prefer a slightly softer, more flexible blade. Forschner/Victorineau and Chicago Cutlery are easy to sharpen, yet maintain an edge well. As a minimum, one should have a 3" paring knife, a 6" boning knife, a 10-12" chef's knife, a 14" -16" butcher knife and a thin, narrow filleting knife. Naturally, a good sharpening steel and a fine grain whetstone are essential.

Once sharpened, knives should never be stored anywhere except in a block, or fitted box, where no metal can touch the edge. After each use, wash by hand and replace the knife in its holder. Don't drop them in the stainless steel or ceramic sink and do not cut through the meat into glass, ceramic or metal.

Used this way, a knife should only need sharpening at 3-5 year intervals. In the meantime, the edge will need to be maintained. Dullness is most often caused by a deformation of a short section of the edge rather than by loss of metal. Restoring alignment eliminates the need to remove metal from the full length of the blade to correct what appeared to be a nick. To do this, draw the edge backward over the steel to roll any turned edges back into place. After the edge is straightened, hit a stroke or two on each side on the steel. Finish up with a few strokes on a ceramic rod or a fine grain, wet Arkansas whetstone. Use water, not oil, when honing. Oil retains the filings, water washes them away to allow cleaner cutting.

Whetstones should be mounted in a holder to allow both hands for handling the blade. Be aware that diamond-impregnated sharpening devices remove metal very effectively, so that the blade of a $75 knife can be quickly converted to small pile of powdered steel.

When a knife does sustain a nick, it needs a serious sharpening. Metal along the full length of the edge must be removed down to the depth of the lost metal. Done right, by hand, this can be a 2 hour job on a long, heavy blade. Some people opt to take it to a professional.

While most cutting boards these days are plastic, I still prefer wooden cutting boards at home. The thinner, lighter plastic boards are more convenient on the road. Recent studies show that feckless flight, from wood to plastic, to have been misguided. Wood has some antibacterial action, as yet unidentified, which is very effective against the malicious microbes. Whichever you use, clean them carefully after each use. Scrubbing with a stiff brush under hot soapy water is the most effective method. Dry them well before storing.

Personal Protective Devices

Working around hot coals and metal, turning hot meat, slopping sauces and grease rationally call for some forms of protection. What you need really

depends upon what you do. Gloves and hot pads are the answer to most. I have used thick white cotton gloves for years to turn ribs and roasts at barbecuing temperatures.

Overly messy folk or compulsive neatniks need an apron. Grill Sox (Tm) is a new arm protector, made of high-tech Aramid fiber, that would be very handy when doing a lot of grilling. It protects the hand up to the shoulder from heat.

Mops and Brushes

Mops and brushes are handier than a spoon for basting. Make certain that the cotton looking mop is all cotton. Synthetic fibers will melt. Before dipping it into your sauce, wet the mop well in water and wring out the excess. Wash any mop well in strongly soaped water to remove all the flavors and let fully dry before storing. Sometimes a bit of chlorine bleach does wonders.

A small hog-bristle paint brush makes a fine tool for basting or painting on a glaze. They are easily cleaned and maintained.

Injectors

Some thirty-something years ago, I began playing with the idea of injecting seasoned oil into venison to counter the lack of natural fat. I found quickly that even the largest human size syringes were inadequate. Hieing down to the livestock supply store, I found a more appropriate tool. By experimentation, I discovered that relatively small amounts of seasoned oil, pumped into scattered spots, seemed to preserve tenderness as well as add flavor.

But there was a problem: the muscles of large animals do not easily separate into neat cavities to hold a foreign substance. It took a lot of pressure just to get a little in and most of that injected was subsequently expelled. The difference didn't seem to be worth the mess and effort. If venison is not over cooked, it is most often naturally tender. I found that flavor could be more easily introduced by stuffing small pieces of garlic and onion into little pockets pierced with a knife. So I dropped the syringe in the back of the drawer of unsuccessful tools.

In the late 80s, the gentleman who invented the Cajun Injection system came by for a visit to introduce me to his new product. Like my old cow-sized syringe, it would inject flavoring, but not as much as everybody wanted to believe. Eventually, the process was bought by a large company and heavily promoted. It would probably have died a slow death except for the sudden discovery of deep frying whole turkeys.

Poultry accepts the injections much more readily than meat of four-legged creatures. Pumping seasonings into a turkey before dunking it in a wash tub of hot oil gave it a surprising burst of flavor. As turkey frying spread, so did injection.

There is now a heavy-duty injector which uses a caulking gun's lever action to provide strong force through a rather large stainless needle. I predict that we shall see a lot of pigs and poultry plumped to an unnatural curvature.

Injection is a technique under development and worth trying if you cook outdoors a lot. I find it most useful in injecting seasoned oil, lard or tallow into game and tougher cuts of beef.

Grill Cleaning Brushes

You could cook a lifetime and never really suffer for the lack of a grill brush. A rake across the top of the hot grates with a spatula and a wipe with a paper towel will normally do the job. But if you insist on having all the gadgets, they are available. Most so-called grill brushes are made of brass. This is entirely okay, probably better if your gas grill has porcelain covered meat grates. My favorite is a stainless steel, pool-cleaning brush — it has fine bristles.

Grill Screens

Screens of a fine stainless steel mesh are handy for small tidbits, like shrimp or scallops, and helpful in grilling smaller fish fillets and vegetables. There are other designs constructed of expanded steel or having holes punched in mild steel. I consider them well worth having.

Grill Wok

There is a new utensil that I have found to be very versatile and useful on the grill. It is a rectangular, wok-sided pan with holes in the bottom and handles on the sides. It is great for vegetables, shrimp and such.

Fish Holders

Some find fish-shaped, hinged wire containers make cooking whole fish or large fillets easier. Fish are less likely to break apart when turning. If you grill a lot of whole fish or large fillets, they are well worth buying and storing.

Rotisseries

Back in ancient times, when my old 'Cue Cart and Atlanta Stove Works were still alive, a close friend and cooking buddy, Pappy Pickens, became enamored of rotisseries. He turned out some "pretty good barbecue" using them. Those just discovering barbecue, need to have that translated. "Pretty good barbecue" is the highest praise that a friend can bestow upon another's barbecue. "Good as I ever tasted" and "Best I ever had" are phrases used only by food writers, raving about restaurant barbecue — which most often is not even barbecue at all.

By putting chicken halves or quarters into a spit-mounted basket, Pappy had eliminated the spitting and balancing, and balancing and spitting, and cursing and balancing, that I detested. He would hit them with his special, jalapeno-laced basting sauce occasionally, and fiddle in his garden, while the rotating chickens kept most of the sauce on their revolving carcasses. He liked the idea so much that he bought — with good reason — spit motors by the six pack.

It's true that the chicken did look sort of like they had fallen naked off the back of an 18-wheeler doing 85 mph on the interstate highway, but they tasted good and required much less attention than if they hadn't been rotating on a spit. I must add that Pappy's pit was fired to a higher-than-normal temperature for barbecuing, but because the birds were turning, they cooked at the proper temperature.

I personally found the rotisserie noisy, and a pain in the pork butt. The meat has to be balanced rather closely, or the motor will be overloaded when trying to lift the heavier side. If the imbalance is substantial, the motor may quickly burn out. While a chicken balances rather easily, driving the spit through the center of a 10 lb. sirloin tip roast is a chore — especially when you come up with an unbalanced load.

My advice is to forego the rotisserie and work on cooking technique. If the temperature is right, the food cooks just as well, and as fast, sitting quietly on the grill. Leave all the electrical cords and noise back in the kitchen.

Jacquard Tenderizers

This is another item high on my list of things I can do without. This is a creative misnomer for a gadget which looks like a short board with a lot of nails driven through it, or a scrub brush, with needles replacing the bristles. When these needles are repeatedly pounded into a tough piece of meat (read brisket) the meat is supposed to become tender. It is named after Joseph Marie Jacquard who invented a loom, about 1801, which used needles controlled by holes punched in cards to weave different designs.

In my estimation, this gadget is worth less in outdoor cooking than the effort it takes to explain it.

Chapter Fourteen

Meat Selection, Safety, Handling and Storage

Meat has long been a favorite food, highly prized for flavor and texture. Its preparation has long held man's fancy. Methods, techniques, seasonings and recipes made men and nations notable. In all societies, meat has always been held in high esteem. Only now, in this abundant land, has the value of meat been questioned, and never has it been more abundantly available.

I have no quarrel with those who choose not to eat meat. That reduces consumption and lessens the upward pressure on prices. I am more concerned that average consumers know much less about meat and its producers than ever before. Much of what is printed is erroneous or misleading. Facts are few and far between. What follows is not meant to be a nutritionist's handbook, but facts about commercially available meat.

Buying meat at regular prices is the wasteful exercise of a spendthrift. If you intend to grill often, it makes good sense to buy those cuts of meat that you normally use when they are on sale and store them properly in the freezer. That way you not only have them ready when you need them but knowing that you paid $1.99 a pound for a rib eye steak that is currently marked $5.99 in the meat case makes it all the more flavorful.

This is not meant to be a definitive book on meat, but the competent cook will learn as much as he can about the raw materials that make up his masterpiece. Therefore, I have included some basic facts about meat as it is normally sold in the US. In this, I have relied more upon information from the U.S. Department of Agriculture, than from the meat people. My attempt over the last two years to get informative photographs of the location on the carcass of different cuts has been typical. The beef people were truly bovine in their response. What I have been able to get from them are fancy photos of finished dishes or retail cuts glistening in glorious presentation. The pork people were no less porcine in their response.

Therefore, I have relied on other sources, some of them very old, some of them very new, some of it handmade, to illustrate.

Even, though the USDA is more committed to supporting the meat producers than is the general public, I find their basic information accurate, and I have shamelessly borrowed from it. They are overly cautious on cooking times, temperatures, to the detriment of taste and texture of the meat, and they are truly paranoid about thawing procedures.

Cooking times are merely rough estimates. Actual times will depend upon the beginning internal temperature of the meat, the temperature of the grill, the shape of the meat and the ability of the grill to maintain the temperature. Use these times as estimates, but check with your thermometer probe at about 3/4ths of the listed times.

General Food Safety

Let's get the safety problems covered up front. Meats may have several bacteria which, if not properly terminated, can cause unpleasantness at a minimum and have the potential for much more serious results. With common sense and a little technical knowledge, man can continue to do safely what he has done for thousands of years; eat meat. Most food-borne illness outbreaks are a result of contamination from food handlers. Sanitary food handling and proper cooking and refrigeration should prevent food-borne illnesses.

First step in food safety is to know your source. Be nosy, be particular about your source of meat. Use all of your senses. Observe the cleanliness of the market and the employees. Is the guy packaging meat hacking and coughing? When he sneezes into his hand, does he go wash it before handling the meat? When you see an employee picking up packages of meat from the display cases and taking them back inside the butcher shop, you can bet your sweet pork butt that these packages will shortly return with a new wrapper and a new date. You might just smell that new package. They didn't change the aroma of the meat.

Get acquainted with the market manager and employees, if for nothing else to get an idea of their attitude about their work. A lousy attitude makes for a lax approach to sanitation. If your state requires inspection results to be posted, make certain that you read the report and take note of the infractions.

I would avoid, like the plague, meat ground in giant factories and sold in patty form. There only a very few people in the world that I would serve that to.

Fortunately, almost 100% of whole cuts of meat are free of harmful bacteria. Harmful bacteria rarely have a natural opportunity to get into the musculature of the animal. It is only during the handling that the surface of the meat may be contaminated by humans. All of these bacteria can be killed by cooking and even their potential for contamination is contained by keeping the meat chilled below 40° until ready to cook.

Safe Handling

Once you have chosen your meat, safety is in your hands and handling. Buy meat last— just before checking out at the register. Put packages of raw meat in disposable plastic bags, if available, to contain any leakage which could contaminate cooked foods or produce.

Take meat home immediately and refrigerate it at below 40° F. If you are not going home directly, or if the trip takes more than 20 minutes, take along a cooler to store meat and other perishables. At home, don't overload the cooling capacity of your refrigerator or freezer. If you have bought a pile of meat that you intend to cook before freezing, it is better to cool some of it rapidly in the freezer than to stack it all in the overworked 'fridge.

As on any perishable meat, fish or poultry, bacteria can multiply rapidly at temperatures between 40°F and 140°F (out of refrigeration and before thorough cooking occurs). Freezing doesn't kill bacteria but they are destroyed by thorough cooking of any food to 160°F.

Bacteria must be consumed in food to cause illness. They cannot enter the body through a skin cut. However, raw meat must be handled carefully to prevent cross contamination. This can occur if raw meat or its juices contact cooked food or foods that will be eaten raw such as salad. An example of this is chopping veggies on an unwashed cutting board, just after cutting a raw chicken on it.

Storage

Meat should be stored refrigerated at 40° or below or frozen. Even at 40°, meat and meat products have a relatively short span where they retain the quality and remain safe. Use within the time period expressed in the section on each type of meat, or freeze it. Properly wrapped frozen meat will retain its quality for long periods.

Thawing

The USDA, bless their bureaucratic souls, insist that all meat and poultry should either be thawed in the refrigerator, in running water or in the microwave. A frozen 20 lb. turkey should be thawed that way because, left sitting in the sink, the exterior would warm to temperatures which would encourage bacterial growth before the center thawed. Likewise, a frozen 15 lb. whole sirloin tip could benefit from a day in the 'fridge before bringing it to the sink for 8-10 hours.

Frozen whole chickens can be thawed swiftly in water in the sink or in a large pot. Of course, if you are boiling the chicken, don't bother— just throw it in the pot. Frozen steak, chops, ribs will thaw safely in the sink. If you are, regrettably, in a rush, and the microwave has a defrost cycle, use it, but then cook the meat promptly. Microwaves, no matter how sophisticated the system, heat up some parts to temperatures that promote bacterial growth, while leaving other parts frozen.

Our protectors are adamant that meat should not be brought to room temperature before cooking. It is not only foolishly wasteful of energy to try to cook frozen food—unless boiling—but it terribly degrades the taste and texture. Frozen meat does not cook like normal meat. It should be a criminal offense to put a steak or chop on the grill which is not at least 65-70° in the center.

From a safety standpoint, I believe that it is much safer to bring chicken to room temperature before putting it on the grill than it is to risk that the still frozen center might not be cooked to 160°.

Cooking

The temperature danger zone is between 40° and 140°. Below 40°, bacteria are essentially inactive: above 140°, most of it has been killed. Bacteria on the outside surface of the meat will be quickly killed by the heat of broiling, roasting or barbecuing. It is only any internal bacteria which presents a potential health hazard. The progression from room temperature to 160° is swift enough in all techniques, except hot and cold smoking that the risk is minimal. Once the internal temperature of meat reaches 160°, all common bacteria are killed.

Those drying, cold smoking and hot smoking need to pay close attention to technique, time and temperatures. For drying and cold smoking cured foods, the cure depresses the bacteria's ability to multiply. Drying and cold smoking without a previous cure, are dangerous. Hot smoking can be a race that you do not want to lose.

USDA recommends cooking turkeys and other poultry to 185°, thus drying it out, even though they know, publish even, that it is safe at 160°. I challenged them on that. I called up the agency representative and asked, "Why?" "It tastes better," I was told. "Says who?" said I. "A panel," they said. I have wall panels that know more about taste and texture.

Pork and poultry cooked to an internal temperature of 160° are much juicier and more tender than those cooked to 185°. Beef and lamb cooked beyond 145° suffer in tenderness and texture. My advice is, "Do not let irrational fears and specious advice destroy the very tastes and textures that we so avidly pursue."

A bogus threat of cancer, resulting from nitrosamines was published a few years ago, creating fodder for the frenzy press. It has been debunked. The threat of getting cancer from nitrosamines is less than getting stoned by a meteorite. The theoretically cancer-causing nitrosamines may occur when meat fat is burned over hot coals and redeposited upon the meat. Even if this were true, it is easily preventable, but, if it weren't, one would have to eat his weight in broiled fat beef each day to reach a danger level. I suggest that one would first die of other reasons.

Nitrates, used in curing meats, came under a vicious, ill-informed attack. Nitrates have been used by man for thousands of years for curing meat. It is essential in preventing Clostridium botulinum from occurring during curing. Nitrites, which the nitrates turn into during the curing process, occur naturally in foods. In the highly favored bacon, lettuce and tomato sandwich, there is more nitrite in the lettuce and the tomato than in the bacon. Foods cured using nitrates are not recommended for infants, however, since their digestive systems are not fully developed.

So much for the fiction: let's look at some facts; these are the most common pathogens:

Escherichia coli can colonize in the intestines of animals and could contaminate muscle meat at slaughter. E. coli O157:H7 is a rare strain that produces large quantities of a potent toxin that forms in and causes severe damage to the lining of the intestine. The disease produced by it is called Hemorrhagic Colitis and is characterized by bloody diarrhea. Like all coli, E. coli O157:H7 is spread by handling and processing, but is easily destroyed by cooking to 160°.

Salmonella may be found in the intestinal tracts of livestock, poultry, dogs, cats and other warm-blooded animals. There are about 2,000 Salmonella bacterial species. Freezing doesn't kill this microorganism, but it is destroyed by cooking. Salmonella must be eaten to cause illness. They cannot enter the body through a skin cut. Contamination can occur if raw meat or its juices contact cooked food or foods that will be eaten raw, such as salad.

Staphylococcus aureus can be carried on human hands, nasal passages or throats. Most food-borne illness outbreaks are a result of contamination from food handlers and production of a heat-stable toxin in the food. Sanitary food handling, proper cooking and refrigerating should prevent food-borne staphylococcal illness.

Listeria monocytogenes is destroyed by cooking, but a cooked product can be re-contaminated by poor handling practices and poor sanitation. The USDA has a zero tolerance for Listeria monocytogenes in cooked and ready-to-eat products such as franks or lunch meat. Observe handling information such as "Keep Refrigerated" and "Use-By" dates on labels.

Trichinella spiralis is a parasite present is some pork. Humans may contract trichinosis by eating pork which has not been cooked to 137°. As a practical matter, most people cook pork well beyond that stage. This parasite may also be killed by a deep freezing process and pork so treated is labeled "Certified Pork."

Much progress has been made in reducing trichinosis in grain-fed hogs and human cases have greatly declined since 1950.

Clostridium botulinum does not occur in fresh meat. This is a deadly toxin which grows in an anaerobic (without oxygen) atmosphere. The greatest danger of exposure in meat is in smoking uncured meats at low temperatures or in cured meats, such as dry-cured sausages. By far, most cases in the U.S. result from low-acid vegetables improperly canned at home.

Infectious Hepatitis, usually called Type A, is a serious viral infection which attacks the liver. It can be spread by improper handling, but is killed by proper cooking. Another reason for not buying pre-ground meat, but for cooking it past 160° if you do.

It isn't necessary to wash raw meat before cooking it. Any bacteria which might be present on the surface would be destroyed by cooking.

Regulatory Controls on U.S. Meat Production and Processing

The U. S. Department of Agriculture (USDA) and its Food Service Inspection Service (FSIS) are responsible for carrying out the regulations regarding food safety.

Inspections

In general, all livestock and domestic poultry is inspected during the processing, either by the FSIS or a state agency with equivalent standards. If approved, each beef, pork and lamb carcass gets a stamp. Poultry may get a tag. In my studied opinion, there are not enough inspectors, especially in poultry plants and those plants processing beyond the primal cut stage, i.e., luncheon meats, wieners.

While we are passing out licks, fish and imported produce get minimal inspection. According to a recent survey, less than 1% of imported produce gets a formal inspection. Seafood inspection, except for some states, is practically non-existent.

In addition to a review of the carcass for wholesomeness, the FSIS also checks for absence of growth hormones and antibiotics. These are allowed during the feeding phase, but the animal must be taken off these drugs long enough prior to slaughter that no residue remains. According to USDA, there are very few infractions.

Labeling

In general, again, whatever is on the label must be accurate. If the label says "fresh," the meat can have no additives, but, if the meat is processed in any way, the label must list the additives.

Labeling for nutrition, lean, extra lean have specifically defined meanings which change from time to time, but must conform the definition *du jour*.

Names like "certified" and "natural" are creations of the producers, not the USDA.

"Use by" dates are not required, nor can they be trusted. Unfortunately, stores readily repackage and re-date meat. Let the Buyer Beware! Except for vacuum-packaged or fully aged beef (that you are not likely ever to see in a grocery store meat market), beef should have a moist surface that is bright pinkish-red consistent color. The bones should be pink, not gray.

Livestock is usually cut into "primal" cuts. These are large chunks such as shoulder, rib section, hind quarter, etc, from which the smaller cuts, like steaks and roasts are cut. The USDA wants the retail package to show the primal cut as well as the final cut. This gives you a little more information.

Beef, Pork and Lamb

Beef

The domestication of cattle for food, dates to about 6500 B.C. in the Middle East. Cattle were not native to America, but brought to the New World on ships by European explorers and colonists. Americans weren't big eaters of fresh beef until about 1870 when the enormous growth of the cattle industry in the west made beef more readily available. The introduction of cattle cars, and later, refrigerated cars on the railroad facilitated distribution of the beef.

"Beef" is meat from full-grown cattle about 2 years old. A live steer weighs about 1,000 pounds and yields about 450 pounds of edible meat. There are at least 50 breeds of beef cattle, but fewer than 10 make up most cattle produced. Some major breeds are Angus, Hereford, Charolais and Brahman.

"Baby beef" and "calf" are interchangeable terms used to describe young cattle weighing about 700 pounds that have been raised mainly on milk and grass. The meat cuts from baby beef are smaller; the meat is light red and contains less fat than beef. The fat may have a yellow tint due to the vitamin A in grass.

"Veal" is meat from a calf which weighs about 150 pounds. Those that are mainly milk-fed usually are less than 3 months old. The difference between "veal" and "calf" is based on the color of their meat, which is determined almost entirely by diet. Veal is pale pink and contains more cholesterol than beef.

Grading is based on marbling, which is white flecks of fat within the meat muscle. The greater amount of marbling in beef, the higher the grade because marbling makes beef more tender, flavorful and juicy. USDA Prime beef (about two percent of graded beef) has the most fat marbling; however, it is higher in fat content. Most of the graded beef sold in supermarkets is Choice or Select. The protein, vitamin, and mineral content of beef are similar regardless of the grade. Although all beef is inspected for wholesomeness, some of it is not graded. The overall quality of ungraded beef may be higher or lower than most government grades found in retail markets and can be had at a bargain if you know what to look for.

All cattle start out eating grass on the range; then three-fourths of them are brought into feed lots where they are fed high-protein feed based on corn or other grains. This penning up and stuffing of the arteries with cholesterol creates the marbling effect. All feeders are treated equally, but just like humans some are more genetically inclined to become Choice rather than Prime.

Aging

Some beef, as well as lamb and game, is aged to develop additional tenderness by allowing enzymes to soften the connective tissue and enhance flavor. If you've ever tasted fully aged meat, you will not forget the difference. Aging is done commercially under closely controlled temperatures (34-38° F) and humidity and can take from 10 days to 6 weeks. Unfortunately, in the drive for profit, speeding meat from the slaughter house to the kitchen is paramount; therefore, most beef is not aged enough. The other consideration, of course, is that beef loses 12-15% of its weight through evaporation during its storage. The USDA does not recommend aging beef in a home refrigerator, nor do I, unless you have, as I do, a refrigerator that can be dedicated to the chore.

Beef muscle meat not exposed to oxygen— in vacuum (cryovac) packaging, for example—is a burgundy or purplish color. After exposure to the air for 15 minutes or so, the myoglobin receives oxygen, and the meat turns cherry red. According to some experts, meat in cryovac packaging does some aging. The red liquid in package is not blood. Blood is removed from beef during slaughter and only a small amount remains within the muscle tissue. Since beef is about 3/4 water, this natural moisture combined with protein is the source of the liquid in the package.

One of the important proteins in meat, myoglobin, holds oxygen in the muscle. The amount of myoglobin in animal muscles determines the color of meat. Beef is called a red meat because it contains more myoglobin than chicken or fish. Other red meats are veal, lamb and pork. This myoglobin's reaction to heat and moisture is largely responsible for the so called "smoke ring" that smoke blowers and neophytes esteem beyond reason.

When beef has been refrigerated about 5 days, it may turn brown due to chemical changes in the myoglobin. If so, it may be spoiled, have an off-odor and be tacky to the touch. A smell should tell. Discard it.

Properly wrapped to protect from "freezer burn," (a dehydrating reaction with oxygen) beef can be frozen for months without appreciable deterioration in flavor or texture. The secrets to successful freezing are simple. Get ALL the air out of the package and seal it. The packaging, of course must be impermeable. The meat must be frozen quickly—starting down, at least around 5°. Don't overload a freezer. It is better to refrigerate part of the meat, freezing a portion at the time, than to overwhelm the freezer and allow large, rather than small ice crystals to form in the meat.

Retail Cuts of Fresh Beef

There are four basic major (primal) cuts into which beef is separated: chuck, loin, rib and round.

Beef Shoulder
chuck roast, steak
cross rib roast

Beef Ribs
Rib and rib eye steaks, rib roast

Beef Loin
club, t-bone, porterhouse
and sirloin steaks

Beef Round

sirloin tip, tri-tip, round,
rump and sirloin roasts

Pork

Fresh Pork

Pork is the meat from hogs or domestic swine. The domestication of "pigs" (young hogs) for food dates back to about 7000 B.C. in the Middle East. However, evidence shows that Stone Age man ate wild boar, the hog's ancestor, and the earliest surviving pork recipe is Chinese, at least 2000-years old—shortly after Bo-bo began burning down the pig parlors.

Hogs were brought to Florida by Hernando de Soto in 1525 and soon were America's most popular meat—thanks, partially, to barbecue. In the 19th century—as America urbanized and people began living away from the farm, "salt pork"—pork that is preserved with a high level of salt—became a staple food, much like salt cod in Europe. Pork has continued to be an important part of our diet since that time.

Pork is generally produced from young animals (6 to 7 months old) that weigh from 175 to 240 pounds. Much of a hog is cured and made into ham, bacon and sausage. Uncured meat is called "fresh pork." Although pork is the number one meat consumed in the world, U.S. consumption dropped during the 1970s, largely because its high fat content caused health-conscious Americans to choose leaner meats. Today's hogs have much less fat due to improved genetics, breeding and feeding. Pork is about 50% leaner than it was 25 years ago. I have had to change my basting recipes to add oil for pork, whereas 25 years ago I didn't feel that the meat needed it.

Pork is a nutritious meat providing essential nutrients like vitamins B1, B2, B6 and B12 and is a good source of the minerals iron and zinc. A 3-ounce portion of cooked lean pork contains about 200 calories, 25 grams of protein, 9 grams of fat and 70 mg. cholesterol.

Pork, "the other white meat," is classified red meat because it contains more myoglobin than chicken or fish. All livestock are considered "red meat." When buying pork, look for cuts with a relatively small amount of fat over the outside and with meat that is firm and a grayish pink color. For best flavor and tenderness, meat should have a small amount of marbling.

Retail Cuts of Fresh Pork

Pork is separated into four basic cuts: **shoulder, loin, side** and **leg**.

Shoulder
From the shoulder, comes the Boston butt and shoulder. Picnic ham and blade roasts.

Side
Spare ribs and back ribs come from the side, below the loin.

Loin
The loin section contains pork chops, bone rib roast, country style pork chops, pork loin and tenderloin.

Leg
 The hind leg, of course, is the source of ham.

Lamb

Lamb is the oldest domesticated meat species. It has been raised by humans since about 9,000 years ago in the Middle East. In many countries, lamb is the major source of meat eaten. Many Americans think of lamb as a springtime food, but it can be enjoyed year round.

Lamb is meat from sheep less than 1 year old. Most are brought to market at about 6 to 8 months old. If the phrase "Spring Lamb" is on a meat label, it means the lamb was produced between March and October, but lamb is available all the time.

Lamb is usually tender because it is from animals less than 1 year old. However, look for good marbling (white flecks of fat within the meat muscle), and meat that is fine textured and firm. In color, the meat should be pink and the fat should be firm, white and not too thick. The USDA quality grades are reliable guides.

A lamb weighs about 120 pounds and yields approximately 60 to 72 pounds of retail lamb cuts, which include bone and fat.

Mutton is meat from sheep more than a year old. It is likely to be less tender than lamb and have a stronger flavor. It takes a special talent to like to eat sheep.

Lamb is separated into five primal cuts: shoulder, rack—which is the rib section—shank/breast, loin, and leg. The hind legs are are often sold as "short leg," which means that the sirloin section has been removed. The so-called American leg has the shank, as well as the sirloin removed.

Goat a.k.a Cabrito

Although popular in many other countries, goat is a much underutilized resource in the U.S. Goats can live on grazing that would starve a sheep and which would make a cow swoon at the mere thought of eating. The goat is a much more effective converter of fodder to protein than the cow so that a flock of goats could thrive on the food required to feed one cow. The meat is not only healthy but tender and delicious when properly harvested and prepared. Young goat, known as cabrito to those of Latin American cultures, can be readily found in markets catering to those of Latin American extraction.

Cabrito, although not quite as naturally tender as lamb, can normally be cooked the same as lamb. It excels as, however, as a subject for barbecue. In my youth, barbecued goat was a family tradition. And although many decline to knowingly even taste it, many have unwittingly devoured it with gusto.

Like game animals, goat has less fat than pen-raised beef and pork. It is, therefore, healthy as well as tasty. I predict that this delicious meat will become much more popular with the grilling and barbecue set.

Poultry

Chicken

Chicken is now the number one meat species consumed by Americans. It is a descendant of the Southeast Asian red jungle fowl first domesticated in India around 2000 B.C. Most of the birds raised for meat in America today are from the Cornish (a British breed) and the White Rock (a breed developed in New England). Broiler-fryers, roasters, stewing/baking hens, capons and Rock Cornish hens are all chickens. Here are definitions for these types:

* **Broiler-fryer** - a young, tender chicken about 7 weeks old which weighs 2 1/2 to 4 1/2 pounds when eviscerated. Cook by any method.
* **Rock Cornish Game Hen**- a small broiler-fryer weighing between 1 and 2 pounds. Usually roasted whole.
* **Roaster** - an older chicken about 3 to 5 months old which weighs 5 to 7 pounds. It yields more meat per pound than a broiler-fryer.
* **Capon** - Male chickens about 16 weeks to 8 months old which are surgically unsexed. They weigh about 4 to 7 pounds and have generous quantities of tender, light meat. Usually roasted.
* **Stewing/Baking Hen** - a mature laying hen 10 months to 1 1/2 years old. Since the meat is less tender than young chickens, it's best used in moist cooking such as stewing or slow cooking as in barbecue.
* **Cock or Rooster** - a mature male chicken with coarse skin and tough, dark meat. Makes good stock.

Chicken is a healthy meat which provides a significant amount of protein. A 100-gram (3 1/2-ounce) portion of roasted breast meat with skin has 197 calories, 30 grams of protein, 84 milligrams cholesterol and 7.8 grams fat (35% of total calories).

To eliminate about half the fat, trim away the skin before eating the meat. It makes little difference in the fat content whether the skin is removed before or after cooking, but the meat is more moist and tender when cooked with the skin on. Actually, the fat cooks out and the crunchy skin of a roasted chicken is to die for.

Color of Skin

Chicken skin color varies from cream-colored to yellow. Skin color is a result of the type of feed the chicken ate, not a measure of nutritional value, flavor, tenderness or fat content. Color preferences vary in different sections of the country so growers use the type of feed which produces the desired color. A range fed chicken will have a much more colorful skin, have a lot more taste and be a good bit tougher.

Dark Bones

Darkening around bones occurs primarily in young broiler-fryers. Since their bones have not calcified completely, pigment from the bone marrow can seep through the porous bones. Freezing can also contribute to this seepage. When the chicken is cooked, the pigment turns dark. It's perfectly safe to eat chicken meat that turns dark during cooking.

Pink Meat

When testing for doneness, rubbery pink meat and pink juices are a sign that the chicken needs additional cooking. However, if the chicken has reached 160° F, the juices run clear and the meat is tender but looks pink, it should be safe to eat. The pink color in safely cooked chicken is due to the hemoglobin in tissues which can form a heat-stable color, especially in the thigh which has more hemoglobin than the breast. Smoking or grilling may also cause this reaction, which occurs more in young birds.

Color of Giblets

Giblet color can vary, especially in the liver, from mahogany to yellow. The type of feed, the chicken's metabolism and its breed can account for the variation in color. If the liver is green, do not eat it. This is due to bile retention. However, the chicken should be safe to eat.

Frozen poultry does not retain its quality as long as beef; therefore, I recommend cycling it through within a couple of months.

Turkey

Domesticated turkey is a large North American bird with white plumage and a bare, wattled head and neck and fewer brain cells than a cockroach. Its name is the result of about as much intelligence. The native American bird was so called because observers mistakenly thought that it resembled the South African guinea fowl, which they also thought came from Turkey; thence, turkey.

Although sharing a distinct deficit in brain power, the Turkey is unrelated to the guinea fowl. This dum-dumb, domestic fowl has been bred for bigger breasts, lighter plumage and smaller brains, (does that seem somehow, familiar?) from the wily, wild fowl.

SEX!

The sex designation of "hen"or "tom" (male) turkey is optional on the label, and is only an indication of size. Toms are larger but both toms and hens should be equally tender. Turkeys of either sex that are less than 8 months of age according to present regulations are considered "young" turkeys.

Ducks and Geese

The white Pekin duck, native to China, is a relative newcomer to America. In 1873, a Yankee Clipper ship crossed the Pacific with fewer than a dozen of them, marking the beginning of America's domestic duck industry. Raised so well and long on Long Island, they became known as the Long Island duck. The domestic goose, bred in ancient Egypt, China and India, arrived from a different direction — across the Atlantic from Europe, where they're immensely popular. Following is basic information on these two poultry species.

Duck

Broiler Duckling or Fryer Duckling - a young duck (usually under 8 weeks of age) of either sex that is tender meated and has a soft bill; ducklings classified as broiler-fryers weigh from 3 to 6 1/2 pounds.

Roaster Duckling - a young duck (usually under 16 weeks of age) of either sex that is tender-meated and has a bill that is not completely hardened; they usually weigh from 4 to 7 1/2 pounds.

Mature Duck or Old Duck - a duck (usually over 6 months of age) of either sex with toughened flesh and a hardened bill; these ducks are usually too old to lay eggs and their meat is used in processed products.

Goose

Young Goose or Gosling - may be of either sex and is tender meated. A gosling weighs about 8 pounds; a young goose weighs 12 to 14 pounds.

Mature Goose or Old Goose - may be of either sex and has toughened flesh. A mature goose is usually a spent breeder and its meat is used in processed products. A gander is a male goose.

Almost all ducks are raised indoors to protect from predators and to manage their manure, which is collected and used elsewhere selectively as fertilizer. Most ducks are now raised in Wisconsin and Indiana since land on Long Island, NY, where most ducks were formerly raised, has become increasingly too valuable for farming.

Geese are raised under cover for the first six weeks of life. Then they are put on the range 14 to 20 weeks where they eat grass and some grain. California and South Dakota are the main geese-raising states.

When buying whole duck or goose, allow about 1 to 1 1/2 pounds of raw weight per person. Raw boneless meat yields about 3 servings per pound after cooking. Estimate 3 to 4-ounces per person for fully cooked products.

Hams and Sausage

Hams

Curing hams is an ancient art originating around the salt beds of the Middle East, where the ancient sea beds contained nitrates as well as sodium chloride. In Greece, Homer wrote of cured hams—almost 3000 years ago. The Romans learned the secrets from the Greeks, and Cato, The Elder (also called Cato The Censor) carefully described the dry curing of ham in his treatise on agriculture, *De agri cultura,* around 160 BC. By the settling of America, the art of curing ham and bacon had become a skill which was essential to the survival of the American pioneer families.

Gone are the days when most folk cure their own hams and we probably eat less ham than our grandparents did. However, hams are plentiful and available in several forms. They can be fresh, cook-before-eating, fully-cooked, picnic and country types. There are so many kinds, let's carve up the information into bite sizes.

Definition

According to the USDA, while, the word "ham" means "pork which comes from the hind leg of a hog, ham can legally be made from the front leg of a hog as long as it is labeled "pork shoulder picnic." Makes sense to me! So called "turkey ham" must be made from the thigh meat of turkey.

Hams may be fresh, cured, or cured and smoked. The usual color for cured ham is deep rose or pink; fresh ham looks just like a fresh pork roast; country hams, tasso (cajun ham) and prosciutto (which are dry cured) range from pink to mahogany color.

Some hams are ready to eat, some are not. Ready-to-eat hams include prosciuto and fully cooked hams; they can be eaten right out of the package. Fresh hams and hams that are only trichinae treated must be cooked before eating. Know what you have and follow the directions for preparation.

Sausages

Summer sausage, kielbasa, bologna, bratwurst, chorizos, Italian and myriad other less known sausages are popular in different locations and cultures. Most of them are good fare for the grill. Until you make your own, here is some basic information on definitions, selection and storage of commercially available sausages.

Types of Sausages

Some sausages can be eaten without cooking; some need cooking. They can be made from red meat, poultry or a combination. Uncooked sausages include fresh (bulk, patties or links) and smoked sausages. Uncooked smoked sausages containing pork must be treated for trichinae.

Ready-to-eat sausages are dry, semi-dry and/or cooked. Dry sausages may be smoked, unsmoked or cooked. Semi-dry sausages are usually heated in the smokehouse to fully cook the product and partially dry it.

It's hard to tell the players without a scorecard!

Reading the Label

Let the label be your guide to sausage selection and handling. It will tell you about needed refrigeration, the nutrient content and the ingredients. All ingredients in the product must be listed by weight in descending order in the ingredient statement. Safe-handling instructions are mandatory in the U.S. for all raw or partially cooked meat and poultry products.

For sausage products packaged under federal inspection, a Nutrition Facts panel is mandatory. If sausages are made and packaged in a local store, the nutrient information on the package is voluntary or may be found out at the point of purchase. The Nutrition Facts information on the label can help you compare products and make more informed, healthy food choices. The label must say "Keep Refrigerated" if the sausage is perishable. Product dating is optional but the manufacturer may have affixed a date.

Definition of Fresh Sausages

Fresh sausages are a ground-meat food product prepared from one or more kinds of meat or meat and meat byproducts. They may contain water not exceeding 3% of the total ingredients in the product. They are usually seasoned, frequently cured, and may contain binders and extenders. They must be kept refrigerated and thoroughly cooked before eating.

Content of Fresh Sausages

* **Fresh Pork Sausages** - May not contain pork byproducts and no more than 50% fat by weight.

* **Fresh Beef Sausages** - May not include beef byproducts and no more than 30% fat by weight.

* **Breakfast Sausages** - May contain meat and meat byproducts and no more than 50% fat by weight.

* **Whole Hog Sausage** - Meat from swine in such proportions as are normal to a single animal and no more than 50% fat by weight.

* **Italian Sausage Products** - Cured or uncured sausages containing at least 85% meat or a combination of meat and fat with the total fat content constituting not more than 35% of the finished product. It contains salt, pepper, fennel and/or anise and no more than 3% water. Optional ingredients permitted in Italian Sausages are spices (including paprika) and flavorings, red or green peppers, onions, garlic and parsley, sugar, dextrose and corn syrup.

Cooked and/ or Smoked Sausages

These products are made of one or more different kinds of chopped or ground meats which have been seasoned, cooked and/or smoked. Water can be no more than 10% by weight. Meat byproducts may be used. Sausages in this category are **salami, liverwurst, hot dogs, bologna, knockwurst, bratwurst, braunschweiger and thuringer-style.**

Cooked salami (not dry) is made from fresh meats which are cured, stuffed into casings and cooked in a smokehouse at high temperature. It may be air dried for a short time. It has a softer texture than dry and semi-dry sausages and must be refrigerated.

Dry and Semi-Dry Sausages

Dry sausages may or may not be characterized by a bacterial fermentation. When fermented, the intentional encouragement of a lactic acid bacteria growth is useful as a meat preservative as well as for producing the typical tangy flavor. The ingredients are mixed with spices and curing materials, stuffed into casings, and put through a carefully controlled, long, continuous air-drying process.

Dry sausages require more production time than other types of sausages and result in a concentrated form of meat. Medium-dry sausage is about 70% of its "green" weight when sold. Green weight is the weight of the raw article before add of substances or cooking. Less-dry and fully-dried sausages range from 80% to 60% of original weight at completion.

Dry sausages include **chorizos**—Spanish, smoked, highly spiced. **pepperoni**—not cooked, air dried. **Genoa Salami**—Italian, usually made from pork, but may have a small amount of beef; it is moistened with wine or grape juice and seasoned with garlic. **Lola or Lolita and Lyons** sausage—mildly seasoned pork with garlic.

Semi-dry sausages are usually heated in the smokehouse to fully cook the product and partially dry it. Semi-dry sausages are semi-soft sausages with good- keeping qualities due to their lactic acid fermentation. **Summer sausage** or **cervelat** is the general classification for mildly seasoned, smoked, semi-dry sausages like **Mortadella** and **Lebanon** bologna.

Health Risks of Dry Sausages

Because dry sausages are not cooked, but fermented, people "at risk" (the elderly, very young children, pregnant women and those with weakened immune systems) might want to avoid eating them. Fermentation is one of the oldest methods of preserving meats. In this procedure, a mixture of curing ingredients, such as salt and sodium nitrite and a "starter" culture of acid-bacteria is mixed with chopped and ground meat, placed in casings, fermented and then dried. The amount of acid produced during fermentation and the lack of moisture in the finished product after drying typically have been shown to cause pathogenic bacteria to die.

Dry sausages—such as **pepperoni, Lebanon bologna and summer sausage,** have had a good safety record for hundreds of years. But in December 1994, some children and adults became ill after eating dry cured salami and sausages from a California plant. Illnesses reported from this outbreak are believed to represent the first time this product has been associated with E. coli O157:H7. These illnesses have raised some questions about the effectiveness of processes for producing dry fermented sausage free of this deadly organism.

Storage

All sausage—except dry sausage—is perishable and therefore must be kept refrigerated. If the sausage has a "use-by" date, follow that date.

Game

The Game Plan

Without getting too gamy, here's the game plan. First, you get some game, then you clean it quickly and thoroughly. Then you have all sorts of options to score with.

There is a slight nip in the air, the squirrels are feasting in the oak and hickory trees, and the bird feeders— and people keep asking for more on cooking game. So, it's time to cover the wilderness scene. While most of this refers to larger game animals, such as deer and elk, the same principles apply to smaller game and wild fowl.

Those who have tasted game properly prepared know that it is deliciously different— although it should not be so different as to be at all offensive to even the most delicate palate. Game animals, unlike their penned and plumped domestic cousins, have little fat interspersed in their muscles. This marbling, as it is called, is what makes beef tender enough to broil and chew without working up a sweat. On the other hand, that fat that the animal has worked to store up for winter has a rather distinctive flavor and, on most game, is removed before cooking or storing.

There are a couple of essential elements to serving good game. First and foremost is that the game must be properly treated after it is harvested. With deer, or any game animal, bleeding, gutting and cooling should be accomplished as rapidly as possible.

A gut-shot deer, dragged out of the woods, loaded on the back, or the hood, of a pickup and flaunted around the territory for several hours before gutting and cleaning is unlikely ever to be fit to eat. It is my studied opinion, however, that the idiots who do this should be forced at the point of a gun, if necessary, to cook and eat the whole carcass! Regardless of how big the rack, if you can't make any shot but the gut shot, let it go! The competent hunter/sportsman will place his shot well or decline to fire.

Immediately after the hunter has made certain that the deer is actually dead, he should sever the jugular vein and elevate the hind quarter to make certain that the deer is bled. Naturally, if he has made a heart shot with a .30-06, bleeding will not be necessary.

Second, he will cut open the abdomen, remove the organs and intestines— and, the trachea. This has two purposes. One, to remove any bacteria-bearing organs and second, to open the cavity for faster cooling. The competent hunter will deposit the tongue, liver and heart in plastic bags which he has wisely brought. True gourmets will also clean and retain the stomach for tripe in Pepper Pot Stew or Menudo and the kidneys as well. At this time, any blood clots would be cut out and, if the stomach or intestines were penetrated, any meat tainted with fecal matter— for the whole path of the bullet. The cavity should be propped open to allow air to circulate. If there is snow, the cavity should be filled with it. **(Note: Persons with sores or cuts should wear rubber gloves.)**

Next step is to skin the animal. If the carcass is warm, the skin can be separated easily by running the hands under the hide, otherwise, a sharp knife is essential. He should be extremely careful to get no more hairs on the carcass than is unavoidable. Once a hair is on the flesh, it seems to turn invisible and multiply. There will be hairs! Therefore, every time the meat is handled, afterwards, he should look for hairs. Hairs contain strong odors and will ruin the taste of meat all around.

Ideally, at this time, the next step would be to cover the carcass, cool it and transport it quickly to a meat locker where it could be aged under proper conditions for 2-3 weeks. This makes the meat much more tender and enhances the taste. As a precaution, the carcass should be marked with indelible ink!!! It shouldn't be accidentally mistaken for the one that has been hauled around on the pickup.

If there is no opportunity to have the carcass aged, it should be cut up. It is a good idea to immerse the primal cuts (large sections) in ice water to which salt has been added to chill them quickly. Meat to be frozen should be wrapped tightly in two individually sealed layers of butcher paper — expelling as much air as possible. Meat stored in plastic bags should have all the air expelled from the bag before sealing. Air oxidizes (reacts with) the meat which causes "freezer burns" and deteriorates the quality. The meat should be cooled down as much as possible before being put into the freezer. Most home freezers cannot adequately handle such an overload and it will take much longer for the meat to freeze. This will cause larger ice crystals to form and the difference is noticeable.

If you don't know how to cut up a food animal and really want to learn, call Merle "The Butcher" Ellis, at 415-383-6585 and see if he still has any copies of Cutting Up in The Kitchen. It is the best I have ever read on the subject and guaranteed to save you twice its price the next time you go on a meat buying trip.

Chapter Fifteen
Building Your Own Grill

One of the most frequent requests that I get, is for grill plans, and "blue prints" This was and continues to be, puzzling. First, in order to build a proper, useful grill, you need some idea of what it will be used for and, at least, an inkling of how to use it. Then, the function provides the basis for the construction plan, with personal preferences filling in the details.

Wanting to build a brick pit or a stainless steel grill, without knowing how to operate one, is similar to wanting to make one's debut at the grill by cooking a whole hog. It is the equivalent of starting a singing career by a booking in the Carnegie.

My advice to would-be whole-hog cookers is to do a few pork butts first. My advice to the would-be grill builder is to learn a little about grilling first. Having a stack of bricks left over from the house construction is not a valid reason to throw up a brick pit. However, you asked for it.

Essential Components

Meat Grill

The only absolutely essential components are the meat grill and some sort of supports for it with the ground serving as the fire pit/box. If the meat grill can be adjusted, in relation to the coals, such a "grill" can be used to broil, roast, barbecue and smoke. This grill can be made of expanded metal, cast iron or fabricated with iron or steel rods.

Fire Grate

A fire grate, constructed of heavier metal than the meat grill, or ceramic, allows air to flow from under the coals, improving combustion, and allowing the ashes to be removed without disturbing the coals. Removing the ashes also improves the flow of air.

Fire Pit

As long as the pit is open, receiving air from all sides, the only control of the rate of burn, which controls temperature, is by adding or removing fuel. Once a fire pit/fire box is enclosed, temperature can be varied by controlling the incoming air flow, but a means of controlling the air flow becomes essential. If it is enclosed, the pit needs a door for providing fuel and removing ashes.

Air vents

Openings for incoming and outgoing air should be large enough to permit adequate air for combustion and have a means of varying that flow. To be most effective, the entrance should be below the fire grate and the control should allow fine-tuning of the flow and be tight enough to shut it off completely if desired. The exhaust vent should also have a means for controlling flow and some means of preventing rain from entering.

Covering

Covering the meat grill, forming a cooking chamber, improves the efficiency of the cooking process and permits more opportunities for controlling temperature. Such a cover needs to be moveable, either hinged or light enough to be removed, and when closed should provide a relatively air-tight seal.

Choosing the Construction Material

Metal or masonry is a matter of personal choice, since both function well, however, a metal grill has the option of being made to be portable. Selection, most likely, will be based more on the personal tastes and skills than on performance.

Masonry Pits

Masonry pits are distinctly non-portable, expensive to build, and more expensive to operate. It takes several times the fuel, to heat up a masonry pit, as it does a metal pit. Most masonry pits wind up as flower or herb beds — a use for which they are well-suited.

The following plans, drawings and illustrations are more for examples than to provide the exact design that you may want, at this moment, in your backyard. You will most likely want to adapt or alter these plans. For that, you need some basic information

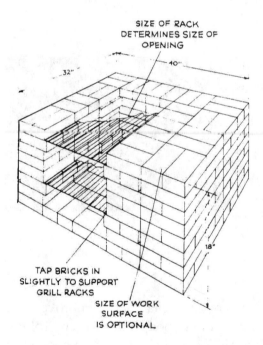

SIZE OF RACK DETERMINES SIZE OF OPENING

32"

40"

18"

TAP BRICKS IN SLIGHTLY TO SUPPORT GRILL RACKS

SIZE OF WORK SURFACE IS OPTIONAL

Masonry pits can be just stacked bricks, stones or concrete blocks or they can be cemented together with mortar. Mortarless construction costs less, and is a whole lot easier to take apart, when the time comes. To mortar, or not to mortar, is one of the first decisions that has to be made, because it effects the dimensions. In either case, the pit should be built on a suitable foundation, or slab, which is strong enough to support the weight, and which extends below the local frost line.

Common brick measures 2 1/4 x 3 3/4 x 8 inches. When mortared with 1/2" joints, the measurements become 2 3/4 x 4 1/4 x 8 1/2 inches. Therefore, if your significant other decides that she wants the top of the grill 36 inches from the walking surface, you will need 16 courses of mortarless brick or 13 mortared courses, shaving 1/12th of an inch off the total.

Fire brick, for lining the fire pit, measure 2 1/2 x 3 5/8 x 9 inches and a 3/8 inch mortar joint is normal. Regular brick can be used, but they will deteriorate from the heat. Concrete, or cinder, block measure 7 5/8 by 7 5/8 by 15 5/8 inches, so that, with a 3/8th inch mortar joint, the dimensions become 8 x 8 x 16 inches.

If you go with stone, make certain that it does not contain entrapped water vapor or you may have some unplanned explosions that could do considerable damage. The rock dimensions are, of course, random, so you will need a skilled stone mason for construction. Any plan, shown in brick or cement block, can be made using any other stone or masonry material.

If you plan to perform the work yourself , my advice is to buy a practical book on masonry construction. This is not a bad idea even if you plan to hire it done. You will be less likely to have chosen impractical designs, and should have a better idea of what to expect from the contractor.

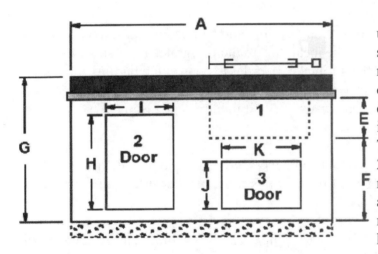

With those building units in mind, let's consider some functional measurements. The standard height of kitchen cabinets and other working surfaces is 36 inches. The normal width is 24 inches. These measurements are not accidental, but are the results of the normal human range of motion.

If you build your grill surface much lower than 36 inches, your back will tell you that you have made a mistake. If your cooking surface is much wider than 24 inches, your back and your arms will make you regret it. Reaching over the hot coals will make you wish for a GrillSox® to protect the flesh Trying to turn a hot, 10 lb. pork butt, at arms length, puts the equivalent stress of 30 lbs. on your arms and back.

If you will be barbecuing whole hogs, where the carcass will only be turned once, the extra width of the grill is not a problem. Broiling Tri-tips, weighing 2 1/2 lbs each, will make you arm weary, unless you can reach the extra width, from either side of an open grill.

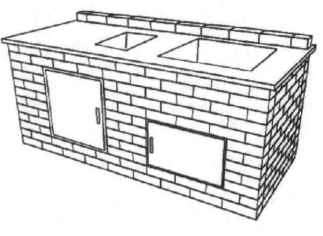

Brick structures which are to form a base, or enclosure, for a drop-in gas appliance, must be built around the dimensions of the unit, and the necessary gas piping. These dimensions will be provided by the manufacturer of the units. Therefore, if you intend to build a gas-fired grill, decide on the unit before you begin construction.

Brick grills to be used for both broiling and barbecuing must have a means of adjusting the relationship of the meat rack to the fire grate. Their should also be some means of controlling the air intake, in order to control the burning rate. And, of course, for efficiency and versatility, the grill should have a movable cover. Wood- fired barbecue pits need an auxiliary pit to burn replenishment wood down to coals.

Hinged parts, such as doors and covers, are hard to find and, unless picked up opportunistically, expensive. I have, at this time, been unable to find a reliable source for new doors and tops.

Fire grates can be fabricated, rather easily, out of re-enforcement steel (rebar) or metal gratings. Meat grills, of several sizes and configurations, can be purchased where replacement parts for grills are sold, or they can be fabricated by welding expanded metal to an angle iron frame.

This is a good time to go back to **Chapter Nine** and review the process of deciding what functions that you want from your grill or pit.

A basic broiling grill of bricks.

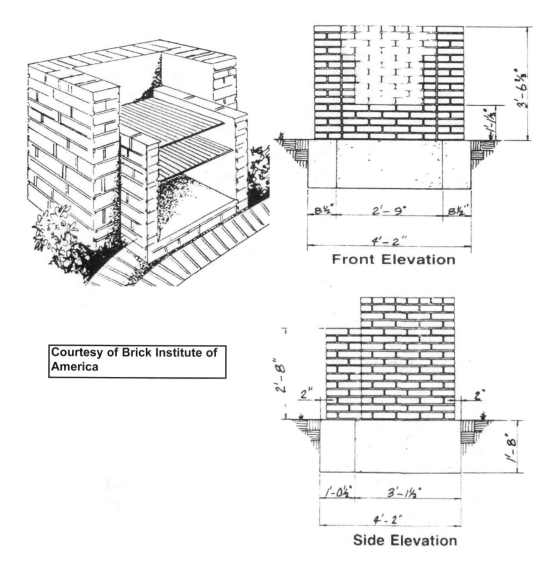

Front Elevation

Side Elevation

Whether built of brick or cement block, the critical measurements remain approximately the same. The following simple pit constructed of cement blocks. Of course, this grill may be constructed of bricks.

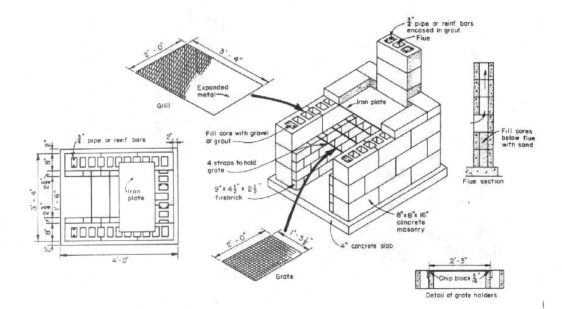

The bare concrete blocks can be dressed up with stucco and adding doors increases the grill's versatility.

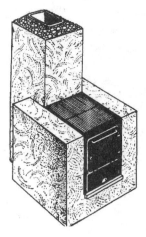

This is a basic brick grill which has been raised to a more comfortable height with additional courses of brick and a chimney added. Sited in the corner of the patio, it will be convenient for broiling, but not practical for barbecuing.

The basic functional part of the grill can be fitted into all manner and size of structures, but no matter how fancy the final construction, the functional requirements remain the same.

For broiling, the meat grill and the fire grate should between 4 to 6 inches. For roasting, without a cover, at least 12 inches and for barbecuing, a minimum of 18 inches. Although, for roasting and barbecuing the temperature can be controlled by the rate of feeding embers under the meat, this requires .such constant attention that it interferes with the essential time for relaxation.

The following is a rather elaborate construction which will satisfy those with and edifice complex, but can do no more than a smaller well designed grill.

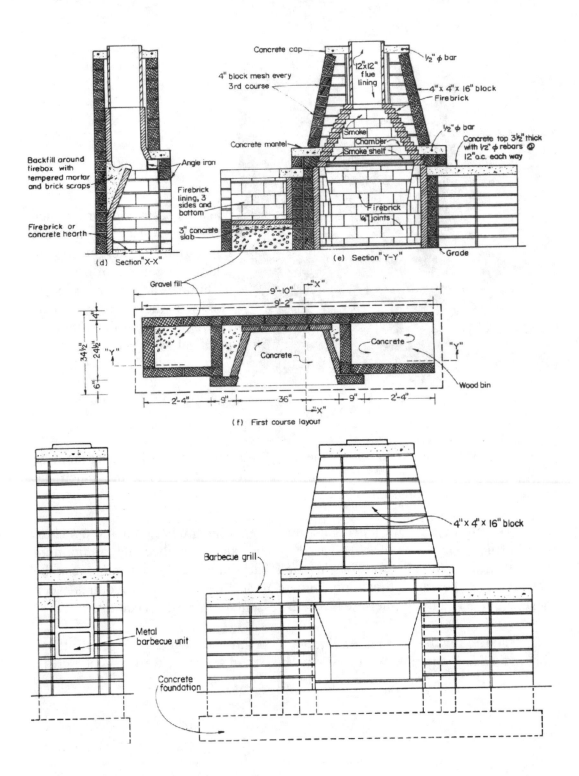

Concrete cap

12"x12" flue lining

½" φ bar

4" block mesh every 3rd course

4"x 4"x 16" block
Firebrick

Smoke Chamber

Concrete mantel

Smoke shelf

½" φ bar

Concrete top 3½" thick with ½" φ rebars @ 12" o.c. each way

Backfill around firebox with tempered mortar and brick scraps

Angle iron

Firebrick lining, 3 sides and bottom

Firebrick or concrete hearth

3" concrete slab

Firebrick ¼ joints

Grade

(d) Section "X-X"

(e) Section "Y-Y"

Gravel fill

9'-10"   "X"

9'-2"

4"

34½"   24½"   "Y"

Concrete

Concrete

"Y"

6"

Wood bin

2'-4"   9"   36"   9"   2'-4"

"X"

(f) First course layout

4"x 4"x 16" block

Barbecue grill

Metal barbecue unit

Concrete foundation

370

Metal pits

Most home-made metal pits started out as something else. The 55 gallon drum has been hacked and sawed and welded into myriad designs. Frequently used large, thicker steel pipe, recycled oil tanks and propane tanks require more work and welding skills but last a lot longer. In any case, the design and construction must satisfy the essential functions in order to be an effective and satisfying grill. The illustration "**Anatomy of a Grill**" provides the elements of a complete design, but lesser grills can perform well..

The basic, horizontal 55 gallon drum has a lid cut from 1/4 to 3/8 of the circumference of the drum and hinged. A fire grate is added, then the meat grate. An air vent is cut in one end and legs of some sort are attached. Fancier ones have a smoke stack. In just a short time, it's ready for the meat.

This Hathorn pit, which I used for illustration, is made of heavier gage metal especially formed into the drum shape and has some other features that improve the grill.

In the right side of the pit is a firebox build of heavier metal and a cast iron fire grate. This protects the grill from an early demise from rust, speeded up by high heat. Some sort of protection from excess heat is essential in the firebox of any grill. The high temperature increases the oxidation of the steel and will destroy it quickly.

The easiest way to prevent this is to provide protection to the body of the grill by metal parts which sacrifice themselves for the good of the grill and can be easily replaced.

371

No matter how thick metal in the firebox of your grill, there should be some protection, a layer of fire bricks if possible, to prevent premature destruction. The fire grates themselves will have to be replaced, even if made of cast iron.

I designed and built these one barrel and two barrel pits, to be constructed without welding. I used on a saber saw for cutting. Both of them allow the meat to be placed directly over the coals for barbecuing (the preferred relationship) with a removable fire box in the bottom. For broiling, there is an another fire grate 4" below the meat grate. The drawings included show a fire brick lining in the bottom and short legs attached.

The lower fire grate is made of expanded metal, which is economical, but will have to be replaced every few years, based on usage and care.

Either can be made in an afternoon and will cook as well as a $5000.00 custom pit.

Vertical One Drum Grill

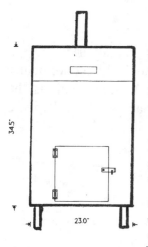

The 55 gallon drum is 23" in diameter and 34.5" high so the grates for several kettle type grills will fit nicely and rest on bolts screwed from the outside into nuts inside.

Draw the lines for the door cuts and the top cut first. Then tape the hinges in place and mark the hole centers with a punch. A saber-saw, jig-saw with couple of metal cutting blades will handle the cutting. Make a starting place with a cold chisel.

The dimensions of the top door are optional but make certain that what will be the front is directly opposite the larger bung hole in the top. That is what you will screw iron pipe into for the exhaust vent. Since the largest thing I ever intended to cook was a 12 lb. turkey, I placed the top rack 12" below the top, and cut the door accordingly. Holes for the bolts for the upper fire grate were drilled 4" below that at 16." This fire grate should be made of heavier bar stock than the meat grate or you could place a circle of expanded metal over a lighter weight grate.

I cut the bottom, fire box door 12"x12" because that seemed about right. The only critical placement is the door bottom. It should be as low as possible so the ashes can be raked out. I lined the bottom with left-over ceramic tiles. The metal removed by the blade cut will prevent an air tight fit and could be closed by bending a strip of thin metal around the cut edge. However, I found it to be just enough air space to maintain temperature at about the right level. When I needed more temperature, I opened the door. The door latch is merely a strip of metal with a hole drilled in one end for the pivot bolt and an ell bend in the other end past the latch receiver. The latch is a short section of lightweight angle iron with a slit wide enough to receive the latch bar.

The fire grate, pictured above was built by a local welder from expanded metal to my specifications 6" high, 10" wide and 18" long on 2" legs.

Two Drum T-Grill

When shooting "The Great American Barbecue Instructional Video" in 1988, I wanted to show a grill that the average person could build economically and that could perform satisfactorily for all the grilling techniques. This is the design that I came up with. I used it for years until I gave it away. My grills were multiplying and I had to make room for more.

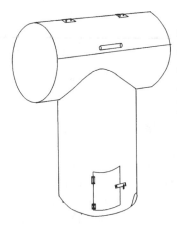

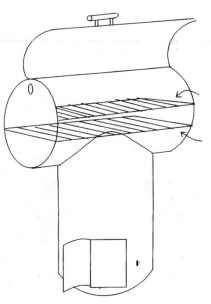

The only tricky part of the construction is cutting out the half ellipses in the vertical drum. The best way that I have found to do this is to draw off the ellipse on kraft paper, slice it down the center of the long axis and tape these to the drum and scribe them off. But, to save you time, the following drawing will allow you to cut the template very quickly. You will need a piece of sturdy paper 12" by 36." Fold it in half, lengthwise, aligning the edges top edges carefully. Draw a grid of 1" squares. Then using the template

374

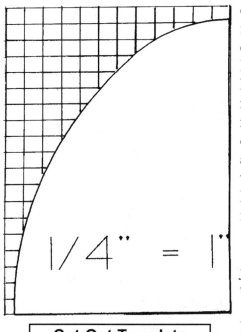

Cut-Out Template

1/4" = 1"

drawing as a reference, mark the intersections clearly on your paper and connect the dots. Child's play. Cut along that line and open up the paper. You should have half of an ellipse with the straight edge measuring 36" and the depth at the maximum measuring ll 1/2". Align the long dimension against the rolled lip of the drum and tape securely and scribe your line. Do the same on the opposite side of the drum. Lines from the two sides should come within 1/8" of meeting.

Follow the line carefully with a jigsaw blade and the two drums will fit together nicely.

Make the cut-out in the horizontal drum centered on one side, but not more than 20" in diameter, in order to leave a 1 1/2 " lip inside to attach the top and bottom drums together with screw clips. Any small 90 degree metal brackets can be used. If you are on a tight budget, cut them out of the waste. Screw the brackets to the vertical drum first with their top slightly below the top of the cut. This way, the screw from inside the horizontal drum will pull the two together tightly.

The grill top lid should be cut from the ends of the drum, leaving the lip attached to the lid, rather than to the body of the grill. As with the one-drum grill, mark and drill holes for the hinges before you cut.

The meat grate may be hinged in the rear, or removable, to permit building the fire for broiling and spreading the coals. The fire boxes for both grills are identical.

A warning for both of these designs: the juncture of lid and grill body are on top and need to be protected from rain or the grill will rust away quickly from the mixture of water and ashes.

A semi-creative guy can use the 55 gal. drum or drum shapes with smaller drums for many configurations.

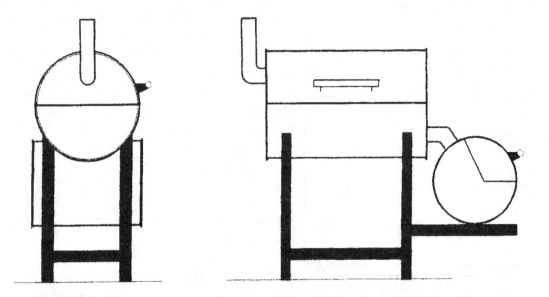

Here a 20-30 gal. drum, connected to one end of the 55 gal. drum to become the fire box. Adding another vertically at the opposite end makes a real smoker.

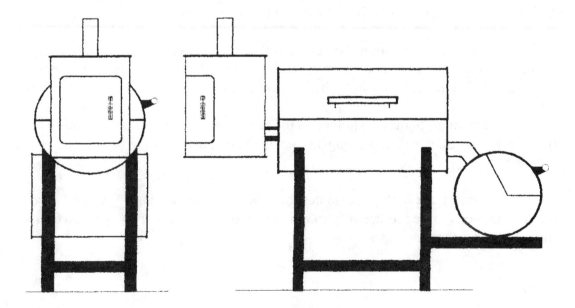

Smokers and Smoke Houses

A smoker can be made of any enclosure large enough to contain the amount of food that one intends to smoke. Hot smoking can best be accomplished on a grill, but a metal enclosure such as a discarded metal clothes locker can be converted for hot or cold smoking.

The recycled freezer illustrated on page 195 is an example of adapting items intended for another use to cold smoking. A 55 gal. drum over a hole in the ground will provide the capacity for two hams or turkeys. Smoke houses are just larger enclosures and can be constructed of wood, masonry or metal. A basic consideration is the necessity for being able to keep the temperature below 90° for sustained periods. For those who want to build a smoke house, the following is a product of the USDA from an ancient bulletin no longer in print.

The drawings depict a 6' x 8' structure of lap siding. More likely, these days the construction would be of exterior wood paneling or plywood. Oriented Strand Board (OSB), metal or masonry would perform as well. Reclaimed boards applied in board and batten fashion offer an economical alternative material.

It is important to note that the fire pit is below and isolated from the interior of the smoke house. My freezer/smoker sits up on a deck with the fire pit on the ground about 15 feet away. I think that if I were to build a smokehouse, I would probably put it up on posts or pilings unless the terrain in the planned location provided the elevation differences required for draft.

However, in the days when smokehouses were essential, and therefore larger, the smoke pit was often in the center of the smoke house. Also, most smoke houses on the farm had packed earth for a floor rather than concrete.

Like everything else connected with cooking and smoking, as long as the function is satisfied, materials and appearance are personal choices.

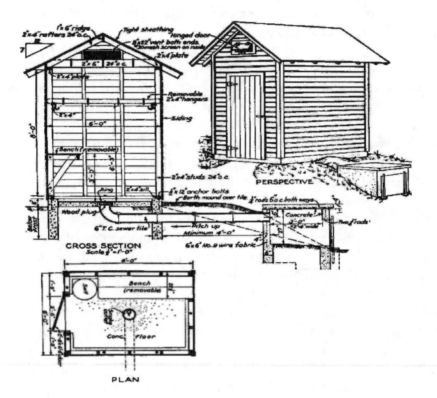

CROSS SECTION
Scale ⅜"=1'-0"

PLAN

My advice is to experiment with smaller smokers before deciding that you really need a smoke house. By then you will also have gained experience in building and maintaining low temperature fires and handling of cured meats. The final design will be one of your making, based on your needs.

Exhibit A-1   (make copy for each grill to be rated).

GAS GRILL DATA SHEET AND RATING SYSTEM

Mfg name:_____   **Model Name**:_____

Model #_____

Mfg suggested uses: grill:___   broil:___   roast:___   barbecue (*)   smoke (*)

* Deduct points from honesty index

Numerical rating: (1-10)   Grill____   Broil____   Roast____

Overall Numerical Rating:_____

Overall dimensions: Ht____   L_____   W_____

Construction

        Body (top & bottom) material_____   Thickness_____   Cast_ Welded__

Screwed_____

  Finish of exterior:_____   Interior_____

  Hinges: size ___x___x_____   Number:_____   Method of attachment ____

_____

   Door handle: __x___x____   Material_____   Method of   attachment___

_____

  Air vent below burners?___   Size of vent   Ht___   L___

   Adjustable?___ From ____2" to ____2"   Method of operation?_____

_____

  Separate burners with individual controls: 1.___   2.___   3.___

  Advertised BTU output:_____ (min. 30M)

  Burner construction material:_____.

  Clean out: All parts of burners visible and easily reached from inside?__

  All parts easily removed with normal tools?_____

  Lighting ease:_____ Piezo?__ Electric____ Flint___

  Warranty period:_____

  Heat sinks: Ceramic briquettes__   Lava Rocks___   Steel baffle__Other__

  Stack diameter:_____ Covered:_____ Damper:_____

Cooking area: Grill dimensions: Ht_____   L._____   W_____

Uses_____

  Computed usable volume in cu"_____

  Grate Construction Material:_____   Thickness:___

  Grate support method:_____   Thickness:___

  Removable:____ Adjustable up or down?____ Distance?_____

                Peripherals

  Thermometer type: _____ Range:_____ Scale size:_____

  Sideboards:_____ Size:_____ Material:_____

  Method of attachment:_____   Dimensions of attach

_____

_____

_____

Exhibit A-1 make copy for each grill to be rated.

GRILL DATA SHEET AND RATING SYSTEM
Wood / Charcoal

Mfg name:_____ **Model Name:**_____ **Model #**_____

Mfg suggested uses: grill___ broil:___ roast:___ barbecue___ hot smoke___

Numerical rating: Grill_____ Broil_____ Roast_____

Barbecue_____ Hot Smoke_____ Cold Smoke_____

Overall Numerical Rating:_____

Overall dimensions: Ht_____ L._____ W_____

Fire Box Ht____ L_____ W_____

  Material_____ Thickness of materials_____ Method of construction_____

  Finish of exterior:_____ Interior_____

  Distance from meat grill:_____ Adjustable?___ From _____ to _____

  Size of door Ht:____ L_____ Thickness:_____

  Hinges: size ___x___x_____ Number:_____ Method of attachment_____

  Door handle: ___x___x_____ Material_____ Method of attachment_____

  Fire grate?____ Ht____ L_____ W_____ Thickness of members_____

  Air vent below fire grate?___ Size of vent Ht___ L___

  Adjustable?___ From _____2" to _____2" Method of operation?_____

  Dimension of movable parts._____

  Clean out provisions: All parts of firebox floor visible and easily reached from door?__

                Bottom of door extends to bottom of firebox?_____

  Fire building ease:_____

  Replenishment/ maintain requirements:_____

  Stack diameter:_____ Covered:_____ Damper:_____

Cooking area:

  Grill dimensions: Ht_____ L._____ W_____ Uses_____

  Computed usable volume in cu"_____

  Grill dimensions: Ht_____ L._____ W_____ Uses_____

  Computed usable volume in cu"_____

  Grill dimensions: Ht_____ L._____ W_____ Uses_____

  Computed usable volume in cu"_____ Computed usable volume in cu"_____

  Computed usable volume in cu"_____

  Grate Construction Material:_____ Thickness:___

  Grate support method:_____ Thickness:___

  Removable:_____ Adjustable up or down?_____ Distance?_____

  Peripherals

    Thermometer type: _____ Range:_____ Scale size:_____

    Sideboards:_____ Size:_____ Material:_____

    Method of attachment:_____ Dimensions of attach:_____

_____

_____

Appendix B - Constituents of Wood Smoke

1993 EPA Report, A Summary of the Emissions Characterization and Non respiratory Effects of Wood Smoke. EPA-453/R-93-036 It can be ordered from the EPA.

Chemical Composition of Wood Smoke

Species	g/kg wood	Species	g/kg wood
Carbon Monoxide	80-370	Phenanthrene	2×10^{-5} -3.4×10^{-2}
Methane	14-25	Anthracene	5×10^{-5} -2.1×10^{-5}
VOCs (C2-C7)	7-27	Methylanthracenes	7×10^{-5} - 8×10^{-5}
Aldehydes	0.6-5.4	Fluoranthene	7×10^{-4}- 4.2×10^{-2}
Formaldehyde	0.1-0.7	Pyrene	8×10^{-4} -3.1×10^{-2}
Acrolein	0.02-0.1	Benzo(a)anthracene	4×10^{-4} - 2×10^{-3}
Propionaldehyde	0.1-0.3	Chrysene	5×10^{4}- 1×10^{-2}
Butryaldehyde	0.01-1.7	Benzofluoranthenes	6×10^{-4}- 5×10^{-3}
Acetaldehyde	0.03-0.6	Benzo(e)pyrene	2×10^{4} - 4×10^{-3}
Furfural	0.2-1.6	Benzo(a)pyrene	3×10^{4}- 5×10^{-3}
Substituted Furans	0.15-1.7	Perylene	5×10^{-5} - 3×10^{-3}
Benzene	0.6-4.0	Ideno(1,2,3-cd)pyrene	2×10^{-4}- 1.3×10^{-2}
Alkyl Benzenes	1-6	Benz(ghi)perylene	3×10^{-5}- 1.1×10^{-2}
Toluene	0.15-1.0	Coronene	8×10^{-4}- 3×10^{-3}
Acetic Acid	1.8-2.4	Dibenzo(a,h)pyrene	3×10^{4}- 1×10^{-3}
Formic Acid	.06-0.08	Retene	7×10^{-3} - 3×10^{-2}
Nitrogen Oxides (NO,NO2)	0.2-0.9	Dibenz(a,h)anthracene	2×10^{-5} - 2×10^{-3}
Sulfur Dioxide	.16-0.24	Trace Elements	
Methyl chloride	.01-0.04	Na	3×10^{-3} - 1.8×10^{-2}
Napthalene	0.24-1.6	Mg	2×10^{-4} - 3×10^{-3}
Substituted Napthalenes	0.3-2.1	Al	1×10^{-4} - 2.4×10^{-2}
Oxygenated Monoaromatic	1 - 7	Si	3×10^{-4} - 3.1×10^{-2}
Guaiacol (and derivatives)	0.4-1.6	S	1×10^{-3} - 2.9×10^{-2}
Phenol (and derivatives)	0.2-0.8	Cl	7×10^{-4} - 2.1×10^{-2}
Syringol (and derivatives)	0.7-2.7	K	3×10^{-3} - 8.6×10^{-2}
Catechol (and derivatives)	0.2-0.8	Ca	9×10^{-4} - 1.8×10^{-2}
Total Particle Mass	7-30	Ti	4×10^{-5} - 3×10^{-3}
Particulate Organic Carbon	2-20	V	2×10^{-5} - 4×10^{-3}
Oxygenated PAHs	0.15-1	Cr	2×10^{-5} - 3×10^{-3}
PAHs		Mn	7×10^{-5} - 4×10^{-3}
Fluorene	4×10^{-5} -1.7×10^{-2}	Fe	3×10^{-4} - 5×10^{-3}
		Ni	1×10^{-6} - 1×10^{-3}
		Cu	2×10^{-4} - 9×10^{-4}

Zn	7×10^{-4} - 8×10^{-3}
Br	7×10^{-5} - 9×10^{-4}
Pb	1×10^{-4} - 3×10^{-3}
Particulate Elemental Carbon	0.3 - 5
Normal alkanes (C24-C30)	1×10^{-3} - 6×10^{-3}
Cyclic di-and triterpenoids	
Dehydroabietic acid	0.01 - 0.05
Isopimaric acid	0.02 - 0.10
Lupenone	2×10^{-3} - 8×10^{-3}
Friedelin	4×10^{-6} - 2×10^{-5}
Chlorinated dioxins	1×10^{-5} - 4×10^{-5}
Particulate Acidity	7×10^{-3} - 7×10^{-2}

1 Some species are grouped into general classes as indicated by italics

2 To estimate the weight percentage in the exhaust, divide the g/kg value by 80. This assumes that there are 7.3 kg combustion air per kg of wood.

Major species not listed here include carbon dioxide and water vapor (about 12 and 7 weight % respectively under the assumed conditions

3 At ambient conditions; V = vapor, P = particulate, and VIP = vapor and/or particulate (i.e., semi-volatile).

4 DeAngelis (1980)

5 OMNI (1988)

6 Lipari (1984), Values for fireplaces

7 Edye et al (1991). smoldering conditions; other substituted furans include 2-furanmethanol, 2 acetylfuran, 5 methyl-2furaldehyde, and benzofuran

8 Value estimated for pine from Edye et al (1991) from reported yield relative to guaiacol, from guaiacol values of Hawthorne (1989) and assuming particulate organic carbon is 50% of total particle mass

9 Steiber et al (1992), values computed assuming a range of 3-20 g of total extractable, speciated mass per kg wood

10 Khalil (1983)

11 Hawthorne (1989), values for syringol for hardwood fuel; see also Hawthorne (1988)

12 Core (1989), DeAngelis (1980), Kalman and Larson (1987)

13 From one or more of the following studies: Cooke (1981), Truesdale (1984), Alfheirn et al (1984), Zeedijk (1986), Core (1989), Kalman and Larson (1987); assuming a range of 7 to 30 grams of particulate mass per kg wood when values were reported in grams per gram of particulate mass. Similar assumptions apply to references 14,15 and references 17-19

14 Core (1989), Kalman and Larson (1987)

15 Watson (1979), Core (1989), Kalman and Larson (1987)

16 Rau (1989), Core (1989)

17 Core (1989)

18 Standley and Simoneit (1990); Dehydroabietic acid values for pine smoke, lupenone and isopimaric acid values for alder smoke and friedlin values for oaf: soot.

19 Nestrick and Lamparski (1982), from particulate condensed on flue pipes; includes TCDDs, HCDDs, H7CDDs and OCDDS

Gas Grill Maintenance and Repair

A majority of grills have grill bodies made of cast aluminum which has traditionally been used because of its resistance to rust and it's ability to hold and distribute heat evenly. Aluminum castings are very durable and often come with 10 year to lifetime guarantees. The quality of the casting varies by thickness and grade of aluminum. Also available are porcelainized steel and stainless steel grill bodies which offer a high level of rust resistance while sacrificing some grill efficiency.

1.   The Body

* Inside the grill - Food grease is extremely corrosive and should be periodically cleaned from the grill. Use a putty knife to scrape and remove accumulated grease, and vacuum the inside of the grill. Left unattended over a period of time, these food acids will actually corrode away the bottom of the grill. Do not use a putty knife on porcelainized surfaces, as this will damage the porcelain and expose the steel to the corrosive food greases.

* White spots - Aluminum is resistant to rust, but extreme temperatures and weathering may cause oxidation to form white spots. It has been our experience that the use of a grill cover will minimize, but not eliminate this problem. Oil or polish will help the situation (see below).

* General cleaning - Use a mild soap and water and wash the grill as you would your car.

* Vegetable oil - A light coating of oil applied with a soft rag will add luster and offer protection to the outside of the castings. Heavier coatings of vegetable oil will have a tendency to build up and appear sticky. Coat the inside of the grill when it is new or when it is clean to give it extra protection from food acids.*** Stove polish** - Is available as a liquid or paste and can be applied with a soft cloth. The polish contains black pigments which will revitalize the finish by adding color, and the wax offers protection from the weather.

* To refinish castings - (body)

> 1. Clean the exterior to remove burned on grease and oils.
> 2. Lightly sand with steel wool, medium emery paper or fine sandpaper.
> 3. Clean off residue with a vinegar and water solution. This neutralizes the finish. Rinse with clear water.

4. Once dry, paint with a high temperature paint. These paints can withstand very high temperatures, and are commonly available where other paints are sold.

5. High temperature paints are cured by heat. After the paint has thoroughly dried, bake it on, by operating grill for 15 minutes on a medium heat.

* **Glass windows** - The glass can be cleaned using a water and ammonia mixture. Windex or other glass cleaners will also work. Abrasive cleaners and pads will scratch the glass surface. Never attempt to clean the glass when it's hot, and do not use cleaners containing lye or oven cleaner. If the glass is removed to clean, be sure to allow a loose fit in the frame which gives the glass room for expansion when heated.

2.   Cooking Grids

Cooking grids come in a variety of styles and materials. The most common are chrome plated and porcelainized rod. Also available, are cast iron, porcelainized cast iron, stainless steel and porcelainized steel. Many grills are also equipped with a warming rack that rests above the primary cooking surface which can be used for both keeping foods warm and as a cooking area when using an indirect method of cooking.

* **Chrome plated** - Generally the least expensive cooking grids. They are subject to rusting and food sticking; however, they should provide several years of satisfactory service. Warming racks are generally chrome plated.

* **Porcelain coated rod** - Their shiny black or gray porcelain coating makes these cooking grids easier to clean and helps prevent the food from sticking. Care must be taken not to chip the porcelain coating which will expose the steel rod and allow rusting. A soft brass bristled brush should be used to clean the grids. Scraping will damage the coating. Porcelain coated grids vary in quality by the thickness of the rod and the thickness of the porcelain coating.

* **Stainless steel** - Offering excellent rust resistance, these grids generally have a wide configuration, allowing easy food-handling and providing wide sear marks. They cool easily, and meats may have a tendency to stick.

* **Cast iron** - Offering the most mass, these grids have excellent searing capabilities, as they retain their heat the longest. They are available with or without a porcelain coating, and because they are so heavy, should last for many years. Non-porcelainized cast iron grids require curing with vegetable oil in a manner similar to curing a cast iron frying pan.

Maintenance Hints.....

* **Cleaning** - Cooking grids can be cleaned by heating them in the grill with the lid closed, much like using a self cleaning oven. A layer of aluminum foil ove the grids will help concentrate the heat. Do not overheat your grill, and do not leave your grill unattended. A maximum of 5 to 10 minutes on HIGH is recommened by most grill manufactures. After baking, brush the loose residue from the grid s with a brass bristled brush. If desired, they can then be cleaned with a mild soap and water.

* **Vegetable oil** - Coat the cooking grids with vegetable oil before cooking. This helps prevent the food from sticking and makes cleaning easier.

* **Rusting** - There is no fix for chipped away porcelain and rusting food grids . Clean away rust and coat with vegetable oil. Do not paint cooking grids or any cooking surface.

3.   **Lava Rock, Briquettes and Heat Plates**

Directly above the burner, the gas grill will generally have a rock grate which is designed to hold a layer of lava rock or ceramic briquettes. This has the dual purpose of spreading the heat from the burner uniformly over the cooking surface of the grill and vaporizing food drippings to give food it's grilled flavoring. Also available are a variety of styles of heat distribution plates which come in a wide variety of materials and designs.

* **Lava Rock** - The most common and least expensive alternative. The light density of the rock offers quick heating with good distribution. It is very porous, which allows grease and char to build-up, and should be changed yearly or when saturated. When not changed or burnt-off regularly, "rock" catches fire causing extreme flare-ups and out of control cooking situations.

* **Pumice Stone** - Similar to lava rock, offering the same quality heat distribution, pumice stone has a less porous surface at a slightly higher cost. The less porous surface allows the stone to be baked off more thoroughly for fewer flare-ups.

* **Ceramic Briquettes** - Baked ceramic briquettes come in a wide variety of shapes and sizes. They are self-cleaning by allowing the heat from the burner flame to bake them clean. Cone or pyramid shapes are designs to allow the grease to roll off without build-up. Replacement is necessary after eventual weakening and crumbling of briquettes. They carry the highest initial cost and vary in cost and quality by the degree of hardness. Through their uniform shape and size, they offer superior heat distribution.

* **Heat distribution plates** - Designed to reduce flare-ups, these plates can be made of aluminized steel, stainless steel, porcelainized steel or cast iron. They concentrate the heat more than lava rock or briquettes; therefore, requiring lower control settings. The plates have holes or slots that are configured to allow heat to rise evenly through the plate as the plate radiates heat to the cooking surface above. Food drippings are burnt and vaporized as they contact the hot plate.

4. **Burners**

The burner is the heart of the barbecue and is subject to great abuse from corrosive food acids, high temperatures and moisture. Although it is common that burner replacement becomes necessary during the life of the grill, burner life can be greatly extended by periodic maintenance and cleaning. In addition, frequent use will actually extend burner longevity by burning away moisture and food acids.

* **Burner shape** - Burners come in a variety of shapes, styles and materials and are described and referred to generally by their shape as viewed from the top. For example, the most common being the H-Burner which is shaped like the letter H, the oval burner which is oval shaped and the bar burner in the shape of a long thin bar. Burner shape or configuration effects the distribution of the flame and uniformity of the heat across the cooking surface. Because combustion air holes molded into the bottom of the castings follow the actual contour of the burner , replacement burners must be of the same shape and configuration as the original.

* **Materials** - Different materials are used in burner construction with some mate rials being more resistant to corrosion than others. All warranty periods below are generally given by the grill manufacturers for the types of material listed. Individual warranties vary greatly among manufacturers and burner life is great ly dependent upon usage, maintenance and environment.

o Aluminized Steel - A galvanized type steel, which is commonly used in lower end grills and sometimes carries a 3- year warranty.

o Porcelain Coated Steel - A baked on porcelain enamel finished steel. Generally carries a 3-year warranty.

o Stainless Steel - The most common material used and can be found in low end through upper end grills. There are different grades of stainless steel, in addition to different gauges or thickness. Warranties range from 3 to 5 years.

o Cast Iron - Solid molded cast iron. Usually carries longer warranties with some up to 10 years. Cast iron is subject to drying and flaking and should be oiled and maintained to enjoy full life expectancy.

o Cast Brass - Solid molded cast brass. The least common burner, only available on several distinct models of upper end grills. They carry the longest warranty, with some up to 15 years.

* Cleaning - Wire brush the burner exterior to remove loose corrosion and excessive residue. Clean clogged gas holes with an opened paper clip. Check burner assembly for corrosion damage or any opening that would emit excess air. Replace corroded or damaged burners.

* Burner Flame -

o New Burner - A new burner may give excessive yellow flame while burning off oils used in manufacturing. After breaking in a new burner and once the oil has burnt away, check the burner flame.

o Inspection - Caution: Grill hood must always be open when lighting. With the grill lid closed and the cooking surfaces in place, observe the burner's flame from below the grill bottom and looking through the air supply holes. A good flame would be blue with some yellow tip coming from the burner holes. There should not be an excessive gap between the flame and the burner. Some yellow tips on flames extend up to 1" in length are acceptable as long as no carbon or soot deposits appear.

o Adjusting Flame - If flames are excessively yellow and irregular, the oil residue may not be completely burnt off, the venturi may not be properly positioned over the orifice or the venturi shutters may not be properly adjusted.

To Adjust Shutters:
1. Loosen screw to air shutter and close shutter.
2. Open slowly until flame is free of yellow. Do not open any further than required.
3. Shut off gas and tighten adjustment screw.
4. Allow grill to cool before proceeding

5.   **Venturi Tubes**

The venturi tubes are the tubes that extend from the burner to the control valves. These have openings at the ends to allow air to mix with the gas as it leaves the control valve. Generally, they are fitted with moveable shutters that allow for air mixture adjustment and with spider guards or small screening to discourage spiders and insects from entering. While checking the venturi, also look for rust. Corrosion starts at the top of the burner, and usually at the seams where food acids accumulate. If the burner is left unattended and not replaced at an appropriate time, the rust will eventually work its way down under the burner to where the venturis attach, requiring venturi replacement.

* **Bugs** - Commonly, spiders and small insects will spin webs or build nests inside the venturi tubes. This especially occurs in late summer and fall before frost, when spiders are most active. These nests can obstruct gas flow and cause a fire in and around the valve at the control panel. Such a fire can cause operator injury and serious damage to your grill. To help prevent a blockage and ensure full heat output, clean and inspect venturi tubes often.

* **Spider Guards** - Screening is often built into the venturi openings to act as a spider guard. Spider guards can be fabricated by wrapping small sections of aluminum screen around the venturi openings and securing with small gauge wire to keep the screens in place. The guards should be cleaned periodically to keep dust from blocking air openings.

1. Remove burner assembly from grill.
2. Look inside lower end of venturi tubes for insect nests, cobwebs or wasp mud.
3. To remove insect nests, cobwebs or wasp mud, use an accessory flexible venturi brush, or bend a small hook on one end of a 20 inch long flexible wire.
4. Use the brush or wire to remove the obstructions from the venturi tubes.
5. Inspect and clean burner if needed.
6. Replace the burner assembly into the grill.
7. Make sure valve orifices are inside venturi tubes.
8. Secure burner to grill.

NOTE: These tubes do not mechanically attach to the valve. Be sure that the valve orifice extends at least 1/4 of an inch into the venture tube.

* **Adjustment** - Moveable shutters are a part of most venturi tubes and have a locking screw which when loosened allows the shutter to be rotated, controlling the air and gas mixture and subsequently the burner flame. Some venturi tubes are factory set and have no means of adjustment.

Twist-lock venturis.

Featured on Sunbeam and new model Charmglow grills, the twist-lock venturi is designed for ease of installation and assembly. The venturis are mounted by placing the venturi into the inlet on the burner and twisting the venturi to a perpendicular position. At that point, there are two small metal lips on the venturi that lock the venturi into place causing a secure seal. It is common that these lips will corrode which will inhibit the venturi from locking securely into place. Although burners of this type are shipped with a collector plate giving additional support to the venturis, we recommend replacement if the locking lips on the venturis show signs of rust .

Flange mount venturis.

The flange mount is the most common type of venturi and has a mounting flange that attaches with two screws or nuts. There is a gasket that goes between the flange and the burner which gives a secure seal. Pitting and rusting of the flange surface may allow gas to escape between the gasket and the flange. If this surface is corroded, we recommend replacement of the venturi. As an added note, universal venturis may not fit on original equipment burners because of a difference in the hole pattern on the flange.

6.   Ignitor Systems

Ignitor systems most commonly consist of a gas collector box, ceramic electrode, wire and ignitor push button. Contrary to popular belief, these ignitor systems are highly dependable and should provide several years of dependable performance. Most ignitor problems that we have encountered are actually burner related problems or a result of excessive grease and char buildup.

* **How they work**. When the gas is turned on at the control knob it begins to flow to the burner and escapes through the burner ports. As the gas escapes, it accumulates in the collector box and is ignited by an electric spark generated when the ignitor push-button is activated.

***Testing**. With the gas shut off, watch the electrode tip inside the gas collector while activating the ignitor. It may be necessary to use a small hand mirror to see inside the collector box. A spark should jump from the electrode tip to the collector box or from the electrode tip to the burner for burner mounted electrodes. If you are getting spark and the grill still will not light, check the venturis for blockage. Gas escaping at the venturis may catch fire at the control valves.

No spark.....

o Check the wire connections for corrosion or looseness. Operate the pushbutton   while watching the connections from the underside of the grill to assure the spark isn't jumping from a connection to the grill body.

o There should be a 2" clearance between the wire and the grill body.

o Check that the electrode isn't cracked or broken. It is normal for the wire to fit loosely in the porcelain.

o Greasy electrode? The spark will track through the grease to the grill body. If this happens, replacement is required.

o Dirt and rust on the electrode wire tip, or the metal surface that accepts the spark, can prevent the electrode from sparking. Remove rust by lightly sanding with emery cloth or fine sandpaper.

o Check that the burner ports are not clogged and possibly preventing gas to enter the collector box.

o The locking nut on the push-button serves as an electrical ground. Loosen it first and re-tighten to assure a good connection.

On models with side burners, check the spark gap on the side burner, along with the main electrode. Both electrodes are in series, which means that if the side burner electrode spark gap is too large, neither electrode will spark. To adjust side burner electrode, first try positioning the electrode closer to the burner. Use caution if trying to bend the electrode wire closer. The porcelain electrode is fragile and will break if bent near the tip.

7.   **Control Valves**

The control valves supply and regulate the gas flow to the burner. These valves have a spring-loaded locking feature and are designed to lock into place when the valve is in the OFF position. The valve must be depressed, by pushing in the control knob while turning to the ON position. If a problem occurs with the valve lock not releasing, check that the valve stem extends sufficiently from the control panel and is allowing full depression of the control knob which releases the locking device.

* Repair parts - Individual repair parts for control valves are not available. Replacement is necessary if a control valve becomes broken or frozen, and replacements for some models are available individually, or may occasionally require replacement as a set. Valve configuration varies widely between makes and models of gas grills and must be ordered specifically for your make and model of grill.

* **Orifice cleaning** - The valve orifice is an integral part of the control valve. Orifices on the valves will sometimes plug from either insects invading through the venturi or from debris inside the supply line. Orifices can be removed for cleaning. Use an orifice cleaning tool or small wire to clear orifice hole. Use caution not to scratch or damage the orifice hole. Do not operate grill without orifice in place. This poses an extremely dangerous fire hazard.

* **Orifice size** - The orifice, in conjunction with the control valve, acts to regulate and restrict the amount of gas delivered to the burner. The hole size in the orifice varies by the gas supply pressure and by the BTU rating of the burner. Grills equipped for LP gas operate at a much higher gas pressure, and therefore have a smaller size orifice.

* **Conversion kits** - Conversion kits are available for changing the grill gas supply from propane to natural gas for some brands of grills. Generally included in the kit are proper sized orifices, a flexible hose and quick connect assembly.

* **Knobs** - Control knobs vary greatly between grill brands. The variances are the knob shaft length, clockwise and counter clockwise bezel and the OFF position. Original equipment knobs guarantee a proper fit and indication. In addition, universal replacement knobs are available that can be set up for most brand grills.

8.   **Pressure Regulator and P.O.L. Valve**

All LP grills are equipped with a pressure regulator which attaches between the grill control valves and the LP cylinder. The pressure output of the tank is much greater than the pressure required to operate the grill, and the regulator reduces this pressure to a workable level. A regulator must be used in conjunction with an LP tank or the risk of explosion will occur. The P.O.L. valve is the connector that goes between the regulator and the tank. New model grills are equipped with a new style P.O.L. valve that is connected to the LP tank with a large Acme type nut.

* **Adjustment** - The regulator is factory set at a specified outlet pressure of 11 inches of water column and is generally factory sealed and not adjustable. Do not try to adjust. The regulator can be checked by measuring the pressure with a manometer.

* Inspection

o Vent hole - There is a vent hole on top of the regulator. Check that it is clear of dirt and debris. If the hole is plugged, erratic and dangerous burning may result.

o O-ring seal - Before attaching the regulator to the cylinder, inspect the rubber O-ring on the P.O.L. fitting. Do not operate the grill if the O-ring is damaged or missing. Seal damage is common, and we recommend replacement of the seal when the burner is replaced or when the seal is damaged. Cracks, splits or distortion will allow gas to escape. Additionally, the seal should be soft, pliable and protrude slightly from the brass P.O.L. valve.

o Chew marks - Critters like good barbecue too! The hose should be kept clean of grease and food drippings which attract squirrels and other animals. The animals will often eat the drippings on the hose and chew into the hose lining trying to get the last taste. Try cleaning the hose with an ammonia cleaner solution to minimize the attraction.

* Test for leaks -
1. Mix a 50/50 solution of liquid dish soap and water.
2. Connect the LP cylinder.
3. Make sure the control valves are OFF.
4. Brush the soap solution over the P.O.L. valve and all piping and hose connections.
5. Turn on the cylinder valve and listen for leaks, and look carefully for soap bubbles being formed at the connections which indicates leaks.

9.   LP Gas Supply Cylinder

LP Gas is short for Liquefied Petroleum Gas. Also called propane or bottled gas, LP gas is highly flammable. It becomes liquid when stored under high pressure inside a cylinder and vaporizes when released.

* **Tank level-** The best way to tell cylinder level is by the weight of the cylinder. Standard cylinder capacity is 20 lb. of propane. Full cylinder weight should be approximately 38 pounds. A full tank is heavy! Accessory options are available which will measure gas flow and give a tank level indication.

* **Connecting the tank-** The standard style valve outlet is a left-hand thread and tightens in a counter-clockwise rotation. Likewise, turning the hex nut clockwise disconnects the P.O.L. valve or regulator assembly.

* Filling the cylinder- Not a self-service operation! The LP dealer will have a qualified person available to run the equipment that fills the LP Tank.

NOTE: A cylinder POL plug should always be used in the cylinder valve outlet when the cylinder is being transported and when the cylinder is not connected to the grill. The cylinder should not be stored in a building, garage or any other enclosed area. Store outdoors in a well ventilated area.

* Tank age- The date manufactured is stamped into the guard surrounding the cylinder valve. (This guard also acts as the carrying handle.) Cylinders should be re-certified after 12 years from this date. Re-certification can generally be done by a local propane distributor. The charge is $5 to $10, and the tanks are tagged and certified for another 5 year period.

* Rusty tank- Cylinders can be repainted with a rust preventative type paint. Remove loose rust with sandpaper or steel wool, and clean away any grease or oils. Do not paint valve assembly and do not paint over warning labels. Mask off valve assembly and warning labels if using spray paint. Use white, or off-white paint with the color specified for propane tanks. Light colored paints will help reflect heat when exposed to the sun.

* New style tanks- These tanks have an internal thread to accommodate standard POL fittings, and also have an external thread to accommodate new grills with the Marshall Type large Acme nut. New style tanks have an internal check valve which prevents gas flow until a leak tight connection is made. Compare local pricing of a new tank, as the cost of the adapter may be nearly as much as the cost of a new tank!

* New style tank with older model grill- You can use a new style tank with an older model standard POL fitting. The new style tank valves have internal threads which allow you to connect the standard POL fitting in a counter-clockwise rotation.

Reprinted by permission of Re-New! 731 Kirkland Avenue, Kirkland, WA 98033
Website **www.grillparts.com**

Resources

Abacus Publishing Company, 8168 Hwy. 98 E. L3, McComb, MS 39648
   Tel:601-684-0001 Fax: 601-684-0052 email:cchale@telapex.com
Barbecue Store, The www.barbecuen.com
Barbecue'n On The Internet, www.barbecuen.com
California BBQ Assoc. 21911 Bear Creek Way, Los Gatos, CA 95030-9497
   Tel: 408-354-4693 or 354-1237 email:frankbbq@slip.net
Central Texas Barbecue Cooker's Assoc. P.O. Box 4566, Temple, TX 76505
Goat Gap Gazette, P.O. Box 800, Brookesmith TX 76827-0800
   Tel: 915-646-6914
Greater Omaha Barbecue Society, 4928 N. 105th, Omaha, NE 68134
International BBQ Cookers Assoc. Tel: 817-469-1579 Fax: 860-7755
   email:IBCALYNN.AOL.com
Kansas City Barbeque Society, 11514 Hickman Mills Dr. KC. MO 64134
   Tel: 800-963-5227 Fax: 816-765-5860 email:KCBS@compuserve.com
Lone Star Barbecue Society, P.O. Box120771, Arlington, TX 76012
   Tel: 817-261-9507
N. Texas Area BBQ Cookers Assoc. P.O. Box 3024, Denton, TX 76201
   Tel: 817-383-1942
National Barbecue News, P.O. Box 981, Douglas, GA 31534
   Tel: 912-384-0001, Fax:912-384-0002 email:joedoc@accessatc.net
National Barbecue Association (NBBQA) P.O. Box 7685, KC, MO 64134
   Tel: 816-767-8311
New England Barbecue Society, P.O. Box 536, Hanover, MA 02339
Pacific Northwest Barbecue Assoc. 4244 134th Ave. SE, Bellevue WA 98006
   Tel: 425-643-0607
Southern California BBQ Assoc. P.O.Box 251 Azusa, CA 91702
   Tel: 626-835-1723

Index

Afterword

This started out as a labor of love, but in the end, deteriorated into hard labor, which can be more aptly described by a four-letter word, "work." It is fun to whip out pithy answers to an individual's question, confident that errors of fact and omission can be easily corrected. Trying to make certain that all information is accurate and complete and understandable for thousands of readers becomes serious business.

Writing this book was a pleasure; rewriting, rewriting, rewriting was not. Recalling rules of grammar and punctuation from a distant, misty past, was challenging, but nothing like removing all the excess of commas which prompted Sandra Lyon, the editor, to dub me a "CommaKazi."

Most frustrating was the fact that, fully aware of my lack of visual creativity, I had sent my sketches and rough plans out to some experts in the field. The professional results were due back in May. By September they were not returned. So I was forced to do a "Little Red Hen" and finish the illustrations myself. I apologize for their shortcomings.

I hope that you will find the book entertaining and informative, but, most of all, I hope that you will be encouraged to discover tastes and textures for yourself; to no longer be bound by someone else's recipe. When you find a sauce or seasoning that you like, learn to recreate that taste, and maybe then, improve upon it.

But the main idea that I would like to convey about barbecuing is: relax, have fun.

Smoky

Order Form

- Fax orders: 601-684-0052
- Telephone orders: 601-684-0001
- e-mail orders: cchale@telapex.con
- Postal Orders: Smoky Hale, 8168 Hwy. 98 E. L3, McComb, MS 39648

Please send the following books:
I understand that I may return any books for full refund for any reason, no questions asked.

Name:_____
Address:_____
City:_____State:____ Zip:_____
Telephone:_____
Softbound: $19.95 + $1.55 S&H. - $21.50
Hardbound: $24.95 + $1.55 S&H - 26.50

Order Form

- Fax orders: 601-684-0052
- Telephone orders: 601-684-0001
- e-mail orders: cchale@telapex.con
- Postal Orders: Smoky Hale, 8168 Hwy. 98 E. L3, McComb, MS 39648

Please send the following books:
I understand that I may return any books for full refund for any reason, no questions asked.

Name:_____
Address:_____
City:_____State:____ Zip:_____
Telephone:_____
Softbound: $19.95 + $1.55 S&H. - $21.50
Hardbound: $24.95 + $1.55 S&H - 26.50

Smoky Hale

Reared in rural L.A. (lower Alabama), C. Clark "Smoky" Hale was barbecuing even before he began bull riding. After losing a vocal cord, coming out a poor second to the bull, in a riding contest, he gave up bull riding to devote more time to barbecuing.

In the early 80's he went out to buy a book on barbecuing for his best boyhood buddy who had just served him gas-grilled chicken blackened on the outside and raw in the middle.

Unable to find a single book with accurate information on authentic barbecue and appalled at the drivel written about it, he decided to write one so the technique could survive. After a couple of years of research and writing, "The Great American Barbeque Book" was published in 1985. It swiftly became the reference book for amateurs and professional barbecue cook-off competitors. He is considered by those in the know to be "the authority" on authentic barbecue.

The book also stirred a fire storm of demand for accurate information on all forms of grilling and cooking outdoors. Smoky began a weekly newspaper column, "Outdoor Cooking with Smoky" which ran for several years. He also appeared on many television shows and conducted seminars on barbecuing and grilling.

Over the years, he has judged all the major barbecue contests and is described, among serious and no-serious barbecue afficionados, as "a legend" even though he denies being old enough to be one. He has been published in several national magazines and is invited to give teaching sessions at barbecue societies and associations from coast to coast.

When he is not out teaching and promoting barbecuing and grilling, Smoky resides deep in the woods of South Mississippi.